# THE GODS OF THE CELTS

# THE GODS
# OF
# THE CELTS

Miranda Green, Ph.D., F.S.A.

1986
ALAN SUTTON
Gloucester

BARNES AND NOBLE BOOKS
Totowa, New Jersey

First Published in 1986 by Alan Sutton Publishing Limited
30 Brunswick Road
Gloucester GL1 1JJ

**British Library Cataloguing in Publication Data**

Green, Miranda J.
  Gods of the Celts.
  1. Druids and druidism — History
  I. Title
  299'.16      BL910

ISBN 0–86299–292–3


First Published in United States of America in 1986 by Barnes and Noble Books, 81 Adams Drive, Totowa, N.J. 07512
ISBN 0-389-20672-5

Designed by Richard Bryant
Cover Design by Martin Latham
Typesetting and origination by
Alan Sutton Publishing Limited, Gloucester.
Printed in Great Britain at the Alden Press, Oxford

*Dedication*

For Stephen: to remind him of chthonic monsters,
ram-horned snakes and famous pigs.

## Acknowledgements

I should like to express my gratitude to the following individuals:

Dr Stephen Green, for reading and commenting upon the book in draft and for his constant encouragement; Mrs Betty Naggar, for many of the photographs; Mr P Lopeman, for some of the figures; and Mrs Sharon Moyle, for typing the first draft of the manuscript. I am grateful for help in providing individual illustrations to Margaret Tremayne, HBMC English Heritage; John Dent, Archaeology Unit, Humberside County Council; Professor Barry Cunliffe, Institute of Archaeology, Oxford, and Keith Parfitt, Dover Archaeological Group.

I wish to thank the staff of the following museums for their help and for permission to publish their material: Augst, Römermuseum; Aylesbury, Buckinghamshire County Museum; Bath, Roman Baths Museum; Bonn, Rheinisches Landesmuseum; Bristol, City of Bristol Museum and Art Gallery; Cambridge, University Museum of Archaeology and Anthropology; Cardiff, National Museum of Wales; Carlisle Museum; Chedworth, Roman Villa Museum; Chester, Grosvenor Museum; Cirencester, Corinium Museum; Colchester and Essex Museum; Copenhagen, Nationalmuseet; Dijon, Musée Archéologique de Dijon; Dorchester, Dorset County Museum; Edinburgh, Royal Scottish Museum; Gloucester City Museum; Graz, Landesmuseum Joanneum; Great Driffield Museum; Leiden, Rijksmuseum van Oudheden; London, Trustees of the British Museum; Museum of London; Luxembourg, Musée de'Histoire et d'Art; Netherhall Collection, Maryport; Newcastle, University Museum of Antiquities; Newport Museum and Art Gallery; Nîmes, Musée Archéologique; Nottingham University Museum; Oxford, Ashmolean Museum; Paris, Musée des Antiquités Nationales, St Germain-en-Laye; Peterborough City Museum; Saverne Museum, Alsace; Scunthorpe Museum; Sheffield City Museum; Shrewsbury, Rewley's House Museum; Stroud District Museum; Stuttgart, Württembergisches Landesmuseum; Torquay Museum; Worthing Museum and Art Gallery.

# CONTENTS

|  | Page |
|---|---|
| PROLOGUE: | 1 |
| CHAPTER ONE:<br>The Celts and Religion | 7 |
| CHAPTER TWO:<br>Cults of Sun and Sky | 39 |
| CHAPTER THREE:<br>Fertility and the Mother-Goddesses | 72 |
| CHAPTER FOUR:<br>War, Death and the Underworld | 103 |
| CHAPTER FIVE:<br>Water-Gods and Healers | 138 |
| CHAPTER SIX:<br>Animals and Animism | 167 |
| CHAPTER SEVEN:<br>Symbolism and Imagery in Celtic Cult Expression | 200 |
| Notes/References | 226 |
| Bibliography | 236 |
| Index | 250 |

# LIST OF ILLUSTRATIONS

1 Late Iron Age bronze boar, Lexden, Colchester. 9
2 Bronze shield with boar motif; second century BC; River Witham, Lincs. 9
3 Gaulish coin depicting stag and boar; near Maidstone, Kent. 10
4 Stone pillar, fifth century BC; Pfalzfeld, Germany. 11
5 Wooden female figure, first century BC; Ballachulish, Argyll. 13
6 Ground-plan of contiguous Iron Age shrines, Frilford, Oxon. 18
7 Ceremonial regalia. 23
8 Lead *defixio* invoking Sulis, from Roman reservoir; Bath. 24
9 Gilt silver cauldron; Gundestrup, Jutland. First century BC. 25
10 Stone pillar with incised severed heads. Third-second century BC; Entremont, Provence. 29
11 Stone squatting figure of warrior-god with hand resting on human head. Third-second century BC; Entremont, Provence. 30
12 Celtic stone head in relief; Carmarthen, Dyfed. 31
13 Bronze seventh-sixth century BC cult-wagon; Strettweg, Austria. 34
14 Stone votive tablets to Mars Olloudius and Romulus; Custom Scrubs, Glos. 37
15 Late Iron Age hoard of wheel-model and boar-figurines; Hounslow, Middlesex. 41
16 Bronze wheel-brooch; Lakenheath, Suffolk. 43
17 Part of hoard containing wheel-model; Felmingham Hall, Norfolk. 47
18 Bronze-wheel-model; France (unprovenanced). 48
19 Bronze figurine of wheel-god; Le Châtalet, France. 51
20 Clay antefixes decorated with human heads and solar symbols. Caerleon, Gwent. 52
21 Bronze mace-terminal depicting god, wheel, eagle, dolphin and three-horned bull's head; Willingham Fen, Cambs. 53
22 Sheet-bronze sceptre-binding from temple; Farley Heath, Surrey. 54
23 Stone wheel-decorated altar; Gilly, near Nîmes. 57
24 Relief of seated wheel-god with *cornucopiae*; Netherby, Cumbria. 60
25 Tombstone decorated with wheel-signs; Saverne area. 61
26 Reconstruction of Jupiter-column; Hausen-an-der-Zaber, near Stuttgart, Germany. 62
27 Inscription recording restoration of a Jupiter-column; Cirencester. Fourth century AD. 64
28 Corinthian figured capital with Bacchic figures, probably from Jupiter-column; Cirencester. 65
29 Plaque of the Triple Mothers; Cirencester. 75
30 Plaque of the Triple Mothers; Cirencester. 79
31 Plaque of Triple Coventina; Carrawburgh, Northumberland. 80
32 Statue-base dedicated to the *Suleviae*, by Sulinus son of Brucetus, a sculptor; Bath. 81
33 Altar to the *Suleviae*, dedicated by Brucetus; Cirencester. 82
34 Relief of Triple Mothers with children; Cirencester. 83
35 Mother-goddess with three apples; Ashcroft, Cirencester. 86
36 Altar to Nehalennia; Colijnsplaat, Netherlands. 87
37 Mother-goddess with palm; Caerwent, Gwent. 88
38 Pipe-clay mother-goddesses and mould; Toulon-sur-Allier and London. 89
39 *Genii cucullati* and mother-goddess, Cirencester. 90
40 *Genii cucullati* and mother-goddess, Cirencester. 91
41 Stone Epona; Luxembourg 92
42 Bronze Epona; Dalheim, Luxembourg. 93
43 Pipe-clay 'Venus'; London. 94
44 Pipe-clay 'Venus' with solar symbols; Allier, France. 94
45 Bronze Sucellus; Lyon. 96
46 Silver finger-ring dedicated to Sucellus; York. 96
47 Tablet depicting Mercury and Rosmerta; Shakespeare Inn, Gloucester. 98

48 Mercury, Rosmerta and Fortuna; Bon Marché site, Gloucester. 99
49 Stone phallic head; Eype, Dorset. 100
50 Bronze shield, first century AD; from Thames at Battersea. 105
51 Bronze horned helmet, first century BC; from Thames at Waterloo Bridge, London. 106
52 Ritually-bent bronze spear models; Woodeaton temple, Oxon. 107
53 Iron Age chalk figurine of warrior; Garton Slack, Yorkshire. 109
54 Two silver plaques dedicated to Cocidius; Bewcastle, Cumbria. 112
55 Naked horned warrior-god with spear and shield; Maryport, Cumbria. 114
56 Statue-base with human and goose-feet, dedicated to Mars Lenus Ocelus Vellaunus; Caerwent. 115
57 Stone tablet depicting triple Mars; Lower Slaughter, Glos. 115
58 Stone relief of horseman-god; Margidunum, Notts. 117
59 Bronze horseman; Westwood Bridge, Peterborough, Cambs. 118
60 Altar depicting Celtic Mars; King's Stanley, Glos. 119
61 Iron Age chariot-burial of young adult female, found with pig-remains and work-box, excavated in 1984; Wetwang, Yorkshire. 125
62 Iron Age pit-burial of male; fifth century BC; Danebury, Hants. 127
63 Iron Age bog-burial of adult male. The man was poleaxed garrotted and his throat cut; 300 BC; Lindow Moss, Cheshire. 128
64 Chalk figurine; found in chamber at bottom of pit; Deal, Kent. 134
65 Votive deposit of ironwork within two cauldrons; late Iron Age/early Roman; from bog at Blackburn Mill, S Scotland. 146
66 Votive bog-deposit of ironwork within cauldron; late Iron Age/early Roman; Carlingwark Loch, S Scotland. 146
67 Aerial view of the site of Coventina's Well; Carrawburgh. 149
68 Iron Age wooden head; from healing shrine at Source de la Seine sanctuary, near Dijon, France. 151
69 Altar to Sulis Minerva, dedicated by Sulinus; Bath. 154
70 Gilded bronze head of Sulis Minerva; Bath. 156
71 *Genii cucullati* and worshipper from well; Lower Slaughter, Glos. 157
72 Bronze deerhound; Lydney, Glos. 159
73 Bronze plaque of dying boar; Muntham Court temple, Sussex. 160
74 Altar to Apollo Cunomaglus; Nettleton Shrub temple, Wiltshire. 163
75 Bronze bull/eagle head bucket-mount; Thealby, Lincs; late Iron Age/early Roman. 169
76 Bronze figurine of Epona; Wiltshire. 174
77 Bronze bull-mounts; Holyhead, Anglesey and Welshpool, Powys. 177
78 Bronze, late Iron Age, stag; Milber Down Hillfort, Devon. 182
79 Bronze stag, found in pit near rectangular temple; Colchester. 183
80 Bronze plaque to Silvanus Callirius, dedicated by a coppersmith. Colchester. 183
81 Jet bear-amulet; Bootle, Lancs. 185
82 Bronze eagle; Woodeaton, Oxon. 189
83 Bronze three-horned bull; Cirencester. 190
84 Pipe-clay three-horned bull, from child's grave; Colchester. 191
85 Silver-washed three-horned bull, with figures of deities on its back, from mid fourth century AD shrine; Maiden Castle, Dorset. 191
86 Stone plaque of Cernunnos and ram-horned snakes; Cirencester. 193
87 Stone altar with ram-horned snake; Lypiatt Park, Glos. 194
88 Iron Age silver coin with head of Cernunnos and wheel-symbol; Petersfield, Hants. 196
89 Horned stone head; Carvoran, Northumberland. 197
90 Plaque of *Genii cucullati*; Cirencester. 201
91 Chalk or limestone janiform figure; Ivy Chimneys, Witham, Essex. 204
92 Schist plaque of Triple Mothers; Bath. 209
93 Triple vase; Chester. 210
94 Three-faced stone head in non-local granite; first century BC – first century AD; (?) Sutherland, N Scotland. 211
95 Sheet bronze relief of ithyphallic deity; Woodeaton, Oxon. 212
96 Incised figure of deity; Cirencester. 213

# LIST OF ILLUSTRATIONS

97 Lead relief of horned god; Chesters, Northumberland.  214
98 Stone relief of Mercury, from well; Emberton, Bucks.  215
99 Stone head from shrine; Caerwent, Gwent.  217
100 Bronze plaque showing opposed human faces; late first century BC/first century AD; Tal-y-Llyn, Powys.  217
101 Face-pot; Caerwent, Gwent.  219
102 Stone figure; the rear view indicates that a kind of pelt may be worn; Cirencester.  220
103 Bronze anchor-model; Woodeaton, Oxon.  221

# PROLOGUE

## Introducing the Celts

The Celts had no tradition of written records and therefore cannot identify themselves to us directly. They are known either archaeologically or through the writing of literate Mediterranean societies. The Celts or *Keltoi* (in the Greek) were first defined as such by the Greeks before 500 BC. The very earliest reference is in an account of coastal travel from Spain and southern France which is quoted by one Rufus Avienus, proconsul of Africa, in a coastal survey (*Ora Maritima*). Around 500 BC Celts are again mentioned by Hecataeus of Miletus. Some sixty years later, Herodotus in his *Histories* talked of the source of the Danube being in the territory of the Celts and stated also that these people were almost the most westerly of all Europeans.

The origin of the peoples called 'Celts' by classical writers has long been the subject of speculation and controversy. But it seems irrefutable that somehow, this group of peoples, whose language and material culture contained sufficient unity to be identifiable to their neighbours, had their roots in the later Bronze Age cultures of Europe. However, the Celts – whether in Britain or mainland Europe – did not suddenly appear from a specific place as the result of a single event but, rather, were people who had become 'Celtic' by accretion in process of time. No one culture or time should be sought as the immediate source of Celtic beginnings. Indeed it could be argued that it is futile to enquire when the Celts first appeared since the people recognised as such by Graeco-Roman authors were in fact the lineal descendants of generations stretching back as far as the Neolithic farmers of the fifth-fourth millennium BC. The process of 'celticisation' should thus be seen as a gradual phenomenon. The classical world, as evidenced by its writers, used the term 'Celts' to refer to the 'barbarian' peoples who occupied much of North-West and Central Europe. It should be realised that this term, perhaps carelessly applied (and at times mis-applied) was employed to describe a multitude of tribes of differing ethnic traditions and varying customs. Nevertheless, as long as this is understood, it is a useful generalisation. Archaeological research has demonstrated that by the fifth century BC large

1

tracts of Europe – from Britain to the Black Sea, and from North Italy and Yugoslavia to Belgium – shared a number of elements. By the fourth century BC the Celts were regarded by their Mediterranean neighbours as one of the four great peripheral nations of the known world. Rapid expansion took Celtic tribes into Italy around 400 BC and in 387 Rome itself was defeated. In 279 BC a group of Celts entered Greece and plundered the sacred site of Delphi; in 278 a splinter-group established themselves in Asia Minor (Galatia). Whilst it is impossible to speak of a nation of Celts, processes of trade and exchange, folk-movement and convergent evolution, caused the peoples inhabiting barbarian, non-Mediterranean Europe to develop a degree of cultural homogeneity. It was this which was acknowledged by Graeco-Roman authors and which caused them to use 'Celts' as a unifying term. If one speaks entirely archaeologically, it is thus possible to state that Iron Age Celts originated in Central and West Central Europe.

In order to place the Celts in their prehistoric context, it is necessary to look briefly backwards beyond the recognisable emergence of the Celtic world. The later Bronze Age 'Urnfield' culture, commencing circa 1300 BC was roughly coincident with the decline of Mycenaean power. In Central Europe new burial rites may be observed at this time, consisting of large-scale cremation-burial in flat cemeteries (giving rise to the term 'Urnfield'). Their very widespread occurrence around the close of the second millennium BC provides a phenomenon sufficiently coherent for some scholars to equate Urnfield peoples with proto-Celts. This European later Bronze Age is of interest in the present context for two main reasons. One is that the spread of cremation-rites suggests changes in belief about death and the afterlife. Secondly, the culture is characterised in material/technological terms by the new ability of bronzesmiths to manipulate bronze into sheets to make such large items as vessels and shields. The vessels were frequently decorated with figural and abstract designs and, along with other paraphernalia, appear to reflect a more mature religious symbolism and more unified methods of religious expression. This prolific sheet-bronze production suggests also both a relatively settled time of prosperous trading and sophisticated organisation of trade-routes. The use of sheet metal vessels (sometimes mounted on wagons) in religious ritual is interesting for, by about 1200–1100 BC, we know that wetter conditions prevailed and it is suggested that this climatic change may be reflected in the water-cults possibly represented by such containers.

The reasons for the rise of the Urnfield people may be sought in the economic turmoil and folk movement, emanating partly from the east, from the region of the Black Sea: such concretions of power as the Hittite and Mycenaean Empires crumbled, giving rise to a consequent diminution of external demand on local European mineral resources. In parallel, skills were being developed by Central and East European metalsmiths. In the eighth century BC the Dorian invasions of Greece ushered in, for the first time in Central Europe, the use of horses for riding rather than merely for traction: this may mark the beginning of pastoral nomadism in Europe. The horse was certainly a symbol of an aristocratic warrior-élite, which was the main feature of later Celtic society. Riding brought with it the rich metal paraphernalia which would naturally accompany such a practice. The new wealth of Central Europe during the early first millennium BC was based partly on metal and partly on salt-mining. Piggott would see the development of Central European sheet metalworking as having association with an early wine-trade with the Mediterranean world. Certainly by the eighth century there was an expansion of peoples from their original Urnfield homelands to what would become the Celtic world incorporating, for example, Italy, the Balkans, France and Iberia.

By about 700 BC new cultural elements may be observed. New metal types associated with horse-harness are present, the distribution of which suggests raiding parties moving rapidly from one region to another. The new material culture is called 'Hallstatt' after the type-site in the Salzkammergut of the Hallein/Salzburg area of Austria. Ironworking on a large scale comes in for the first time in this period. The metal was known and utilised as an exotic material before this date but by the end of the eighth century BC iron was commonplace in continental Europe and, somewhat later – by about 600 BC – in Britain and Ireland. The Hallstatt culture is characterised in Central Europe by rich inhumation burial, in wooden mortuary houses under earthen barrows or mounds, with four-wheeled wagons or carts, sometimes partly dismantled. The grave evidence suggests a warrior-élite with members of the ruling class (men and women) elaborately buried. The frequent presence of not two but three sets of horse-trappings in such graves suggests the possible representation not only of the wagon-team but also of the chieftain's own charger. From the seventh century the main item traded from the

3

Mediterranean to the Celtic world seems to have been wine – reflected archaeologically by wine-vessel imports. The main trade the other way would certainly have included salt.

In about 500 BC the centres of power appear to have shifted North and West to the Rhineland and Marne. There is still evidence for the presence of the warrior-aristocracy, but now the burial-rite of the élite generally consisted of two-wheeled vehicle-burial, reflecting the use of a light chariot or cart. Warrior-accoutrements abound in the archaeological record, as do luxury objects often decorated for the first time with specifically Celtic art-designs. The La Tène, as this first truly Celtic culture is called (after the type-site of La Tène in Switzerland), is characterised also by the presence for the first time of what may be termed proto-towns – large sprawling fortified settlements, permanently settled hillforts or *oppida*, like Danebury in Britain, Alesia in France, Manching in Bavaria or the Dürrnberg in Austria. These *oppida* were scattered across the whole of the Celtic world from Iberia to Galatia.

We have reached the point where classical sources and archaeology converge on the Celtic peoples of the later first millennium BC and may now look in more detail at the kind of society represented by this evidence, a society basically heroic, strictly hierarchical, based on kingship and with a martial aristocracy. The evidence of archaeology, classical written sources and some of the early Irish material (pp 7–17) gives us a fairly detailed picture of swaggering heroes continually fighting and proving their ferocity and valour to their peers; squabbling over who should have the champion's portion of pork (traditionally this went to the best warrior, along with the right to carve the chief carcase of the feast). Feasting is evidenced archaeologically in Britain: at Danebury, cauldron-hooks and spits are recorded together with remains of joints in midden deposits. The accoutrements of such warriors were spears, a long iron sword and body-covering shield and, above all, a war-chariot. Cattle-rearing (and raiding) would have been the main occupation in Ireland at least, with cattle the staple form of wealth, along with metal treasure; the unit of value was the cow. Irish sources tell us of kings and sub-kings, nobles and lesser nobles, freemen (landowners, priests, artists/craftsmen) and serfs. The basic unit of social structure was the *derbfine* or extended family, groups of these making up the *tuath* or tribe. Kings and sub-kings were bound to each other by oaths of allegiance; and clientdom or vasselage was an important form of relationship between

4

higher and lower social classes. Certainly by the last few centuries BC the Celts had established a deeply stratified social structure in which craftsmen and religious specialists had their place. It is suggested that this may have been stimulated partly by long-distance trade and exposure to the wealth of the classical world which could have brought about a shift from inherited to achieved status. This increase in markets may have facilitated the client-patron relationship between the lower echelons of society and the aristocracy. Kinship-links may have weakened and political ties may have become stronger. We have hints, indeed, that the hierarchical nature of barbarian society had its roots further back in prehistory. We have already seen a warrior-élite at the very end of the Bronze Age, and Burgess would see the deepening of social stratification as early as the later second millennium BC. The client-patron relationship is especially important within the context of Celtic art. This is the main medium through which we are able to study Celtic religious expression certainly in the La Tène and Romano-Celtic periods. In the first place, in a heroic society, the aristocracy would stimulate wealth in the form of met-alwork, and give it away as part of the important host-guest relationship between people of equal rank. For the most part, Iron Age Celtic art, and predominantly metalwork, was an aristocratic phenomenon and this obviously distorts any picture gained from it concerning expressions of religious belief. Craftsmen themselves would frequently have been peripatetic, serving a number of patrons at one time and this, together, with the hoarding of items for gift-exchange, means that art-transmission from area to area was fluid. It is necessary, within this context, to realise that whilst peas-ants may have reflected continuity over a long period, aristocratic art-ideas and traditions may quickly and easily have been transmitted over long distances within Europe. One further thing should be said at this stage: there are two main schools of thought concerning the nature of Celtic art. The first view, represented by Megaw is that Celtic art is basically religious. The second, argued by Powell is that it was essentially decorative and that whatever symbolic implications there may be, embellishment is the prime concern. We shall examine the function of Celtic art later, in Chapter One.

A final point needs to be made concerning the nature of our evidence for the religion and gods of the Celtic peoples. By the last two centuries BC, if not somewhat before, Celtic society was localised and fragmented. This is demonstrated by the lack of any unifying style among later Celtic art, including coin-design. Interestingly for us, it is the very divergent nature of god-representation which in the Romano-Celtic period is such an essential feature of Celtic religion.

# CHAPTER ONE: THE CELTS AND RELIGION

## THE NATURE OF THE EVIDENCE

The nature of our information about the Celts and their religion comes from a number of different sources, all of which have to be treated with a degree of caution, for reasons which will become apparent. The evidence is composed first of contemporary literature written, however, not by the Celts themselves who had no tradition of a written language, but by their Mediterranean neighbours. Second, there is archaeological material pertaining to the pre-Roman (which I term 'free Celtic') and Romano-Celtic world. Third, there exist vernacular written sources in Irish and Welsh. The problem is that none of these sources comes under the category of direct information. That would only be the case if the Celts had written in detail about themselves. Every piece of Graeco-Roman and vernacular literature is in a very real sense second-hand: first, because comments were made by an alien people far removed in cultural terms from the object of their remarks; second, because the post-Roman literature is separated spatially and temporally from the Celts of the later first millennium BC and the Roman period. The evidence of archaeology is at best incomplete and ambiguous; at worst, it is misleading and confusing. The survival (or lack of it) of the evidence is one problem; its interpretation is another. As Piggott so rightly points out there is great difficulty in interpreting – especially in the area of religious beliefs – by archaeology alone; any attempt at an explanation of Celtic religion must at best be extremely speculative – a construction rather than a reconstruction.

The evidence of archaeology for the prehistoric Celtic period (roughly sixth-first century BC depending on geography and the timing of the Roman conquests) may be divided into that of cult-sites including votive/ritual deposits and evidence of sacrifice, and shrines and natural features; burial rites; and iconography, including pre-Roman coins. During the Romano-Celtic period, evidence is augmented by inscriptions, an increasing number of substantial religious structures and a vastly increased iconography – mainly in stone. Sometimes archaeological and written sources are in concert but frequently they conflict, as we will see later, and

this makes for difficulties. Of the different kinds of archaeological evidence, some may be more unequivocal in terms
of religious interpretation than others. Inferences may be
made about cult activity on the ground in the form of
suggested shrines and votive deposits – but since we have
no dedications to the gods in the free Celtic period, we can
only argue as to the likelihood of ritual function from the
seemingly irrational nature of such material. For instance,
we may infer that some later Bronze Age hoards may have a
ritual purpose, perhaps because the contents have been
deliberately and carefully laid out, as at Appleby, Lincs or
because there is evidence of ritual breakage. Similarly, it is
possible to infer that certain structures, as occur in such
pre-Roman fortified settlements as Danebury, Maiden Castle
and South Cadbury, may be sanctuaries, since they do not
fit into any patterns of secular activity.

Iconography in Celtic art likewise conveys ambiguity in
terms of purpose. In some instances, like the few pieces of
Hallstatt or La Tène-period figure-sculpture from
Württemberg and the Rhineland, it is fairly evident that
religious personages are being represented. But where, as on
most pieces of Celtic metalwork, human or animal figures
are part of an overall decorative design, it is much less easy
to be sure of anything other than ornamentation. It is
worthwhile here to look in slightly more detail at Celtic art
and iconography to examine the forms in which possible
evidence for deity-representation are present. Figural bronzework of a possible religious character occurs, in non-
Mediterranean Europe, in the later homelands of the Celts,
from at least the later second millennium BC. The Danish
Trundholm 'sun-chariot' (strictly speaking outside our geographical area) with its solar disc and horse-team, dates to
around 1300 BC. From the twelfth century BC, small in-the-
round bronze water-birds appear in Central Europe and
seem to possess some form of talismanic significance.
In the later Urnfield period repeated motifs on sheet-
bronze include aquatic birds, sun and ship-symbols in
association. Early Celtic art really begins with the rich
burials of the Hallstatt trader-knights. Birds, horses and
cattle appear on bronzework; and one may point to the
unique gold bowl from Altstetten, Zürich, which may be a
cult-vessel decorated with sun, crescent-moon and beasts.
La Tène metalwork is predominantly decorative as we have
seen but it is a matter of opinion as to whether the,
sometimes grotesque, faces which peer out from abstract
and stylised foliage-designs on bracelets, like the gold one
from Rodenbach with flowing Celtic moustache, or the

1  Late Iron Age bronze boar, from rich tumulus; Lexden, Colchester. Copyright: Colchester & Essex Museum.

bronze example from la Charne, Troyes have any religious significance. Megaw argues that La Tène art employs iconography which endows even the simplest items with symbolism (Megaw 1970, 38). Whilst Britain is less orientated towards humans and animals in its art, the later La Tène material is more definitely representative, both in insular and continental contexts. In Denmark, Celtic cauldrons from Brå and Rynkeby, were both probably votive

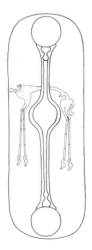

2  Bronze shield with outline of boar motif; second century BC; River Witham, Lincs. Illustration: Miranda Green. British Museum.

offerings and quite possibly originally the possessions of priests. The latter dates to the first century BC and is ornamented with a human head and ox-heads. Buckets like those from Aylesford, Swarling and Marlborough bear human heads which presumably have symbolic significance. The Witham Shield (Fig. 2) depicted a boar-motif, albeit stylised but unmistakeably an isolated boar-figure. The iron fire-dogs found in tombs of the immediately pre-Roman period, like those from Barton, Cambs., bear unequivocal bull-motifs. On the Continent, figural bronzework becomes relatively common in the immediate pre-Roman period: boar-figurines are plentiful, illustrated by the large example from Neuvy-en-Sullias; and human bronze figures are not unknown – as for instance the cross-legged god from Bouray. Before we leave metalwork, we should look briefly at pre-Roman Celtic coinage, since this sometimes portrays figural representations. Allen argues that such items may well have a symbolic function simply because their primary purpose was as largesse and as a gauge of wealth. He rightly points out that in terms of an art-form, coins stand apart from the

3  Gaulish coin depicting stag and boar with over-large antlers and bristles respectively; near Maidstone, Kent. Copyright: National Museum of Wales.

mainstream because of limitations imposed both by size and mass-production; indeed, from the middle La Tène period, coins were issued by the million. What is of especial interest is the tracing of iconographic links between coins and other Celtic religious art. An example of this is the coins of the Aulerci Eburovices of the Evreux region whose motifs link closely with the sculpture of man and boar from Euffigneix. The coins show a boar-motif superimposed on the neck of an anthropomorphic representation and the stone depicts a torced human figure with a boar carved along its torso (Allen 1976a and 1980).

Pre-Roman Celtic stone iconography is rare. Two main continental clusters exist – an early group in Germany and a somewhat later set (fourth – second century BC) far away in Provence. One of the earliest Celtic figures is from a late Hallstatt tumulus at Hirschlanden, north-west of Stuttgart, where, possibly originally positioned at the summit of the mound, is a huge sandstone figure dating to the end of the sixth century BC and wearing a helmet, torc, belt and dagger. Also from Germany are a janiform (double-faced) pillar from Holzerlingen, whose heads are horned, and stone heads from Heidelberg and in relief on the Pfalzfeld Pillar. From further east comes a moustached, very Celtic-looking head from Mšecké Žehrovice in Czechoslovakia.

4  Stone pillar, fifth century BC; Pfalzfeld, Germany. Copyright: Rheinisches Landesmuseum, Bonn.

11

The southern French material is especially interesting partly in the amount and variety of sculpture present, but also in the fact that a number of cultural/ethnic forces were at work. Fortified *oppida* in this area belonged to Celtic tribes having associations on the one hand with the Ligurians of south-eastern France and with Greek colonists from Marseilles, on the other. There was certainly Greek influence in the establishment of built shrines and in the use of stone depictions, but the style and content of the iconography is undeniably Celtic. For purposes of this introductory survey it will be sufficient to look briefly at two key sites – Entremont and Roquepertuse. Entremont was the capital of the Saluvii, sacked by Rome in 123 BC. The shrine stood on the highest ground and possessed limestone pillars with incised carvings of human heads (Fig. 10), and other sculptures mostly again associated with disembodied heads. At the cliff-sanctuary of Roquepertuse, located not far away, three stone pillars formed the portal to the shrine. These columns had niches containing human skulls, and a great stone bird stood poised on the cross-beam. Squatting warriors, one bearing a Celtic torc, and a Janus-head held in the beak of a huge bird, are among the repertoire of this southern Gaulish mountain-temple. It is probable that most of the sculptures in the Provençal group date from the fourth – second centuries BC, with a *floruit* perhaps during the third century.

In pre-Roman Celtic iconography of the La Tène period as a whole, figure-sculpture is usually relatively simple and human and animal forms are subservient to the overall design especially in metalwork, as in the Waldalgesheim bronzes but also exemplified by the Pfalzfeld stone pillar where human heads present a fluid, stylised appearance entirely in keeping with the surrounding scrollwork pattern. A representative style did not fully develop until the period of Roman rule which stimulated figural por-trayal, albeit largely ignoring the 'heavy hand of Roman classicism'. Romano-Celtic stone iconography, influenced by Roman art-formulae but exhibiting religious forms and themes alien to the Mediterranean world, demonstrates that before the conquest there must have existed local and tribal gods, each with a name (four hundred different Celtic gods are named on Romano-Celtic inscriptions) and each with specific qualities. Indeed, some non Graeco-Roman symbols appearing in the Roman period are known before – for example the horned head exhibited on the Holzerlingen sculpture, and the emphasis on human heads and animals. We will see in later chapters that isolation of iconographic

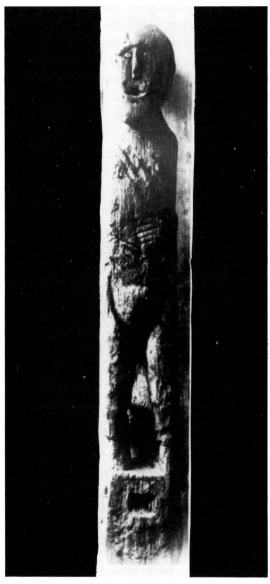

5  Wooden female figure, from wicker structure, first century BC;
   Ballachulish, Argyll. Copyright: National Museums of Scotland.

types during the Romano-Celtic period is one of the best
ways of classifying cult-objects, even though this must
necessarily contain an element of arbitrariness.

Before we leave iconography, the use of wooden
sculptures should be mentioned. Pre-Roman figure-carving
seems sparse indeed when we look at the medium of stone.
But the chance survival in water-logged conditions, as at the
Seine sanctuary near Dijon (pp 150–151), shows that there

13

was a tradition of pre-Roman figure-sculpture not confined to the few stone pieces mentioned. This is of particular note when we consider the passage of Lucan where the presence of wooden effigies to the gods in a Gaulish sanctuary is specifically mentioned.

## The Evidence of Literature

As commented upon above, two kinds of literary record exist for the Celtic world, Graeco-Roman and vernacular Celtic. The Celtic world and its customs – including religion – was discussed and described in varying detail in writings of Mediterranean authors, the main ones being Caesar, Strabo, Pomponius Mela, Pliny, Athenaeus, Tacitus, Dio Cassius, Diodorus Siculus, Ammianus Marcellinus and Lucan. Four of these writers base their evidence (acknowledged or unacknowledged) upon earlier but lost writings of Posidonius: Strabo (63 BC – AD 21), Diodorus (writing circa 60 – 30 BC), Caesar (in the mid first century BC) and Athenaeus (circa AD 200). These writers are in general more useful and detailed about Druids and ritual than about the gods themselves. For instance, Caesar speaks as if the Celts' deities were identical with those of Rome and gives them Roman names, whilst Lucan (second century AD) talks of three Celtic gods – Esus, Teutates and Taranis – as if they were really important, a suggestion not supported by epigraphy which names these gods very infrequently. Classical writers have to be used with caution; they are biased by what interested them, by choice or chance of recording and by cultural separation, ignorance and consequential misinterpretation. Caesar on the Druids, for instance, must be seen in the light of his deliberate embellishment of an alien priesthood for politico-propaganda purposes. However, most Celtic ritual, alien though it was in detail, was explicable to the Roman mind, for Mediterranean peoples too were fettered by the concepts of correct and contractual appeasement and propitiation. Only weird and obscene rites – head-hunting, human sacrifice, divination by ritual murder – were curious and distasteful enough to be commented upon in detail. Where classical writers are particularly valuable is precisely in areas where their evidence marries with archaeological data: for instance both demonstrate the existence of human sacrifice and of head-collection. With deities themselves there is less comfort. The vast wealth of iconographic evidence for Celtic gods during the Romano-Celtic period is a subject upon which Graeco-Roman authors are virtually silent.

The other major body of literature is itself Celtic, so it does not suffer the cultural alienation of classical sources. However, it brings with it its own set of problems based partly on temporal separation and partly on its being specific to the fringes of the Celtic world during the thousand years (fifth century BC – fourth century AD) of pagan celticism. As we have seen, there are no indigenous literary references to the La Tène or even the Roman period. There is a danger even where Gaulish archaeological evidence appears to match the insular data since the two types of source are separated by at least several centuries in recording. The Irish evidence may sometimes be specific to Ireland: for example, the religious festivals of Samain and Beltine are related to stock-rearing and pastoralism, not necessarily relevant to lowland Britain and Gaul. We have to bear such constraints in mind when assessing the vernacular material. When Britain and Gaul were under Roman rule, Ireland possessed a heroic society, basically prehistoric-Celtic in terms of developmental stage, whose exploits are discussed in ballads and poems of which the earliest began to be written down sometime in the eighth century AD. For our purposes the group of prose tales known as the Ulster Cycle is of most use. These describe in epic form a series of events pertaining to a specifically Homeric-type heroic, aristocratic, warlike and hierarchical society. Jackson sees this as definitely related to Iron Age Ireland, though Champion wonders if these tales might not be conscious imitation of Homer in early Christian times. Archaism is evident both in the political status of Ulster and in the political structure, customs and material culture described, which all apparently belong to a period some centuries earlier than the time at which they were first written down. The stories centre around the King of Ulster and his followers at a time when Ulster was a large and powerful kingdom with its capital at Emain Macha near Armagh and whose over-king was Conchobar. The opponents of Ulster were the Confederacy of the rest of Ireland led by Ailill of Connaught and his warlike and dominant queen Medb. The main activities appear to have been fighting, cattle-raiding and feasting. The proof that the background to these tales was earlier than the introduction of Christianity in the fifth century AD is based on a number of arguments. By the fifth century, the whole political framework of Ireland had altered: by now Ulster was much smaller and insignificant, its greatness having been

15

smashed by the family of Niall (who died in about AD 404). Thus events in the Ulster Cycle are arguably older than this change. Likewise, though Christianity was established in the fifth century, the heroes in the stories swear not by God but by the gods of their tribes. Jackson dates the formulation of the body of narrative material recorded around the third or fourth century AD embodying tradition going back perhaps to the second century BC; thus the Ulster Cycle would describe events in late La Tène Ireland. But doubt has recently been cast on this *terminus post quem* for Celtic culture to Ireland. Champion argues that the society described could date much earlier than the second century BC.

Other Irish and indeed Welsh sources must be acknowledged, though their value for the period in question must be minimised by their lateness in compilation and by their very nature. References to religion and mythology in later Celtic literature cannot safely be used to illuminate a subject which is essentially pre-Christian and a part of prehistoric Europe. But it is true, nevertheless, that however late the manuscripts (mostly eleventh – twelfth century AD) they do contain a vast amount of non- and therefore pre-Christian material. For example, many deities occur in the Irish sources – such as Nuadu and Lug – who can be traced also in the Romano-Celtic record (Nuadu may well be the Nodens of Romano-Celtic Britain, and Lug's name is enshrined in various town-names, like Lugdunum (Lyon) and Luguvalium (Carlisle). The later Irish material exists in such works as the 'Book of Invasions', the 'History of Races', and the Fionn Cyle, all of twelfth century date. Wales also had a Celtic oral tradition which was rich but poorly documented for the early period. Of the extant tales, the four Branches of the Mabinogi, of late eleventh century date, and the Tale of Cwlhwch and Olwen are perhaps of greatest interest. But though, for example, the Druids of Caesar and other classical writers play a large role in these late literary works, it is evident that medieval Irish and Welsh antiquarians/historians were fairly ignorant of the actual beliefs of the people about whom they wrote. If we look closely at these works, mythology abounds but there is little tangible evidence for religion apart from the names of certain gods. The message of this medieval Celtic literary material, then, is 'examine with interest but use with extreme caution' any possible direct link with the later first millennium BC and the early centuries AD.

The similarities between the archaeological and literary records (both Graeco-Roman and Irish) should be highlighted, since the links do strengthen the authenticity of each, and serve also to counteract the Ireland-specific constraints mentioned earlier. Some similarities between the sources are very significant indeed. The aristocratic society itself, with its hierarchical division into nobles, free landowners and landless men; the system of clientship; the pugnacity, boldness and vanity of the champions are all recorded by classical and later Celtic writers; and the importance of feasting, of pork and otherworld banquets is borne out archaeologically as well. Comments on clothing and weaponry tally and above all the use of the war-chariot is faithfully recorded in all three sources. More important for our purposes, classical and Celtic writers agree on the three learned classes of Druids, Vates and Bards, and on the ritual of head-hunting – the latter being also corroborated archaeologically.

Lastly, in assessing our sources of evidence, we should glance at epigraphy, a group of data relevant only to the Romano-Celtic phase (roughly first century AD onwards). Though god-names were inscribed on monuments through the Roman tradition, they very frequently allude to specifically Celtic god-names and it would be implausible to imagine that these names did not exist orally before Roman influence on Celtic lands.

## THE NATURE OF CELTIC RELIGION

We have looked already at the character of the Celts and their society and at the type of evidence used to construct a picture of religious beliefs and practices. In this section, I wish to touch very briefly on the essence of Celtic religion as projected by this evidence. Detail is unnecessary at this stage since succeeding chapters will examine the most prominent themes at some length. Here my aim is to introduce the kind of religion with which we shall be concerned, and to set the scene by surveying the types of context within which cults were enacted.

### Religious Sites

Let us first look at places of worship, whether built sanctuaries or natural *loci consecrati*. It is generally considered that the Celts did not normally construct permanent, roofed temples. Certainly, except for the curious Provençal shrines (pp 10–12) stone-built

17

sanctuaries are rare in the pre-Roman Celtic world. However, there is a steadily increasing body of evidence for wooden temples preceding Roman examples both in Britain and on the continent. One of the most interesting insular shrines is Frilford in Oxfordshire (Fig. 6). In the Roman period, there were two contiguous buildings here – a circular structure and a shrine of Romano-Celtic type (with rectangular cella and surrounding portico). Beneath both of these, there were Iron Age sanctuaries, a round one under the Romano-Celtic temple and a structure represented by a penannular ditch under the rotunda. The evidence for the former as a ritual site is circumstantial, but inside the penannular ditch were six postholes associated with the votive offerings of a ploughshare (perhaps a foundation-deposit) and a miniature sword and shield. Frilford is important because of its specific Iron Age evidence for cult-activity, and in the presence of two contiguous, perhaps complementary, sanctuaries in both the pre-Roman

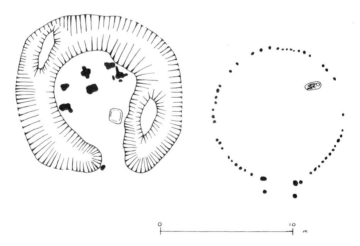

6   Ground-plan of contiguous Iron Age shrines, represented by penannular ditch and circular pattern of postholes, respectively; Frilford, Oxon (after Drury 1980, 61, fig 3.6).

and Roman periods. That Frilford may have been a cult-centre of some significance, at least in the Roman period, is supported by recent field-surveys which have revealed the presence of a small Roman town with an amphitheatre situated close to and perhaps actually within the temple-precinct. The Romano-Celtic shrine at Worth, Kent, was probably also preceded by an Iron Age temple for pre-Roman material beneath the cella included three Iron Age model shields. At Muntham Court, Sussex, the circular Romano-British temple, which was associated with a cult-well and with evidence of a healing cult, may have had a free Celtic precursor represented by Iron Age pits and postholes. At Haddenham, Cambs, where there was cult-activity from the Bronze Age to the Roman era, a Romano-British shrine first built in the first or second century AD, overlay Bronze Age cremations in a barrow, the Roman *temenos* embracing the barrow itself. Adjacent to this was an Iron Age penannular ditched enclosure. The Roman shrine was associated particularly with cult-activity involving sheep or goat sacrifices. Hayling Island was a pre-Roman shrine with a sacred enclosure surrounding a circular building which may or may not – like Frilford – have been roofed. A central pit possibly held a ritual stone or post. Here the cult-activity was concentrated not on the temple itself but on the outer *temenos*, where votive deposits of metalwork – including martial gear and cart or chariot-equipment – were offered to the gods, much of the material being first ritually damaged. Many so-called Iron Age shrines have been defined as such simply because they cannot readily be explained in terms of secular function. Small buildings in a number of hillforts are thus interpreted: such is the case at Danebury and South Cadbury where Alcock stresses that the Iron Age town was not only important as a centre for trade and industry but that 'the focal point of the whole settlement was religious'. At Maiden Castle the only certain religious evidence for a late Iron Age circular building is an infant-burial just outside the door, but it lay under a late Roman round building and near to a Romano-Celtic shrine, and so its context is ambiguous.

There are continental parallels to these British Celtic shrines. In Austria, St Margarethen-am-Silberberg may be compared with the Frilford sanctuaries; the Romano-Celtic temple at St Germain-les-Rocheux (Côte d'Or) had an Iron Age predecessor; and, in the Marne region, small Iron Age shrines were associated with Celtic cemeteries. The evidence for enclosed temple-buildings should not be overstressed. Many rites were performed in the open air, not necessarily involving buildings at all. It is significant that where structures are present, they rarely occupy the central position within the *temenos*. Thus, at Hayling though there was a building, the main rites seem to have taken place outside. It is important too to realise that in the Iron Age there were few 'purpose-built' shrines and Henig rightly points out that the sacred buildings at Hayling and Maiden Castle were little more than large huts, and perhaps served as no more than a focus – rather like a stone, pit or tree.    19

One exception to this is at Heathrow where, in the fourth century BC, a building with cella and portico appears to anticipate the much later and 'mass-produced' Romano-Celtic shrine-type. It should be remembered also that although temples following the fairly rigid architectural *schema* of concentric squares, circles or polygons, to define inner cella and outer ambulatory, predominated in Romano-Celtic western Europe, yet simple circular and rectangular temples – such as those at Brigstock, Muntham and Frilford – were built and used right through the Roman period.

Thus, the important role played by open-air enclosures, as opposed to roofed structures, should not be underestimated. The Frilford shrines may have been open to the sky, and there may have been several other small British sacred enclosures. On the Continent, the pre-Roman trend was towards large communal ritual open-air sites. The enclosures at Aulnay-aux-Planches (Marne) and Libeniče (Czech) are strikingly alike though widely separated in space and time (the French site dates to the tenth century BC and Libeniče to the third century BC). Both consist of sub-rectangular enclosures three hundred feet long containing evidence for possibly sacrificial human and animal burials. The Czech site contained the remains of two burnt upright timbers once adorned with neck-rings, as if they represented images of gods. Two German enclosures, the Goldberg and Goloring, both probably of sixth century BC date, follow an essentially similar pattern: the latter contained a huge central post, evidence of a similar cult-focus to those of Libeniče and Hayling, and perhaps symbolic of a sacred tree or column.

Ritual shafts or pits (discussed in detail in Chapter Four) may likewise have represented man-made foci of worship. In Britain the emphasis seems to have been on late Iron Age south-eastern Britain, but Bronze Age examples at Wilsford and Swanwick indicate the presence of a longstanding tradition. In Germany, certain enclosures or *viereck-shanzen*, dating to the late La Tène if not earlier, contain shafts which were foci of cult-activity: at Holzhausen an enclosure contained three shafts: one, eight metres deep, with a wooden pole at the bottom surrounded by traces of flesh and blood, echoing an almost identical occurrence at Swanwick much earlier, at about 1000 BC. The inference at both places is that a human sacrifice may have been tied to the stake and offered to a deity, perhaps of the Underworld.

Actual cult-offerings at pre-Roman shrines are sparse compared with Roman evidence, and this is what makes the interpretation of free Celtic cult-sites sometimes ambiguous. Human and animal sacrifices are sometimes suggested, as at Cadbury, Aulnay and Maiden Castle; model objects, so common in Romano-British shrines (below, pp 220–222) appear at Frilford and Worth; and deposits of metalwork were offered at Hayling. Celtic gold coins were consecrated to the deities of Harlow and at Hayling coins were covered with gold to present a glittering show to the god. Perhaps some of the most curious offerings are those of an 'antiquarian' nature: a tradition was established in pre-Roman sanctuaries in Britain and Europe where Neolilthic axes were offered to Celtic divinities. An additional practice in Gaulish shrines was ritually to smash these axes, and both here and in Britain, the implements were collected for votive purposes both by free and subsequent Romano-Celtic devotees.

Apart from deliberately constructed sanctuaries, the Celts made great use of natural topographical features. The Celtic word 'nemeton' denoting a sacred grove may be traced in derivative form in Celtic place-names from Britain (Aquae Arnemetiae at Buxton for example) and Spain to Galatia in Asia Minor (Drunemeton). The Irish for 'nemeton' is *fidnemed*. A number of classical authors, too, refer to sacred groves. Strabo speaks of the reunification of three Galatian tribes in a grove of sacred oaks, at Drunemeton for the purpose of discussion on government matters. Tacitus speaks of the forest-clearings of Anglesey as the last Druid stronghold against Rome. Dio Cassius refers to a sacred wood where human sacrifices to a war-goddess Andraste were carried out and Lucan refers to grim sacred woods in southern Gaul, which were sprinkled with human blood. It is possible that in some instances the term 'nemeton' may have been used loosely as synonymous with 'sanctuary'. Later commentaries on Lucan say that the Druids worshipped gods in woods without the use of temples. Romano-Celtic epigraphy informs us that deities dwelt in natural features such as mountains, rivers and springs. Allied to this, the archaeological evidence for votive deposits points to the offering of precious objects, frequently of a martial nature, to gods asssociated with the ground or underworld (Chapter Four) or with water (Chapter Five). It is interesting in the context of aquatic and warrior offerings that such practices are endorsed by Graeco-Roman authors on the Celts. Strabo mentions the treasure of gold ingots at the sacred lake belonging to the Volcae Tectosages at Toulouse in 106 BC; and Caesar remarks on dedications of weapons and booty heaped on the ground in honour of the god of the winning side; the sanctity of the hoard was such that it was left unmolested and did not need to be guarded.    21

### The Sanctity of Natural Features

The preceding discussion of shrines and sanctuaries leads logically to examination of a very significant trait in Celtic religion, that is the endowment with sanctity of natural features – a river, spring, lake, tree, mountain or simply a particular valley or habitat. The gods were everywhere, and this is expressed during the Romano-Celtic period, by god-names which betray this territorial association. The same kind of worship is found in rural Italy during this time, culminating in the relatively sophisticated Roman *Genius loci*, but it is in the Celtic milieu that topographical features assume particular emphasis. We have already alluded to votive deposits in or linked with water, and this is evidenced epigraphically. Water welled from springs in the ground and rivers flowed without obvious cause; many Romano-Celtic divinities were closely associated with water-veneration (Chapter Five), especially in its healing capacity. Trees and clumps of woodland too were revered. We looked earlier at the role of groves in the context of sanctuaries, and it is interesting that names of deities often reflect the sanctity of forests and trees: Nemetona (goddess of the Grove) is recorded at Altripp near Spier, and the name of the tribe in whose territory she was worshipped was the Nemetes. Single trees too were important: such tribal names as the Eburones (yew-tree) and Lemovices (elm) recall the essential rapport with trees. Epigraphy in Gaul also relates to individual trees or tree-species; and dedications were made to Fagus (beech-tree) in the Pyrenees, and there are many other similar examples of tree-reverence. Pliny comments on the association of oaks and Druids and it may be that the large timbers associated with such sites as Hayling (p 18) and Ivy Chimneys reflect the use of trees or tree-substitutes as cult-foci.

Other topographical names demonstrate the close link between divinity and the land. The god Alisonus (Côte d'Or) recalls the town-name of Alesia. Mountain-deities such as Vosegus of the Vosges, or Pyrenean dedications simply to 'mountain' reflect this territorial awareness. This veneration of natural phenomena extends, too, to animals (Chapter Six). In this context it is enough to mention epigraphic allusion where it is asociated with territory: the tribe of the Taurini and the place-name Tarva (Tarbes) in southern Gaul display the importance of the bull to the Gauls. Likewise the bear-goddess Artio of Muri in the Berne area of Switzerland, and the place-name Artomagus are significant; Arduinna the boar-goddess is etymologically linked with the forests of the Ardennes.

## Priests and Ritual

In the free (pre-Roman) Celtic phases, there is little archae-ological evidence specifically related to priests and associ-ated with ritual. During the Romano-Celtic period, apart from temples themselves and inscriptions referring to pri-ests, we have evidence for regalia and ceremonial equip-ment. Crowns and headdresses, as have been found at Hockwold, Norfolk and Cavenham, Suffolk, suggest that local clergy did wear liturgical garb, and it may even be that the gold chains with sun and moon-like symbols from such sites as Backworth in Durham and Dolaucothi, Dyfed (Chapter Two) were badges of office. Objects best defined as sceptres occasionally occur, for instance at Willingham Fen (Fig. 21) and Farley Heath (Chapter Two Fig. 22), and *sistra* or rattles may be evidenced at Brigstock, Willingham and Felmingham Hall, Norfolk. The curious object from Milton, Cambs may be a similar item of ceremonial: here a long-shafted bronze terminates in a flat oval with two perforations and may have supported bells for jangling in processions; the shaft is decorated with incised signs

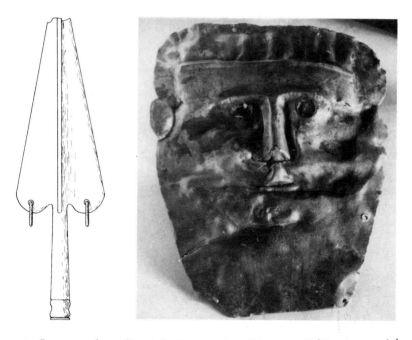

7   Ceremonial regalia. Left. Bronze tip of Romano-Celtic ceremonial stave with rings, possibly for the suspension of bells; from hoard of religious bronzes at Felmingham Hall, Norfolk. Illustration P J Lopeman; copyright: Miranda Green. British Museum. Right. Pew-ter mask from culvert of baths; Bath. Photograph: Berry Naggar. Roman Baths Museum.

including St Andrew's Crosses, which could be sacred symbols. A fragment of what may be a similar object, consisting of a bronze rod marked with diagonal crosses, has recently been found in Chelmsford. Some other regalia is of interest since particular attention is paid to the human face, and we know that the head held a religious fascination for the Celts. Metal face-masks, like those from Bath and Tarbes could have been made for the priest to hold in front of his face during religious ceremonies; perhaps, on certain occasions, it was forbidden to look on the face of one so close to the divine, or alternatively, the priest could have been shielding himself from the presence of the deity. The Tarbes mask may date as early as the third century BC. In the context of masks, a large one, reputedly from East Anglia is particularly interesting; it was made of gold and, in typical Celtic style, has round eyes and prominent brows. This mask was not worn; perforations in the gold suggest that it was nailed up, perhaps on the wall of a shrine, to

8  Lead *defixio* invoking Sulis, from Roman reservoir; Bath. Copyright: Bath Museums Service. Roman Baths Museum.

represent a god. All over the Roman world metal plaques, often feather or leaf-shaped in bronze or silver, were made with a similar function of adorning shrines with the image or dedication to the resident deities. Conversely, lead *defixiones* or curse-tablets were employed with the more sinister purpose of condemning a wrongdoer in the eyes of the gods.

Little is known about the objects used in Celtic liturgy. Perhaps the most famous category of item is the ritual vessel or cauldron. Cult-vessels were being used from the Middle/ late Bronze Age in Europe, and it is suggested that there could be a connection with water-cults (pp 145–147). Celtic cauldrons are ubiquitous in archaeological and historical records, but the most famous vessel is the great gilded silver bowl from Gundestrup in Denmark. This cauldron is referred to repeatedly in this book, and the mythological scenes on its silver plates are much-discussed. There is some controversy as to whether the vessel is Celtic or not and whether its origins lay in the Gaulish world. Caution must be exercised in any interpretation: certain motifs – like the carnyx or war-trumpet and shields – are definitely of La Tène type; but the silversmith had access to and used a wide range of symbols, some of which have no parallel in the western Celtic repertoire of iconography. Indeed, Collis has pointed out that the closest artistic parallels lie in

9  Gilt Silver cauldron; Raevemose Bog, Gundestrup, Jutland, Denmark. First century BC. Copyright: Nationalmuseet, Copenhagen. 69cm diameter.

Romania and argues that the cauldron may have been made there. I believe that there are Celtic elements in the religious imagery as well as in weapon-types; here the stag-horned god is surely the Celtic Cernunnos, and the ram-horned snake is too idiosyncratic a beast to belong to more than one culture. Still, the cauldron's iconography is an amalgam and its provenance in Jutland should also not be forgotten.

## The Druids

The most famous (or infamous) priesthood in the Celtic world was the Druidic. A number of Graeco-Roman authors, including Strabo, Diodorus Siculus and most notably Caesar describe the Druids, but these three derive their information from a single source, Posidonius, and so the common ground between them is not itself significant. There is no need to be surprised at the existence of a powerful religious leadership within the context of Indo-European society, but there are varying views as to the real importance of the Druids in the Celtic world. Tierney and Harding argue that their significance may be more apparent than real in that Caesar confines his remarks to a small part of Book VI of de Bello Gallico. Nash points out that the influence of the Druids was perhaps largely social rather than political and that in this role they were probably very powerful indeed.

It appears that once the main aristocratic hierarchy of Celtic society disintegrated under the impact of Rome, the Druids lost their national influence, for they must have been heavily dependent upon tribal chiefs in terms of status and support and even without Roman persecution, the Druids' power would naturally have dwindled. Historical evidence indicates that Druidism was tolerated in Augustan times as long as Roman citizens were not involved. Tiberius opposed the priesthood, and Claudius tried hard to eliminate it. The Druids enjoyed a brief comeback in the Gaulish rising under Civilis in AD 69–70, but thereafter history is silent until the third century when Druids are recorded as being associated with prophecies against Severus Alexander and Maximin. In the fourth century the Druids reappear, and the Bordeaux poet Ausonius refers to two famous Druids and the tradition of succession from father to son.

There are recurrent references to Druids, as prophets and soothsayers, in the Irish sources; perhaps the most prominent was Cathbad of Ulster. Our evidence for Druids in the free Celtic world comes from Graeco-Roman literary sources. Whatever the precise nature of their influence, there is no doubt that they were a national religious force in Gaul and Britain. Caesar informs us that their main cult-centre was in Britain and that they originated there. The Druids were certainly magicians, if nothing else, in whose power was the entire oral tradition of religion and ritual. Caesar, our most prolific source, says that the Druids officiated at the worship of the gods, regulated sacrifices and gave rulings on all religious questions. On a fixed date every year they assembled in a sacred place in the territory of the Carnutes (near Chartres); and they were no doubt responsible for the fertility cycle and all its associated cult-activity. Pliny tells of a feast prepared on the sixth day of the moon, involving the Druids who climbed a sacred oak, cut off a mistletoe bough using a 'golden' sickle and caught it in a white cloak; two bulls were sacrificed. The importance of the Druids in divination cannot be over-estimated; in both classical and insular sources, they are recorded as being not only priests but also prophets. The importance of omens is demonstrated by the existence both in Ireland and Gaul of unlucky and lucky days. The Coligny Calendar, found near Bourg-en-Bresse (Ain) is probably Augustan: the bronze sheet bears epigraphic evidence for the division of each month into a good and bad half, there being an appropriate time for each act. In the Ulster Cycle of prose tales, the importance of omens is shown by the episode of Queen Medb of Connaught who was prevented by the Druids from commencing battle for a fortnight in order to await an auspicious day.

The main fascination of Graeco-Roman historians for the Druids was their role in human sacrifice, an emphasis which may have been designed deliberately to disgust their readers as a practice typical of outlandish barbarians. The literature makes it clear that as far as the Druids themselves were concerned, the main aim of human sacrifice was not so much the propitiation or appeasement of the gods but divination. Diodorus and Strabo describe the custom of stabbing victims and foretelling the future by observing the death-throes. Evildoers were imprisoned for five years and then killed by impaling: prisoners of war were used as sacrificial victims together, on occasions, with their beasts; the victim could be burned alive in a huge wicker man-shaped image, or shot with arrows (interesting since archery was not a normal method of fighting at this time). British human sacrifice is attested by Tacitus on the island of Anglesey where, in a grim sacred grove, altars were drenched with human blood and entrails (a grisly reminder of the stakes at Swanwick and Holzhausen) which were consulted by the Druids for divinatory purposes. Lucan mentions that the Druids, living deep in the forests, claimed to understand the secrets of the gods. The poet comments that they 'resumed the barbarous rites of their wicked religion', and describes the Celtic deities Esus, Teutates and Taranis, whom the Gauls propitiated with human sacrifices. Commentators on Lucan's text elaborate on this, describing the appeasement of Taranis by burning, Teutates by drowning and Esus by hanging from a tree (perhaps the elements of fire, air and water were deliberately represented). Later in the poem itself Lucan refers to a *nemeton* at Marseille where altars were heaped with hideous offerings and every tree sprinkled with human blood, and Lucan mentions that even the priests were wary of entering the grove at certain times.

Certainly the interpretation of human sacrifice suggested by Caesar is that the power of the gods could only be neutralised or controlled if one human life were exchanged for another. Thus if Gauls were threatened by illness or battle, then the Druids organised human sacrifice; if criminals were not available, then the innocent would have to supply that life for a life.

*Human Sacrifice and Head-Hunting*

We have seen that the Druids were fundamentally concerned with human sacrifice. According to historical testimony, they always officiated at such events. In this connection, it may be significant that the murdered bog-body, Lindow Man (below, pp 128, 144) was found to have mistletoe in his stomach; it is not impossible that he was a Druidic sacrifice. Strabo mentions that the Cimbri likewise despatched their victims and observed their dying struggles for divinatory purposes; this Teutonic (not Celtic) tribe cut the throats of its victims, collected and then examined the blood which was caught in cauldrons. The distaste of classical authors for human sacrifice is evident from their writings (though it was not so many centuries since it was practised in the Mediterranean world). Archaeologically, there is some evidence for this grisly rite. The suggestive remains at Bronze Age Swanwick and Iron Age Holzhausen have already been referred to, and from the later free Celtic phase in Britain comes fairly clear evidence that human sacrifice was practised on occasions. The infant buried at the Maiden Castle shrine may have been deliberately killed; and at Danebury three male corpses in a pit at the bottom of a quarry hollow, buried when the rampart was built, may have been offerings to the gods of the territory on which the hillfort was constructed. Some of the bodies at Danebury were weighted down with stones perhaps to prevent their spirits rising, and dismembered skeletons suggest ritual body-exposure to allow the spirits time to depart. It is possible here that the burial evidence relates specifically to unclean or sacrificial death. There is other evidence from Iron Age Britain too: burials at, for instance, Wandlebury and Hayling Island (Chapter Four) were maybe the result of some rite involving human sacrifice, and the young man crammed face down in a pit under the rampart at South Cadbury was probably a foundation offering.

Most striking, both in terms of archaeological and written evidence, is the emphasis on human heads. At Danebury, there was a preponderance of adult male skulls, placed in the bottom of storage pits, presumably to bless the corn, unless the pits were being used secondarily as rubbish/burial pits. At the Iron Age *oppida* of Bredon Hill, Worcs, and Stanwick, Yorks, the position of human skulls suggests that they had been attached to poles at the fort-gates; and this evidence is echoed at the Celtiberian *oppidum* at Puig Castelar in northern Spain. Shrines too bear witness to the dedication of heads to the gods. A number of the pre-Roman Celto-Ligurian sanctuaries of southern Gaul display the grim tradition of offering the heads of sacrificial or battle-victims. In many of these shrines, from as early as the fourth century BC, skulls were placed in niches cut in the stone structure for their insertion; niches were present at, for instance, St Blaise,

10 Stone pillar with incised severed heads. The mouthless faces and closed eyes are suggestive of their portrayal of dead enemies. Third–second century BC; Entremont, Provence. c 2.57m high (after Benoit 1981, 54).

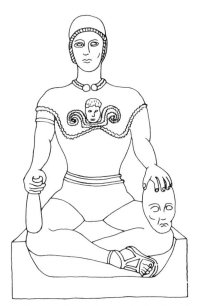

11   Stone squatting figure of warrior-god with hand resting on human
     head. Third–sevond century BC; Entremont, Provence. c 1.5m
     high (after Benoit 1981, 87).

Entremont and Roquepertuse (all in Provence). The
Roquepertuse skulls probably date to the third century BC,
and are interesting in that they are the skulls of strong men
in the prime of life, and this may suggest that they represent
war-dead. One of the Entremont skulls nailed onto a wall,
actually had a javelin-head embedded in it. The presence of
carved stone heads as well as real skulls, implies that the
head was an essential offering: perhaps if the human supply
dried up, then symbolic representations would do instead.
A shrine of Roman date in Britain demonstrates ritual
remarkably similar to those of southern Gaul: at Cosgrove,
Northants, a simple rectangular shrine had a human head
buried in one wall.

   The tradition of head-hunting or head-collecting and
ritual implied by archaeology, is mentioned again and again
in both Graeco-Roman and vernacular literature. Livy
remarks on the killing of a Roman general Postumius in 216
BC by the North Italian tribe of the Boii, who cut off his
head, cleaned it out, gilded it and used the skull as a
cult-vessel. Several writers attest the practice among the
Celts of collecting the heads of enemies in battle, fastening
them to their saddles or impaling them on spears. Livy
speaks of the Senonian Gauls doing just this in 295 BC
when they defeated a Roman legion at Clusium, and
Diodorus and Strabo inform us that the heads of important

victims were embalmed in cedar oil and cherished above all treasures. The placing of heads in temples, attested archaeologically as we have seen, is supported by the literature.

Both Irish and Welsh sources support the Celtic reverence for the human head, and indeed the practice of human sacrifice. The Ulster hero Cú Chulainn collected the heads of the vanquished and placed them on stones. Another Ulster warrior, Conall Cernach, boasted that he slept every night with the head of a slain Connaught man under his knee, and the Irish sources attest the making of a collection of brainballs as battle trophies (the brain was extracted, mixed with lime and allowed to harden to a cement-like substance). The magical properties of heads are referred to in Welsh and Irish literature: in the Mabinogion Bran is mortally wounded and at his request his companions cut off his head and carry it with them on their travels as a talisman; the head of the Ulsterman Conall Cernach, too, had magic powers and it was prophecied that the men of Ulster would gain strength from using this head, which was of supernatural size, as a drinking-vessel.

12   Celtic stone head in relief; Carmarthen, Dyfed. Copyright: National Museum of Wales.

The importance of head-ritual is unequivocal. Human sacrifices were made and the head preserved as being of the greatest cult-significance. Battle-victims, whether killed in warfare or after capture, were decapitated and their heads enshrined. The cult-importance of heads manifests itself throughout Celtic religion; in looking at death-ritual (Chapter Four) we will see that the dead were sometimes beheaded; and in iconography (Chapter Seven) the head is frequently exaggerated or it may be used by itself to symbolise the whole body. Why the human head was so

31

important can never be entirely understood, but it was the means of identifying an individual, and was recognised as the power-centre for human action. I refute any suggestion (Chapter Seven) that the head itself was worshipped, but it was clearly venerated as the most significant element in a human or divine image, representing the whole.

## The Celtic Gods and Belief

Caesar comments that the Gauls were a very religious people; and this is endorsed by the seeming presence of the gods everywhere – in rivers, mountains and in each corner of Celtic territory, as well as by taboos and ritual. The all-pervasive nature of Celtic religion is demonstrated at Camonica Valley where some of the Iron Age (and earlier) carvings occur on rocks in the middle of remote forest. But what form did these gods take? The picture we get – from pre-Roman iconography, literary sources and what we can glean from the Mediterranean gloss on Romano-Celtic evidence – is confused and muddling. Were there many localised gods or was there one main deity with a number of aspects? The evidence points both ways. A glance at the epigraphic record of the Romano-Celtic period reveals about 400 god-names, over 300 of which occur once only; this argues for disparateness, and certainly demonstrates strong localisation. One problem is in the pairing or twinning of Celtic and Roman names: for instance, Mars is linked with several different Celtic epithets. This may indicate no more than the uneasiness of any attempt to equate the strictly functional order of Roman gods with the shadowy, multi-functional character of Celtic deities. It is a mistake to place the elusive Celtic divinity into methodical Graeco-Roman boxes: this is 'certainly to misunderstand the aggressive individuality of Celtic society. . .'. Sjoestedt would argue that Celtic tribes were too disunited to share a common pantheon. However, there are arguments for some degree of mutual belief or way of looking at the supernatural. The Druids, in matters of ritual at least, may have had a unifying role in the annual council held in Carnutian territory. This commonality is supported to an extent by the widespread distribution of some iconographic god-forms – for instance horned deities; mother-goddesses; triplism; animism and many more – during the Romano-Celtic period. Certain recurring themes, such as the veneration of natural phenomena – especially water – may be traced back into the Iron Age and beyond. In the Romano-Celtic phase some definite iconographic patterns may be established: for example, the horseman-god riding down a giant (Chapter Two) appears to have been a favourite among the tribes of North East Gaul; the hammer-god Sucellus was worshipped principally in the Rhône and Saône Valleys; the three-headed form in Belgic Gaul, especially among the Remi; Cernunnos (the stag-antlered god) in Central France; and divine couples among the Aedui. Because of the paucity of pre-Roman Celtic iconography, we have no means of knowing how far these patterns existed earlier. One should not however seek an organised pantheon for the Celts; their prime concern (as with all prehistoric non-Mediterranean European peoples) was to constrain and control supernatural powers to a beneficent end. Lambrechts argues a view opposite to that suggested by the multiplicity of god-names and forms, and postulates one great, ill-defined, multi-facetted deity. All we can say with any confidence is that by the Roman period, with sharper definition and formalisation, both major and minor gods were acknowledged. Before that time the animistic aspect of cult is the most pronounced, together with certain ritual behaviour concerned particularly with sacrificial offerings and with attitudes to the afterlife. The vernacular sources do not help us a great deal but at least two general features may be isolated. One is the tribal emphasis: Irish gods, like the Dagda, were tribal gods, and in the Ulster Cycle the heroes swear by the gods of the tribe; indeed it has been pointed out that, in general, Celtic male deities were usually tribal and females were invariably types of mother-goddess. The other feature found in the vernacular sources is shape-shifting, the ability to move at will between different human and animal forms. This may, archaeologically, account at least in part for the curious faces and pseudo-faces which leer out from Iron Age metalwork; moreover it may also explain the very fundamental importance of animal iconography in the Celtic world (Chapter Six).

## Features of Celtic Cult-Expression

Certain characteristics of physical cult-expression may be isolated as distinctive of celticism, even allowing for the iconographic influence of the Roman period. This may be done by looking at the pre-Roman phases and by examining features which are essentially alien to the Mediterranean world. By the later Bronze Age representations of birds, bulls and wheel-like symbols imply some kind of pre-Celtic

European cult-expression, quite widespread, and probably connected with fertility, power and the sun. This symbolism continues into the Hallstatt period. When we come to the full Celtic La Tène, a new, specifically decorative Celtic art, based mainly on metalwork, appears at first glance to shut out man and to be essentially aniconic. Compared to the man-obsessed Mediterranean world this may be true, but we have seen that Iron Age representations of deities do occur in this period. Lucan speaks of wooden images of deities crudely hewn on tree-trunks. Wooden figures such as that from a wicker hut at Ballachulish, Argyll (Fig. 5), which may be of first century BC date or earlier, may testify to the truth of Lucan's observation, though the dating of isolated images is notoriously problematical. Whilst stone Iron Age god-images are rare, we have seen that in Germany and southern Gaul (pp 10–12) they are not unknown. Figural depictions in bronze occasionally appear as early as the Hallstatt period, exemplified by the seventh-sixth century cult-vehicle from Strettweg in

13  Bronze seventh-sixth century BC cult-wagon; Strettweg, Austria.
Copyright: Landesmuseum Joanneum, Graz.

Austria where a wheeled platform bears a central female figure carrying a bowl above her head and surrounded by horsemen and foot-soldiers with spears and shields. But human figures *per se* are rare among the free Celts and here the remark of Diodorus Siculus concerning the Gaulish king Brennus in the early fourth century BC may be relevant 'Brennus the king of the Gauls, on entering a temple (at Delphi) found no dedications of gold or silver, and when he came only upon images of stone and wood, he laughed at them (the Greeks), to think that men, believing that gods have human form, should set up their images in wood and stone' (*XXII* 9, 4). There is a higher incidence of animal-figures in the free Celtic phase, especially on the Continent. In the Hallstatt metalwork repertoire, the Urnfield water-bird and associated sun-sign still survives, and horses and cattle are common (Fig. 1) motifs. In the La Tène, boar images were fairly common and in the first centuries BC and AD blacksmiths made fire-dogs with bull-head terminals, probably possessing at least some symbolic or quasi-symbolic significance.

If we look at features during the Romano-Celtic period which are alien to the Graeco-Roman world, we can see that whilst the Roman stimulus in method of cult-expression is obvious and influential, the very nature of gods represented is often entirely new. Mother-goddesses, the horse-goddess Epona, the conquering horseman, are but few examples of a new and varied repertoire. Of particular interest is that during the Romano-Celtic period, we see coming to representative fruition ideas whose roots may be traced, sometimes faintly, during the Iron Age. The wheel-god (Chapter Two) existing in full human form by the second century AD, was worshipped by the wheel-symbol alone long before; indeed on the first century BC Gundestrup Cauldron, he may appear for the first time as a human image. Horned gods, ubiquitous during the Roman period, though not Roman, may be portrayed much earlier, at Holzerlingen. The animal-emphasis, absent in that fundamental form in the Mediterranean world, occurs from the Urnfield period around 1200 BC right through to the Roman phase. Portrayals of gods as heads alone may be traced in both periods, and there are other examples of recurring themes which straddle later prehistory and the period of Roman influence on Celtic lands. Whether or not the Celts used any kind of uniform system of religious symbols the continuity is there, sometimes overt, more often implied. The Celtic reluctance to construct images of deities should not blind us to the existence of symbolism,

35

and the Roman stimulus in cult-expression, whilst sometimes confusing, serves not only to enhance the impoverished record of the Iron Age but also to display the fertile religious conceptuality already in existence in the free Celtic phase.

## 'Interpretatio Romana' and 'Interpretatio Celtica'

The influence of Roman religious stimuli on the Celtic world took the form both of physical expression, iconography and epigraphy, and of thought-processes applied to the rigidly functional and universal character of Roman gods as exported to Celtic lands. The interaction between the shadowy, multi-functional and more localised gods of the Celts and the more formal Roman pantheon produced a hybrid religious culture which is as fascinating as it is full of problems of interpretation. The normal Roman representative guise (the naturalistic human form) may conceal a deity who is completely alien and Celtic in character. Epigraphy is equally confusing. Bober puts the problem succinctly in her comment that, on the one hand, the vacuum of Celtic aniconism produced in the Roman period cult-art which was heavily biased towards the classical (the same being true of epigraphy). On the other hand, it appears that the Romans naïvely assumed that Celtic gods were Roman ones. It is worthwhile to look at a few examples of this hybrid and ambiguous cult-expression. The Roman Mars was popular in Gaul and Britain, but he is known by numerous *different* Celtic surnames or epithets, so we do not simply have equation of a Roman deity with a Celtic god assumed similar enough to be twinned with a suitable Roman counterpart. A dedication may be to Mars, but sometimes equated with a native healer-god – like Lenus Mars at Trier; or the dedication might be to Mars, but the accompanying representation might depict a peaceful, rural divinity with cornucopiae, as at Bisley in Gloucestershire. The implication is that union between Roman gods, defined strictly by function, and the ill-defined local spirits of the Celts is an uneasy and muddling one, though such equation occurred spontaneously, for whatever reason. In the case of Mars or Mercury (where twinning most frequently occurs) the process may well have happened because Mars had an Italian aspect of agricultural/protective divinity, in addition to his war-role, which appealed to the Celts with their emphasis on territory. Likewise, the Roman fertility/prosperity facet to Mercury's cult may have struck a chord

14 Stone votive tablets to Mars Olloudius and Romulus; Custom
Scrubs, Glos. Photograph: Betty Naggar. Gloucester City Museum.

in Celtic belief. The occasional confusion between Mars and
Mercury noted in the Celtic world – as on a Uley curse-
tablet – may be explained in terms of the prosperity-
interpretation of both. This may also account for the
apparent contradiction in the Lucan commentaries where
Esus and Teutates are each linked in turn with Mars and
Mercury. What is very interesting is the Celtic fondness for
divine couples, alien to the Mediterranean world. Mars
Loucetius ('Brilliant') has a wholly Celtic consort Nemetona
at Bath and at Mainz. Mercury possesses a Celtic spouse,
Rosmerta 'The Good Purveyor'), who enhances Mercury's
Celtic fertility-function. It is interesting that where couples
are present, the goddess is the more likely to retain a Celtic
name, whilst the male deity adopts a Roman title. This may
reflect the essentially territorial role of Celtic goddesses.

Very frequently, a Roman art-form is borrowed to portray
deities who are totally Celtic in character and do not appear
in the Mediterranean world. The form may owe much to
Graeco-Roman mimesis (see Chapter Seven) but there
Roman influence ends. Examples are the triple mothers,
Epona, Sequana of the Seine, Artio of Berne and Arduinna
of the Ardennes. The evidence, as I see it, is not that the
Romans transformed Celtic gods into civilised Roman ones,
nor of suppression by the conquering power. Rather there is
indication of active encouragement of such Celtic divinities

37

as Nemausus of Nîmes and Sulis of Bath whose pre-existing spring-sanctuaries were positively embellished by the Romans. Indeed the very alien nature of some Celtic iconography should not be forgotten (Chapter Seven). Many North British gods owe little to classical realism, and the three stylised mother-figures from Bath (Fig. 92) would have been curious cult-objects for a romanised Briton. Finally, in assessing romanisation, we should remember that many lower class rural Celts, at any rate in North and West Britain, were probably not Latin speakers, particularly outside military areas, and one would expect their cults and beliefs to have been little altered by the presence of Rome.

# CHAPTER TWO: CULTS OF SUN AND SKY

## Introduction

Celestial phenomena and, in particular, the apparent miracle of the rising and setting sun, must have inspired human awe and reverence from early prehistoric times. The reappearance of the sun, moon and stars by day and night, and the phenomena of lightning, thunder and rain, must have been seen as irrefutable evidence of the existence of supernatural power from the beginning of man's existence as a sentient, self-conscious and world-conscious being. The emanations of the sky (especially sun and rain) symbolised life, particularly to the early farming societies. One may assume, even in earlier prehistory, a considerable pre-occupation with natural forces and events.

It is, of course, impossible to have any real idea of when man in Europe first endowed sun and sky with the properties of a formalised deity nor when he first envisaged such an entity in human form. The earliest anthropomorphic cults seem to have been more concerned with female fertility (pp 74–78). By the Romano-Celtic period in western Europe, both Romans and Celts possessed celestial gods and the Roman divinity, Jupiter, combined the functions of sky and father-god. Jupiter was traditionally represented in iconography as a majestic, bearded, mature male and was accompanied by the emblems of eagle, sceptre and thunderbolt. Each attribute symbolised an aspect of the divinity's role: the eagle reflected the vast expanse of the firmament; the thunderbolt, the power of the thunder-clap wielded by a sky-lord; and the sceptre represented Jupiter's role as chief of the Roman pantheon. Among the Celtic peoples, where religious development had not proceeded as far as in the Roman world, celestial symbolism was less formalised. Its most important feature was its solar aspect (missing from the Graeco-Roman cult), typified by the sun-disc, usually portrayed as a spoked wheel, which is a regular feature both of pre-Roman and Romano-Celtic cult-imagery. This motif is a natural and understandable choice since it combines concepts both of the motion through the sky and physical similarity – the nave or hub representing the sun itself, the spokes the sun's rays and the rim or felloe the surrounding nimbus of light.

In the later first millennium BC in Europe, it is possible to trace a celestial, predominantly solar, cult symbolised by the existence of wheel-motifs, which may fairly be interpreted as solar signs. Representations of gods in human form are extremely rare at this time. I will confine my survey of the prehistoric evidence for sun and sky symbolism to the period of the full Celtic Iron Age during the last five centuries before Christ, but the roots extend further into the prehistoric past, as the following examples show. The Trundholm Chariot from Denmark dates to circa 1300 BC and comprises a bronze model horse drawing a bronze disc, gold-plated on one side, carried on a base set with three pairs of wheels; this is usually interpreted as a solar-disc. Objects from the Hallstatt Iron Age, dated between 700 and 500 BC, illustrate with great clarity the continuing practice of solar cult-expression at this time. The Hallstatt cemetery in Austria produced sheet bronze vessels bearing imagery in the form of sun-wheels flanked by water-birds, as on the container from Grave 507. The continuing occurrence of these motifs can be recognized throughout the Celtic Iron Age and Roman periods. Most vessels of this period bearing cult-iconography are of beaten bronze, but an important exception is the pure gold chased bowl from Zürich-Alstetten, Switzerland which depicts not only stylised beasts but also sun and crescent-moon motifs. Solar symbols are present too on armour and weapons, presumably with a protective or apotropaic function; a Hallstatt grave, for instance, contained an iron dagger with a ornamental gilded hilt in the form of two adjacent wheels.

## SKY-SYMBOLISM IN THE CELTIC IRON AGE

As in preceding later prehistoric phases, metalwork is by far the commonest medium for symbolic expression. Jewellery, weaponry and, for the first time coinage, all imply that the cult of sky and sun remained dominant. Quantities of wheel-models occur together in archaeological contexts, and it is possible to see the emergence of a pattern of material evidence which was later to become firmly established during the subsequent period of Roman occupation of Celtic lands. From now on wheel-miniatures or models play an increasingly significant role in symbolism. Whilst it is not possible to establish their precise function, it is justifiable to assume a talismanic purpose when model wheels were worn on the person. Miniature spoked wheels, usually of bronze or lead, occur from Britain in the West to

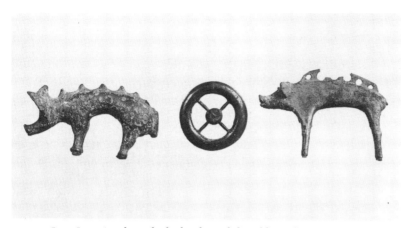

15  Late Iron Age hoard of wheel-model and boar-figurines; Hounslow, Middlesex. Copyright: Trustees of the British Museum.

Czechoslovakia in the East, and appear on settlement sites, graves and, very occasionally in shrines. The Hounslow find of a wheel and bronze boars of late Iron Age type may imply the presence of a temple; but at Villeneuve au Châtelot (Aube) huge numbers of (mostly lead) wheel-models have been found at a temple which was established as early as the late La Tène and carried on into the Roman period. Here at least, a sacral function for these models is not in doubt, and the numbers suggest that they could have served as a kind of religious currency for devotion to the sun-god. Occurrence of wheel-miniatures in sepulchral contexts also argues for a religious significance. For instance, a belt-fragment with a suspended wheel amulet comes from a Swiss grave in the Valais region; at Diarville (Meurthe & Moselle), a man was buried wearing a torc (or necklet) and with a wheel-shaped ornament positioned behind the head; and a series of late Iron Age interments at Basle were each buried with a simple four-spoked miniature wheel. The Dürrnberg hillfort near Hallein in Austria has produced several wheel-models from graves: one grave, that of a small boy dated circa 400 BC, contained jewellery including a realistic wheel-model; another grave, the tomb of a young girl, contained a miniature wheel and model axe. This is especially interesting since bone-evidence indicates that, though she was about eight or ten years old, she was very stunted; she obviously needed her talismans for her journey to the afterlife. It seems reasonable to believe that, where such miniature items occur in graves, they were buried with the dead as talismans against the evil of death and an unknown otherworld. If, by this period, sun-symbols were associated in religion with a specific,

41

celestial, solar god rather than a mere amorphous supernatural power, then this may be evidence of the invocation of such a deity as a protector of the dead, a light in dark places. Apart from graves, wheel-models are frequent finds in *oppida* or Celtic towns, from France to eastern Europe. At Alesia models and moulds for their manufacture survive. At settlements in the Argonne, tiny lead wheel-models were cast in long strips. Chenet postulates the charming idea that these may be explained as Celtic 'rosaries' but a more prosaic, perhaps more likely interpretation is that multiplicity enhanced potency and that the ownership of several cheap lead models was sometimes considered as more efficacious than the possession of a single bronze solar amulet. Another context is that of rivers: over 200 miniature wheels of Iron Age or early Roman date have been found in the Loire near Orléans. Water-deposition was a common cult-act among the Celts (Chapter Five); the reasons are obscure, but objects may have been cast into water for many purposes. The act may have defunctionalised them for the gods, invoked specific water-spirits, or the wheels may have accompanied corpses committed to water for burial.

The solar sign appears as a jewellery motif in the Celtic Iron Age (possibly once again with talismanic significance); and it occurs too as an apotropaic (protective) sign on armour. In the Marne region of eastern France necklets or torcs from, for example, Pogny and Catulauni bear frontal ornamentation in the form of wheels flanked by water-birds, an association of symbols continuing from the tradition of Late Bronze Age and Hallstatt metalwork of at least 500 years before. *Fibulae* or safety-pin brooches, like those from the Marne region and that from Hradiste in Czechoslovakia bear attached wheel-pendants. Sculptural evidence proves that the wheel-sign could form part of helmets and body-armour. The Roman arch at Orange (Vaucluse), probably dating to the second half of the first century BC depicts a range of La Tène weapons including several bull-horn helmets decorated with wheel-symbols, and cuirasses with pectoral wheel-pendants. Sprockhoff suggests that the occurrence of the wheel-motif on Celtic helmets seems almost like the emblem of a secret society. Weapons as well as protective armour bore celestial imagery. A La Tène burial at Hallstatt (Grave 994) was accompanied by a sword-sheath of bronze and iron bearing a curious and complex iconography which may well possess religious significance. Its imagery includes horsemen, wrestlers, and two pairs of men each holding between them a rayed solar

16   Bronze wheel-brooch; Lakenheath, Suffolk. Photograph: Miranda
Green. Cambridge University Museum of Archaeology & Anthropology.

wheel; a dagger from Mainz encrusted with gold solar and
lunar motifs may also be of Iron Age date. One is reminded
of Caesar's remark concerning German religion: 'they count
as gods . . . . Sun, Fire and Moon' (VI, 21).

The role of solar and sky symbolism on Celtic pre-Roman
coinage is of the greatest interest and significance in relation
to later Romano-Celtic iconography. Coinage was copied
and adapted by the Celtic peoples from Greek and Roman
prototypes as early as the third century BC. In northern Gaul
and Britain especially, horse and associated sun-wheel
motifs are particularly important in view of the later
Romano-Celtic links between both solar and equine
religious symbolism. Allen is convinced that the imagery of
Celtic coinage possessed profound religious significance
(Allen 1980). On some coins, one may find the wheel
beneath the horse, in which case it probably represents a
chariot (many Celtic coins were stylistic degenerations of
prototypes of Philip of Macedon with the head of Apollo on

43

the obverse and a charioteer on the reverse); but where a naturalistic spoked wheel is positioned on coins above the horse, it must surely be interpreted as a solar sign. The presence of realistic wheel-representations as suns on Celtic coins in an otherwise frequently abstract, degenerate art-medium demonstrates the significant role of the object as a symbol. Wheels, crescents and swastikas (pp 55–56) are all common on coins. On the obverse of some Armorican issues an anthropomorphic head is accompanied by a wheel-motif, presumably to identify the head as that of the sun-god, and on a coin from Petersfield, Hampshire, a stag-antlered deity displays a solar wheel between his horns.

One final object remains to be looked at in a pre-Roman Iron Age context. This is the Gundestrup Cauldron (Fig. 9) the large silver cult-bowl from Denmark, beyond the Celtic areas, but believed, because of its iconographic decoration, to be of second-first century B.C. Celtic origin. The metal of the cauldron is almost pure silver; it is massive and was externally gilded; it must certainly have been an item of great significance in religous ceremonies, though its purely Celtic origin is open to question. The vessel is composed of five inner and seven outer plates depicting Celtic mythological scenes; on one inner panel the bust of a bearded god is apparently being offered a wheel held by a diminutive but complete human figure, possibly a devotee or attendant, wearing a short tunic and a bull-horned helmet. Only half of the wheel is portrayed but when whole it would have been a sixteen-spoked highly realistic Iron Age cart or chariot wheel. It is possible that we have here a depiction of a solar god in human form. The helmet of the accompanying individual immediately recalls the wheel-bearing helmets carved on the Orange Arch, arguably of similar date to the cauldron.

This summary of the evidence for a sky-cult from later prehistoric Europe seeks to demonstrate that the wheel as a solar symbol was not suddenly introduced when we find it linked to the Roman Jupiter's cult in Gaul and Britain. Important points which emerge include the consistent, recurring use of miniature wheels as talismanic elements, the association of the sun-motif with, for example, horse, bull and water-bird; and the occasional glimpses of anthropomorphic representations, possibly deities, connected with solar symbolism. Whether one may trace genuine continuity of trends and ideas between the Celtic Iron Age and the Romano-Celtic period is open to some doubt. The most that can be said is that there are traces of a sky-cult, using the wheel as a symbol of solar power, sometimes associated with other specific motifs, which recur over several centuries and over wide distances.

## SKY-SYMBOLISM IN THE ROMANO-CELTIC WORLD

In examining the archaeological evidence for Romano-Celtic sky-symbolIsm, it is possible to identify a number of constantly recurring motifs. Of these the most prominent is the solar sign of the wheel, as mentioned above, but other celestial symbols include the swastika, rosette, circle, thunderbolt, double-axe and S-sign (the last three probably being thunder-motifs). Whilst most of these images would appear to be of Celtic or Roman origin, one at least – the swastika – possessed an importance to people beyond the European (and even the Indo-European) world.

The close contact between Celtic and Roman peoples after the initial occupation of Celtic territory caused the juxtaposition of celestial beliefs belonging to both cultures. The Romans introduced the cult of Jupiter or of Jupiter Best and Greatest, at one and the same time the head of the pantheon, a celestial deity and the focus of fealty of the Roman peoples to the spirit and concept of Rome. It should be stressed that this divinity was not a solar power. Evidence has been cited to show that pre-Roman peoples of non-Mediterranean Europe worshipped a sky-god of their own, probably originating long before the Roman, and quite possibly even before the Celtic era (above, pp 40–45). The main sphere of this non-Roman god was that of the sun, hence the consistent symbolism of the spoked wheel. Before the appearance of Roman influence, this Celtic power was, in terms of physical cult-expression, an amorphous being, with shadowy human identity, and manifesting itself for the most part only by means of the solar symbol. During the Roman period there appears to have been interaction between the two entities. The physical form of Jupiter appears to have been adopted by the Celts to represent a mixture or fusion between Celtic and Roman divine power; thus the Celtic solar wheel occurs as an attribute alien to the classical divinity. Other types of imagery appear for the first time during the Roman period but in forms likewise alien to classical cult-expression. Indeed, it would seem as though indigenous celestial beliefs found, for the first time, a physical outlet through the stimulus of Graeco-Roman traditions of human portrayal.

45

## Sun-Symbolism in small cult-objects

The examination of evidence for a Romano-Celtic sun and sky-god is best introduced through study of small personal cult-objects, since most of the pre-Roman cult-material we have looked at is in the form of small portable items, and it is interesting to look at similarities and contrasts from the one period to the other. The material may be divided into miniature wheel-symbols, human representations associated with the motif, and miscellaneous objects. I will begin with models since these maintain a tradition already established during the pre-Roman Iron Age.

True wheel-models and, for the first time, brooches actually in the form of wheels (Fig. 16), are numerous finds in Romano-Celtic Europe. Many give as little indication of a genuine cult-purpose as do the Iron Age examples, but some, by virtue of context, association or intrinsic features, demonstrate a ritual significance and a connection with a sky-cult. Grave-finds of models are still common; for example one may cite the cemetery at Wederath near Trier, where several simple four-spoked models, each about two cm in diameter, are recorded. Again, as during the Iron Age, important finds occur in the Marne, Oise and Seine rivers and elsewhere. The cult-significance of these objects is shown above all by their occurrence as temple-finds, at such sites as Gusenberg and Dhronecken in the Hunsrück near Trier. The evidence from Augst in Switzerland is of particular interest for here a large number of wheels comes from one very small area within the Roman town, indicating the possible existence of a shrine. One of the models is an unequivocal cult-item in that it bears the remains of a votive inscription. In Britain, too, the context is sometimes informative: the large twelve-spoked wheel-model from Felmingham Hall, Norfolk is part of a votive hoard, deposited in a pot in the middle of the third century AD, and associated with a bronze head of Jupiter and a mask of an oriental sun-god. Three gold wheel-models with necklaces and bracelets from Backworth, Durham come from a ritual deposit including a silver *patera* dedicated to the Celtic mother-goddesses, which contained the models, chains, coins and five finger-rings of gold, one dedicated to the 'Matres Coccae' (the Red Mothers). A wheel-model and wheel-brooch from Icklingham, Suffolk were found with the fragment of a statuette of an eagle, emblem of Jupiter. The intrinsic features of some wheel-models are worth noting: gold miniatures forming part of necklaces, like the Backworth examples and other similar ones, bear lunar crescents associated with the sun-

17 Part of hoard containing wheel-model; Felmingham Hall, Norfolk.
Copyright: Trustees of the British Museum.

wheel; a necklace from Balèsmes (Haute-Marne) bears wheel, crescent and double-axe (thunderbolt) symbols together. The other important feature is one of decoration of the wheel itself. On some examples, like brooches from Trègnes in Belgium and Nijmegen, there is incised ornament on panels of enamelling in the form of rayed sun-signs.

An interesting question arises as to what extent wheel-models may definitely be ascribed to a Romano-Celtic sky and solar cult. The first point is of course that the shape of the object resembles the sun; second, we have unequivocal solar decoration on some models; and third, association is sometimes significant. The presence of wheels and crescents together seems to indicate association of sun and moon images; the Balèsmes necklace with the added double-axe could imply the presence of sun, moon and storm imagery. Certainly the double-axe, a very ancient symbol of sky-power in Greek contexts and a consistent associate of non-classical sky-powers – such as the Syrian Dolichenus and the Nabataean Hadad – may well be a thunder-bolt sign. The idea may be that a double-edged weapon faces both ways and contains elements of a link between sky and earth. Other wheel-models have a very firm association with the Roman Jupiter. At Felmingham Hall, the model is associated with two representations of sky-gods; the Icklingham models were again so associated. But the object which perhaps best demonstrates the link between wheel-models and sky-symbolism is the lead object from Plessis-Barbuise (Aube) which is composed of a miniature wheel with, inside it, a figure of a standing Jupiter with his thunderbolt and sceptre.

Having established the essential sky-symbolism of at least some wheel-models, we should look briefly at the function

47

18  Bronze wheel-model; France (unprovenanced). Photograph:
Miranda Green. Musée des Antiquités nationales, St Germain-en-
Laye.

of models *as models*. Where they occur in shrines one may
perhaps assume that they were votive offerings; the same
may be true of water-deposits. Grave and secular finds may
imply talismanic significance and the wearing of a wheel-
model as a good-luck charm. A Celtic warrior carved on a
stone at Fox Amphoux (Var) wears a six-spoked wheel-
pendant on his chest; a similar figure comes from Metz; and
on the arch at Orange body-armour bears amuletic wheel-
models. Bertrand sees the wearers of 'solar' brooches as
possible priests of a sky-cult, and it requires little
imagination to see the Backworth gold wheels and chains as
badges of office akin to mayoral chains. Cook suggests that a
bright bronze wheel-model (when new, bronze would have
shone like gold) strung on a double thread and spun would

quite clearly resemble the sun. I discuss the whole function of miniature objects in religion later (Chapter Seven).

The Hallstatt Iron Age produced ritual vessels associated with a sky and solar cult; the Gundestrup Cauldron of the Late La Tène phase was a large, presumably ceremonial, vessel. The custom of making containers appropriate to a specific ritual is reflected also in the Romano-Celtic period, but with smaller, cruder vessels of clay or glass. French pots from the Pyrenees and other regions, for example Rouen, bear single wheel or swastika-signs, scratched on after the vessel was fired. The fact that the motif is present in isolation and not as part of a decorative pattern probably enhances its interpretation as a symbolic image. Such pots may simply possess the sign as a good-luck motif, but they could have been used in some kind of ritual connected with an offering, perhaps of wine, in a sky-ceremony. British vessels, like that from Silchester or Manchester bear repeated wheel-decoration; the Silchester pot is of particular interest in the presence of alternating wheel and S-motifs. It is difficult to be certain of the precise symbolism involved, but it does recur both on a miniature wheel from Grand-Jailly (Côte d'Or) which has three tiny S-signs soldered on, and a figure of a wheel-bearing god from Le Châtelet (Haute-Marne). This representation is discussed later, but the presence here of S-shaped items hanging from the god's shoulder is frequently interpreted as representing spare lightning-flashes (Fig. 19). Other vessel-fragments with applied wheel-symbols survive from Britain, as at House-steads on Hadrian's Wall, and Malton in Yorkshire. Little Houghton, Northants produced part of a glass bottle bearing a moulded wheel-sign. It is not easy to be sure whether such essentially utilitarian items bear solar signs for a formally religious, perhaps sacramental, purpose, or are merely 'blessed' with a protective sign; I myself think that the former is the more likely, since they are so relatively few in number.

We do possess some instances of unequivocally secular objects but with an apotropaic sign added. Such must be the explanation of the tiles bearing incised solar symbols from Hainault and from Toulouse. Legionary tile-stamps of Legion XXII, based at Mainz display swastikas and it is interesting that soldiers of this legion, working the Roman military quarry at Bad Dürkheim scrawled graffiti and carvings including images of 'matchstick-men', horses, wheels and swastikas. This particular legion may well have contained recruits from Celtic provinces. It is a reasonable assumption that, as may be the case with some wheel-models also, the solar sign is being used as a vaguely symbolic, talismanic, image – with the underlying, maybe almost forgotten, concept of a sky-god symbolising the triumph of light over darkness and of good over evil.

The most evocative group of small cult-objects are those which actually represent a divinity associated with celestial motifs. There are few parallels in the earlier Iron Age phases since the portrayal of gods in human form owes most of its presence to Roman influence. The evidence for a Romano-Celtic sky-god takes the form both of personal possessions and of items which may imply more corporate involvement. Taking individual objects first, the largest group is that of pipe-clay (or china-clay) figurines of a wheel-god, manu-factured by mass-production in the Allier district of Central France. Such factories produced large numbers of cheap clay ex votos, probably bought by poorer people as their offerings in shrines or for use as personal, domestic objects of devotion. One point of interest is that such figurines seem to have been made specifically for a Romano-Celtic clientèle; they were marketed only to Celtic provinces. We know of two main 'Jupiter' types, one where the god is accompanied by an eagle and thunderbolt, the other by a wheel and thunderbolt. This is significant since it looks as though eagle and wheel are interchangeable as images of the sky – the one appealing perhaps to a more romanised client than the other. The wheel on the more Celtic repre-sentations is held in the god's right hand, either by his right ear or down by his side. Some of the figures are accompanied by a second, much smaller human figure kneeling or standing by the god's left side, with the hand of the deity resting on its head; sometimes the arms of the diminutive being are upraised as if to support the weight of the divine hand (and often the face of the little being displays a somewhat dolorous expression). Some large stone monuments, described below, seem to represent a similar theme. It is possible only to speculate upon inter-pretation, but the relative sizes of the deity and the other being are important, as is the gesture of the god; it looks as if a sky-god, represented by eagle/wheel and thunderbolt, is accompanied by an image of earth or the underworld; the hand on the head, the small size of the companion, may well represent domination of sky over earthly forces.

Some other clay objects, all from Britain, are of different type. The first is a baked clay mould made for the production of appliqué clay representations of a wheel-god, from Corbridge, Northumberland. The mould shows a bearded god wearing a tunic and helmet, and holding a

19  Bronze figurine of wheel-god; Le Châtelet, France. Photograph:
    Miranda Green. Musée des Antiquités Nationales, St Germain-en-
    Laye.

legionary's shield and a large knobbed club; an eight-
spoked wheel rest by his left ankle. This portrayal of the
divinity differs from those looked at so far in that the
sky-god here is a military figure, appropriate to an army
supply-depot like Corbridge. The other clay depictions are
antefixes; these are triangular fittings designed to fit onto the
gable-ends of roof-tiles. They bear human heads, crudely
modelled in relief, together with wheel-suns at the apex;
night and day are depicted – sometimes sun, moon and stars
are present (Fig. 20). The antefixes come from the legionary
fortress of Caerleon, Gwent, a military location recalling the
similarly military context of the Corbridge wheel-god. At
Caerleon the idea seems to have been the blessing of a
Roman army installation by the appeasement of a Celtic
sun/sky-god as a permanent, indigenous watchman over an
alien military establishment. At Corbridge the god himself

51

20 Clay antefixes decorated with human heads and solar symbols; Caerleon, Gwent. Copyright: National Museum of Wales.

is a fighter, perhaps against evil and negative forces. This theme is reflected powerfully in some stone images, looked at later (pp 61–65).

The presence of bronzes of the Celtic sky-god implies a different category of worshipper, in that bronze was a much more costly and highly prized material than clay. Two Gaulish figurines, from Le Châtelet (Haute-Marne) and Landouzy-la-Ville (Aisne), might equally have been personal possessions or temple-furniture. Two other bronzes are sceptre-fittings and must have formed part of priestly ceremonial regalia. The two figurines each represent a naked, bearded god accompanied by the solar symbol of the wheel. The Landouzy figure is a grim-faced deity holding a wheel over an altar, with a dedication inscribed on the basal plinth ('to Jupiter Best and Greatest and the Spirit of the Emperor'), providing firm evidence of a collation or fusion between the Roman sky-god Jupiter and the Celtic wheel-god. It is especially interesting that the dedication is entirely Roman, so Roman indeed that the Emperor himself is mentioned; yet the wheel is Celtic and the mien and style of the god are alien to classical forms of representation. The Le Châtelet god (Fig. 19) is different in that he is long-haired and curly-bearded, like conventional images of Jupiter; he bears both wheel and thunderbolt but a curious addition is a ring slung over his shoulder from which hang nine S-shaped objects, interpreted, as I have indicated above, as spare lightning-flashes for the immediate use of the sky-god; it is a charming suggestion which can neither be refuted nor endorsed, and based upon the fact that the thunderbolt itself appears to be composed of S-shaped strands. Of relevance here are the associated wheel and S-signs both on

21 Bronze mace-terminal depicting god, wheel, eagle, dolphin and
three-horned bull's head; Willingham Fen, Cambs. Copyright:
Cambridge University Museum of Archaeology & Anthropology.

the Silchester pot and on the Grand-Jailly wheel-model
already discussed.

The two sceptre-fittings, both from British sites, could not
be more different from each other in artistic treatment. The
only feature they bear in common is the possession of
composite iconography, reflecting a complex mythology.
Both fittings incorporate depictions of a god associated with
a solar wheel as integral parts of ritual regalia. The
Willingham Fen sceptre is a well-modelled object of cast
bronze whereon a young naked god bearing thunderbolt or
club is accompanied by an eagle above a wheel, a dolphin
and the head of a triple-horned bull. The god rests one foot
on the head of an individual being crushed into the ground.
Eagle and wheel appear to be images of Roman and Celtic
sky and sun symbolism; the head at ground-level seems to
represent the sky-god's dominion over earth and
underworld powers (just as in the case of the pipe-clay
figurines discussed earlier). The dolphin and bull are more
enigmatic, but the dolphin could be a death-image as it has
that role in the classical world. The bull is frequently
associated in classical contexts with Zeus and Jupiter and
may here be a further sky-sign (two bucket-mounts from
Thealby, Lincs bear the juxtaposed motifs of eagle and
bull-head). The multiplication of the horns to three may be
explained by the fact that 'three' was a sacred and magical
number for the Celts (Chapters six and seven). New evidence from Willingham suggests that a shrine in the
southern peat fens, four kilometres away from where the
hoard was found, may have once housed this piece of

53

temple-furniture. It is interesting that the shrine was built on what was evidently sacred ground as early as the Bronze Age.

The other sceptre fitting is from the temple-site of Farley Heath, Surrey, (Fig. 22). It consists of a sheet-bronze strip, the binding for a wooden stave, bearing very schematised punched 'matchstick' figures in human and animal form. A human face associated with a sun-like wheel shares the strip with other human images, boars, ravens, stags and such inanimate emblems as hammers and tongs. The mythology reflected here is closed to us, and it is impossible to reconstruct the story behind the images. It is possible, however, to recognise a sun-god, a deity with tongs and a hammer-god, maybe the Gaulish Sucellus (Chapter Four), and what may be other gods in animal form or sacrificial beasts. If a life-death, sky-earth interpretation is appropriate, then the chthonic (earthbound) element could be seen either in the ravens (associated with death as carrion-eaters) or in the smith-deity (connected with iron ore and thence earthly properties). The apparent lack of attention to detail and realism could well reflect either the absence of need for naturalistic representation (since the message could as well be transmitted by stylised, short-hand images) or deliberate attempt at obscurity (see Chapter Seven).

22 Sheet-bronze sceptre-binding from temple; Farley Heath, Albury, Surrey. Copyright: Trustees of the British Museum.

## Sun and Sky Symbolism on stone monuments

The Celtic sky and solar god is represented by about two hundred stone monuments. He occurs as a wheel-bearing Celtic sun-god, but sky-symbolism is represented on stone in other ways as well; in addition to solar power, thunder-symbolism is important; and the triumph of light over darkness, good over evil and sky/life over earth/death is recurrent and significant.

### The Solar God

There is a great deal of variety in the forms of representation of a sun-divinity on monuments connected with Celtic sky-worship. Sometimes the god himself is depicted in various guises; at other times, epigraphic allusions accompany such celestial emblems as the wheel; or portrayals of the solar emblem alone without dedication occur. The most interesting conclusion to emerge from a study of these monuments is the breadth of function of the Celtic solar-sky god who appears to embrace not only sun and sky, but war, fertility and death as well. It is the stone monuments, far more than most of the small bronzes and other items, that provide us with the detailed information necessary to construct a picture of Celtic sky-religion.

It is important to remember that on stone depictions not only is the wheel itself used as a solar image, but derivative symbols also occur – the most important of these being the swastika, but including also the rosette and concentric circle. The swastika merits special investigation. It is widely considered that the swastika, like the wheel, represents rotary movement. Whilst the wheel appears to depict the sun by means of its physical similarity, the significance of the swastika must lie in the suggestion of movement given by its form. There are sufficient occurrences of wheels, swastikas and dedications to a sky-god in association for us to assume a genuine link between the two symbols.

Several important groups of stone monuments on which the wheel-god is represented solely as a sky-divinity can be recognised. Bearing in mind the importance of the swastika, one of these is a homogeneous group of small altars from the Pyrenean region of south-west Gaul. These are roughly carved little stones which may bear a dedication to Jupiter, an incised wheel or swastika or any of these in combination. An altar from Montmaurin (Haute-Garonne) bears a four-spoked wheel and swastika and another from Begnères (Hautes-Pyrénées) bears a swastika alone. At Le Mont Saçon a probable shrine produced both swastika-decorated altars and identical ones with dedications to a sky-god. This suggests that the swastika and dedication are here mutually replaceable. An additional feature of these small altars is the presence on them of a palm-branch or conifer-image, which could be a fertility-symbol, or may – as in the case of some monuments discussed later – reflect links between sky and underworld. Two points of particular note concern this Pyrenean group of stones: one is that swastikas are endemic only to this region; wheel monuments are numerous in other areas (Provence for example) but no swastikas occur. The swastika-symbol was therefore particularly popular for sky-god worshippers in this area of Gaul. The second point is the direct appositeness of a sky-cult in a high mountainous region such as the Pyrenees.

A second group of altars bears epigraphic dedications to Jupiter in association with Celtic solar symbols. With the Pyrenean group, the existence of a sky-cult can only be based upon informed speculation. Here the symbols are linked directly to the Roman sky-lord, and a true marriage between Roman and Celtic cult-expression seems present. A large number of these monuments come from the area of Provence, centred on the Lower Rhône Valley around Nîmes and Montpellier, exemplified by stones from Collias, Aigues Mortes, Lansargues and Tresques. Examples from other areas include those from Cologne in the Rhineland and a northern British group. The dedications are always to Jupiter, but the Celtic wheel, appearing on the altars of all the regional groups, demonstrates the truly Celtic nature of the cult.

The southern Gaulish group was probably set up by native bands of local people; we know the dedicants of the Collias stone to have been two local Gaulish clans – the Coriossedenses and Budicenses. A common theme involves the combination of Celtic and Roman symbols, as at Lansargues, where the Celtic wheel is positioned between two thunderbolts, emblems of the classical Jupiter. The Tresques altar is of especial interest in having on one side a seven-spoked wheel and on the other a seven-petalled rosette, arguing a close association between the two symbols (again there may be juxtaposition of Celtic and Roman imagery, the rosette being a common Graeco-Roman motif). The Lansargues stone is notable in that it is possible to see traces of deliberate attempts at erasure of the symbols, perhaps the work of Christians. Some stones link the

23    Stone wheel-decorated altar; Gilly, near Nîmes. Photograph:
      Miranda Green. Nîmes, Musée Archéologique.

sky-cult with that of other powers. At Clarensac the cult of
the Celtic sky-god was associated with Mother Earth, a
fertility element which will be developed later. The stone
from    Aigues-Mortes    displays    great    complexity:    its
dedication is to Jupiter and Silvanus (the Italian woodland
god), and the iconography includes hammers, pots and a
billhook (symbols of the local Celtic Silvanus cult), two
thunderbolts and two wheels (symbols of the Romano-
Celtic sky-god).
   The altars from the Rhineland and Britain are very
different from the Provençal group, being characterised by
their extreme romanism which betrays military dedication.
The Cologne example is superbly carved, with a high
quality inscription to Jupiter above a naturalistic wheel.
The British altars, from the area of Hadrian's Wall, are
similar    and    the    dedicants    consisted    of    Tungrian
(Castlesteads), Dacian (Birdoswald) and Spanish (Maryport)
auxiliary cohorts. The curious feature here is the actual

presence of such a Celtic religious motif as the wheel on otherwise perfectly classical military monuments. The altars at Birdoswald and Maryport are, in each place, only one of over twenty dedications to Jupiter (the others being without the Celtic solar motif).

Where actual anthropomorphic depictions of the Romano-Celtic solar-sky god are present, the Roman element is manifested by the guise of Jupiter, the Celtic by the solar emblem of the wheel. There is some variety here and I will look at one or two examples of each type. First, it is possible to recognise portrayals where, without the wheel, the representations could be mistaken for those of the Roman god. These include the stones from Alesia (Côte d'Or) and Alzey (Rheinland-Pfalz), where the god sits on a wheel-carved throne, accompanied by an eagle. A stone from Bordeaux shows a god wearing a cloak and holding a wheel and a thunderbolt. At Tongres in Belgium Jupiter and Juno are seated side by side, and it is the goddess who holds the wheel. A second type portrays the god as an armed warrior (an unclassical role for Jupiter) bearing both Celtic and Roman sky emblems. The most important of these comes from Séguret (Vaucluse), where the god is depicted in the guise of a Roman general, but with eagle, thunderbolt, and a large wheel by his side. In the background is an oak (symbol of the classical god) with an encircling snake (alien to Jupiter but possibly adopted by the Celts as an underworld or earth sign). The warrior-image is a curious one (it has already been noted on a small portrayal of the wheel-god from Corbridge (above, p 50) but it may be associated with the concept of the triumph of light over darkness.

The warrior-element in the Celtic sun-cult ties in with certain representations of a wheel-bearing god on horseback bearing down a monster with snake-limbs. The whole concept of the sky-horseman is discussed later in this chapter (pp 61–65) as an essentially separate issue, since most examples are not associated with the solar symbol. Those which do possess such an attribute are interesting mainly because of the link that the wheel-motif provides on the one hand between the horseman-group and the other wheel-bearing images and, on the other, between the wheel and the horse. Where the sky-horseman (who, it is argued below, appears to symbolise the dominion of life over death) is represented with the solar wheel, he normally holds the object as if it were a shield, in his left hand, with the wrist threaded through the spokes to hold the reins of his mount. Such depictions occur, for instance, at Butterstadt (Hessen) and at Obernburg (Bayern) on the German *Limes*, and at Luxeuil and Meaux in Gaul. At Quémigny-sur-Seine the solar emblem is in physical appearance half-way between a wheel and a shield (oval in shape but with spokes or rays). All sky-horseman groups share the elements of rider, horse and chthonic monster being ridden down by the deity's mount; both wheel and horse are probably sun-symbols here. In this context a few related groups may be mentioned. At Champagnat and Dompierre the monster, god and wheel are present but the horse is absent. At Mouhet and Tours only the monster and wheel are depicted. The Mouhet 'giant' kneels, hands behind the back in the attitude of a captive, balancing a wheel on his back. In all these instances, it seems as though the wheel is a substitute for the horse; this in itself enhances the view that the horse is a sun-symbol, as suggested, for example, by its occurrence on Celtic coinage in company with solar motifs.

The third main wheel-god type is associated not with war but with fertility (again an alien concept for Jupiter). The Celts, as a rural, agricultural and pastoral people, appear to have been preoccupied with fertility-veneration which pervaded all aspects of their religion (Chapter Three). Sky and fertility-symbolism are not closely connected in classical mythology but are naturally associated through sun and rain both of which are essential for life and crop-growth. This may account for one or two stone representations of the Celtic sky-god accompanied by fertility emblems. At Naix, a seated wheel-god is depicted with two *cornuacopiae*. At Netherby in Cumbria (Fig. 24), a figure resembling a classical *genius* with cornucopiae in one hand is seated like a Mother-goddess but bears a wheel over an altar instead of the offering plate or *patera* which is the usual attribute of the *genius*. In this connection, we may recall the Clarensac dedication to Jupiter and Terra Mater (and the Backworth association betweeen the Mothers and wheel-models (pp 46–47)).

So far we have examined stone representations of the Romano-Celtic wheel/sky god in basically classical art-form, even if alien, non-classical elements are present. Two totally contrasting sculptures are interesting in that they represent the most unromanised element in Romano-Celtic society. A stone from Bremevaque (Haute-Garonne) depicts a roughly modelled, ithyphallic god with spear, snake and swastika. The relief from Churcham in Gloucestershire displays other Celtic features; here a god wearing a long tunic, is accompanied by two wheels. A non-Roman feature, additional to the fairly rough artistic treatment, is the head

59

24   Relief of seated wheel-god with *cornucopiae*; Netherby, Cumbria.
Copyright: Carlisle Museum.

of the god which is huge in proportion to the body and,
moreover, bears traces of horns; both over-emphasis of the
head and horns are native religious characteristics (pp
214–220), the one representing the Celts' belief that the
head was especially significant, the other the fertility-
element and preoccupation with animal-symbolism
endemic to Celtic religion.

One final group of wheel-monuments remains to be
discussed, that of funerary stones. Most important are what
are known as 'stèles-maisons', house-shaped tombstones
from the cremation-cemeteries of the Alsace region. The
great majority come from the area around Saverne. One
example in Saverne Museum bears Celtic names and three
incised wheel-symbols. On some, wheels and concentric
circles or rosettes are associated. The other region where
funerary monuments decorated with solar motifs occur is

25   Tombstone decorated with wheel-signs; Saverne area. Photograph: Miranda Green. Saverne Museum.

the Pyrenean area of south-west Gaul, especially the
Comminges region. Death and sun seem at first glance to be
a strange association but we should remember the
sepulchral context of some pre-Roman wheel-models (pp
41–42). In Graeco-Roman religion the sun was thought of as
an essentially moving object lighting the earth by day and
the underworld at night; the presence of a Celtic sky-symbol
on tombstones would fit well with the idea of rebirth after
death.

## The Fighter Against the Darkness

The sky-horseman groups, considered above in the context
of solar symbolism, may now be examined in more detail
as a specific phenomenon relating to Romano-Celtic
celestial religion. The sculptured equestrian group is only
one part of an elaborate, composite type of monument set
up in honour of the Celtic sky-god in western Roman
provinces. These monuments are generally known as

61

26  Reconstruction of Jupiter-column; Hausen-an-der-Zaber, near
Stuttgart, Germany. Copyright: Württembergisches Landesmuseum, Stuttgart.

Jupiter-columns or Jupiter-Giant columns. About 150 are
recorded, mainly in eastern Gaul and the Rhineland. They
each consist of four- and eight-sided stone bases carved
with figures of gods (generally connected with sun, moon
and planets) and inscribed with dedications to Jupiter or his
consort Juno. On top of the eight-sided plinth is a tall pillar,
often decorated with foliage-like patterns as if to represent a
tree; this in its turn is topped by a Corinthian capital. It is at
the summit of the column that the sky-horseman rides. The
entire structure must have been extremely impressive; the
complete column from Merten was fifteen metres high.

Jupiter-Giant columns present a prime instance of the conflation of Roman and Celtic sky-worship. The column-bases are outwardly romanised, with carvings of deities identifiable as Roman and even the dedication is to a Roman-named god; but the pillar itself and the sculptured summit-group are foreign to classical religious concepts. The column may be plain or decorated with tree-patterns like the Hausen-an-der-Zaber monument which was carved with oak-leaves and acorns. The oak was sacred to Jupiter, but the image of a tree in stone may relate to the Celtic reverence for trees as objects of sanctity. The symbolism of the tree/pillar is interesting and may reflect a number of ideas; it could represent a 'cosmic pillar' to hold up the sky; it might serve the purpose of raising the sky-god as high and as close to his celestial realm as possible; or the column/tree could reflect links between the upper and lower worlds. Powell postulates (1958, 136) that Jupiter-columns had native fore-runners in wood with, as the ultimate prototype a growing sacred tree. Whatever the precise significance, it is well to recall the wheel-bearing altars of southern Gaul which repeat the tree/sky motif in their imagery of conifers.

The horseman-group at the summit of Jupiter-columns is the most complex and potentially the most illuminating element. The iconography consists of a warrior on horseback rearing over, riding down or being supported by a humanoid monster (the ambiguity here may be deliberate) whose legs are in the form of snakes. The subject-matter may reflect Greek mythology where the Battle between the Olympian Gods and the earthly Titans portrays these earthbound giants with snake-limbs. In Celtic iconography there is an association between the sky-god and serpents seen, for example, on the Séguret stone where an armoured god appears with eagle, wheel, oak and snake. Another stone, a small altar from Lypiatt, Glos., bears a wheel and a snake twined round the stone. Whatever the origin of the horseman-group art-form, it is a Celtic religious theme which is being portrayed; the classical sky-god is never depicted on horseback. The horse here is a celestial, solar, symbol – like the wheel – and the representation appears to be Jupiter as a Celtic sky-lord, image of sky, light, good and life, in dualistic and interdependent combat with an earthbound, dark, and perhaps evil monster. This dualism in the cult-group may represent positive and negative forces, day and night, light and darkness, and the higher and lower aspects of Celtic mythology; perhaps simulta-neously too both the antithesis and interdependence of life

63

and death. Seen in this context, the other chthonic, funerary elements in the cult of the solar god spring into focus.

Classical mythology may have provided Celtic patrons and sculptors with iconographical ideas, but the argument for an authentic Celtic religion gains credence from a number of factors apart from the equestrian nature of the sky-god himself. First, the distribution of these monuments is entirely Celtic. Second, two classical literary allusions may be relevant. In the second century AD Maximus of Tyre stated (*Logoi* 8, 8) that the Celtic image of Zeus was a high oak tree. Valerius Flaccus (*Argonautica* 6, 89) remarks that the tribe of the Coralli (who were probably of Celtic origin) worshipped effigies of Jupiter associated with wheels and columns.

No Jupiter-columns have definitely been identified in Britain but one fragmentary monument from Cirencester, Glos, may have been part of such a structure. Here are present both an elaborate Corinthian capital and a rectangular base with a curious dedication; this inscription refers to the restoration, 'under the old religion' of a statue and column to Jupiter by a Governor of Britannia Prima.

27  Inscription recording restoration of a Jupiter-column; Cirencester. Fourth century AD. Photograph: Betty Naggar. Corinium Museum.

28  Corinthian figured capital with Bacchic figures, probably from
Jupiter-column; Cirencester. Photograph: Betty Naggar. Corinium
Museum.

The governor, whose name was Lucius Septimius was a
citizen of Reims. The date must be after AD 296 (when
Diocletian divided Britain into four provinces), and it is
quite possible that the 'old religion' refers to a pagan lull in
the Christian period, perhaps during Julian's Apostasy in
the mid fourth century AD.

The main point which strikes us about Jupiter-columns is
their sheer size. Though the cost must have mitigated
against private erection of such monuments, and though we
do know that many were set up in cities at public expense, a
number come from private estates and others have been
found in remote sanctuaries. A final word should be said
about the present condition of some pillars: most are very
fragmentary and some betray signs of possible deliberate
destruction. If this is so, then Christians may have been
responsible for smashing and scattering these pagan
edifices, just as a Christian fanatic may have tried to 'rub
out' the solar image on the Lansargues stone.

### Taranis, the Thunderer

In addition to light, sky and sun aspects of a celestial cult, the Celts possessed a thunder-god, known both from archaeological and literary evidence. In his *Pharsalia* , an account of the Civil War between Pompey and Caesar, the poet Lucan – writing in the early second century AD – mentions three Celtic divinities encountered by Caesar's army in Gaul (I, 444–446); one of these is 'Taranis' whose worship Lucan describes as 'crueller than the cult of Scythian Diana', and to whom the Celts offered human sacrifices. Two later commentaries on the Lucan manuscript found at Berne, but ranging in date from the fourth to the ninth centuries AD, each equate or link the name of Taranis with that of a Roman god, one with Dispater (god of the dead), the other with Jupiter; the commentaries describe Taranis, moreover, as 'presider over warfare', and inform us that human sacrifices were offered to him by being burnt alive in tree-trunks.

Archaeological evidence for the cult of Taranis or Taranus is sparse but widespread. The root 'Taran' means 'thunder' in modern Welsh and Breton. Seven dedicatory inscriptions survive on stone altars. Examples from Chester, Tours and Orgon dedicate the stones to 'Thunder', as if the elemental force of thunder itself is being invoked in Celtic form. Others from Böckingen and Godramstein in the Rhineland, and from Scardona in Yugoslavia bear inscriptions to a 'Thunderer'.

The concept of a Celtic thunder-deity raises a number of questions. The first is whether Taranis really was a great Celtic divinity, as Lucan implies. Powell asserts that the obscurity in location and paucity of dedications deny Taranis' universal importance. On the other hand, the widespread distribution of the altars argues the worship of Taranis over a very wide area. Caution must be used in our interpretation of classical sources: Lucan did not himself travel in Gaul and it is often suggested that the historical source for the epic poem lay in the lost books of Livy. His ethnographic and geographical information may then have come from these and therefore need have no meaning in the historical and topographial context in which he places it. All we can say here for certain is that Taranis is a god in his own right and it is not a mere descriptive epithet attached to a Roman god. Though he is linked with Jupiter on some dedications, on others he appears alone.

A further question involves the equation of Taranis with the Roman sky-god. In speaking of such equation, complete identification or oneness of identity is normally understood. One Berne commentator equates Taranis with Jupiter, a claim endorsed by three inscriptions, from Scardona, Chester and Thauron. Alone the commentators need not carry much weight; they need not have been particularly familiar with the details of Celtic mythology, and so the archaeological evidence is vital here. In considering the problem of collation between Taranis and the Roman sky-god, the most important thing to remember is that with 'Taranis' we are defining a deity purely by the name 'Thunderer', which has functional implications. So the name 'Taranis' implies nothing more than a noisy lord of thunder, weather and storms. The linking of Taranis with Jupiter on dedications is the result of conflation between a Celtic entity and one aspect only (the thunder-wielding role) of the Roman god. Taranis may embody a power-struggle in the sky, with overtones of battle and fertility, but thunder is only one of Jupiter's attributes and instruments. Jupiter himself possesses a much wider role as all-powerful ruler of the immensity of the luminous atmosphere. Taranis cannot escape from his name-definition to assume this broader mantle. So the situation seems similar to that of the wheel-bearing solar god of the Celts, where there occurs partial identification of Celtic elemental entities (existing before the Roman era) with relevant aspects of a celestial Roman deity.

Finally there is the question of the equation, in the Berne commentary, between Taranis and Dispater. It is not inconceivable that Taranis also should bear such a chthonic element, as the Celtic sun-god has been seen to posssess an underworld role (in wheel-bearing tombstones, for instance).

## A High Mountain God of the Celts

One manifestation of a Celtic sky-lord is represented entirely by inscriptions. In the mountainous regions of the Celtic world, dedications to Celtic mountain deities associated with the sky and particularly the weather are asssociated with Jupiter. Celtic surnames for this particular Roman divinity are otherwise rare, and in these hilly regions, the epithets themselves are generally tied to specific, topographical, descriptive concepts. For instance, Jupiter Brixianus at Brescia in Cisalpine Gaul was a local god defined by a particular locality. Celtiberian deities of the north-western Spanish mountains – such as Jupiter Ladicus, the spirit of Mount Ladicus – were assimilated

67

with the Roman sky-god. Other Gaulish local names include Jupiter Beisirissa at Cadéac (Hautes-Pyrénées), and Jupiter Poeninus in the Alps around the Great St Bernard Pass, to whom there was a sanctuary in the important pass as early as the Iron Age, and where votive plaques were offered to Poeninus. This phenomenon does not occur only in Gaul; the Norican peoples of Austria were Celtic and here again mountain-spirits were collated with Jupiter. On the highest peak of Koralpe (between the Lavant and Mur valleys, 2000 metres above sea-level), a votive inscription was set up to a native god, Latobius, identified with Jupiter. Uxellinus (the uxello- root means 'high') was another such deity. The same practice occurs in the mountainous regions of Pannonia (modern Hungary), and on the borders of North-East Dalmatia (Yugoslavia) and Upper Moesia (Bulgaria) Jupiter was known as Parthinus, possibly connected with a local tribe or clan known as the Partheni.

So, in widely separated areas of the Celtic world, Jupiter occurs with native surnames referring generally to topographical spirits frequently associated with high places. This must imply that such place-spirits were recognised and identified by the indigenous population before the period of Roman influence. Deities of mountain-summits may well have been storm, weather and celestial entities, as is the case with many eastern mountain Baals – such as Dolichenus of Mount Doliche in Syria, and Hadad of the Nabataean hills. Such spirits would be easily and naturally conflated with a Graeco-Roman sky-god when subjected to classical traditions. But the conflation is not between Celtic sky-entities and the fully developed political religion of the Roman State god Jupiter Best and Greatest. Instead the worship of a Jupiter appears – as it were frozen in time – a Jupiter akin to the original high god of Latium before he became formalised as a city and later imperial deity. The Celtic Jupiter is associated only with natural phenomena of sky, weather and fertility through sun and rain.

## Religion, Ritual and Mythology

The material which has been examined in this chapter is, for the most part, the physical manifestation of cult-expression pertaining to a deity or deities connected with Celtic sky-religion. It is impossible to have any real idea of exactly what cult was involved nor how people regarded the divine entities they recognised in natural phenomena.

However, there are ways in which it is possible to get closer to the concepts expressed both in material remains and in the literature, by isolating and assessing the different elements apparently associated. The iconography both of the sculpture and of certain of the smaller items, added to the evidence both of epigraphy and, to a lesser extent, of literature, shows repeated characteristics over given areas, which point to common mythology and cult-practice.

The main feature of the Celtic sky-cult is that, during the Roman period, it becomes very closely associated with, and to some extent, assimilated to the cult of the Roman Jupiter. This Mediterranean sky-deity becomes, on his introduction to Celtic lands, identified with at least three different indigenous aspects of sky-religion, namely the cults or sub-cults of sun, sky-conqueror and thunder-power. Iconographically, it is the Celtic solar element which is the dominant feature in sky-symbolism, and it is this element which can be traced far back into Celtic prehistory. When during the Roman period, the classical art-form of Jupiter is commonly used to express Celtic solar symbolism, a purely indigenous solar god is sometimes, albeit rarely, represented. The Churcham carving, with its wheel, huge head and horns, is surely one such manifestation; the Caerleon antefixes, with wheels and crudely-modelled human heads, appear to be another.

One striking feature in Romano-Celtic sky-religion is its apparently dualistic character. There is abundant evidence for a death/darkness and underworld element. This is indicated by the monsters of the horseman groups; the occurrence of wheel-models in graves; the presence of sun and associated moon-motifs; the wheel-carvings on tombstones; and perhaps also the dolphin on the Willingham sceptre and the ravens on the Farley Heath stave (and in the Felmingham hoard); and, finally, by the evidence of Lucan's commentator that Taranis was equated with Dispater. This dualism is enhanced by the warrior-image of the sky-god, triumphant over the lower elements in the divine world. Such an image may be the reason why the Celtic sky-god seems to have been beloved of Roman soldiers serving in the Celtic provinces.

A curious aspect of the cult is that of fertility. This is evidenced by the association of sun-wheels with the Celtic Mothers at Backworth in North Britain and, allied to this, a carving of the Mothers from an unprovenanced Cotswold site bears a wheel at the apex of a triangular niche in which the goddesses are seated. This association gains credence from the presence of Gaulish clay figurines, made in the

69

Allier area, of a Celtic Mother decorated with celestial signs. A fertility aspect of Celtic sky-symbolism is demonstrated also by the presence of *cornuacopiae* on some wheel-bearing monuments, and other links with fertility-images have also been discussed.

One feature which is very prominent in this, as in so many other Celtic cults, is zoomorphic or animal-imagery. In the iconography associated with the Celtic sky-god bulls, horses, water-birds, snakes and many other creatures make their appearance. It is difficult to interpret these beasts in terms of symbolism and/or mythology. The horse, as we have seen, is probably a solar animal; the bull could be connected with sky, fertility or invincibility. Snakes and aquatic birds are more of a problem. In classical religion, snakes could represent death, fertility, healing or general well-being; on the horseman sculptures earth or death are probably represented, but a fertility aspect is possible, for instance at Séguret, where a snake curls round an oak. Water-birds are very interesting, since they occur associated with solar symbolism in Celtic prehistory, and because they may possess links with other sky-water associations (see Chapter Five), including the deposition of votive wheels in rivers and sacred springs, and the association of certain Jupiter-columns with water. The water-element in sky-religion is obscure but may either incorporate fertility-worship (the Celtic Mothers are frequently linked with water) or embody the rain-element in celestial cults which, like thunder, would serve as a link between sky and earth.

Finally, there is the question of the mythology of sun and sky-veneration in the Celtic world. One or two objects, like the British sceptres, and some of the sculptures, depict a number of associated themes which indicate considerable complexity in myth and therefore also in ritual. The major features which may be identified concern the sky-god himself and his role in a Celtic pantheon. The god seems to be composed of a single but multi-facetted being or of a number of sub-deities. His sphere of influence includes the sky (and other high places) such as tree-tops and mountains, the sun, other celestial bodies (such as moon and stars), thunder and rain. The cult is associated also with fertility and death. A tentative interpretation suggests the emergence of a dualistic religion in which a celestial high god has dominion over, but is inextricably linked to, the earth and underworld. The combined elements of sun, sky, weather, fertility and death imply a mythology based on the earth's seasonal cycle. In any event, the religion involved the whole spectrum of Romano-Celtic society. At the apex, we may infer the existence of a priesthood from the sceptres, ritual vessels (especially the Gundestrup Cauldron) and the gold chains. In this context, the spectre of human sacrifice hinted at in the literature adds a sombre note. The abundance of large and small stone sculptures betrays a degree of corporate devotion by Roman soldiers serving on the frontiers, and by civilians. Small votive objects, both costly and cheap, are represented by figurines of bronze and clay. Finally, symbols of the sky-cult were worn around the neck or as cloak-fasteners in fulfilment of a talismanic function, or were scrawled for good luck on roof-tiles. The cult of sky and sun must be seen as an integral part of Celtic society and culture.

# CHAPTER THREE:
# FERTILITY AND THE MOTHER-GODDESSES

## Introduction

A preoccupation with fertility symbolism was an entirely natural phenomenon in a society whose everyday survival depended upon the behaviour of the earth, the seasons and the fecundity of crops and livestock. As an essentially rural, farming people, the Celts shared this preoccupation with the other non-industrial societies of past and present. The reproductive capacity of flocks and herds and the crop-yield was of primary concern; the success or failure of the earth's fecundity meant very immediate prosperity or hardship – literally life or death.

Fertility rites must have dominated Celtic cult activity and we have evidence that a number of deities possessed primary or ancillary fertility associations. It is interesting that whilst the Mediterranean civilisations of Greece and Rome possessed goddesses of wisdom, love, war and the sky, the majority (if not all) of the Celtic female divinities appear to have been strongly associated with the reproductive cycle and prosperity, in addition to any other functions. In this chapter, we are particularly concerned with deities whose principal sphere was procreation. Our main evidence is archaeological, specifically iconographic, but this is supplemented by the vernacular tradition of Ireland which supports the material evidence of the pre-Roman and Romano-Celtic world.

The divine fertility-element in Celtic society is most obviously and clearly seen in the various types of Mother-Goddess whose presence and worship is represented archaeologically during the Romano-Celtic period, especially in Gaul and Britain. Images of a goddess associated with life and abundance are physical manifestations of a community endeavouring to control the behaviour of the seasons and to appease and propitiate the forces who imposed the cycle of life and death. We will see that the Celtic Mother was a complex being, like the great fertility deity of Neolithic Europe, in that her cult possessed connections inextricably intertwined between the living and the dead. The divine Mother is represented with the symbols of life and abundance, but her images were buried in tombs with the dead, and moreover, she has a destructive element in having very direct associations with warfare. The Celtic Mother may well, like her Neolithic predecessor, have been the product of a sedentary, perhaps matrilinear community and, while we have insufficient evidence to be able to argue this with confidence, some points of evidence do support this suggestion. First, we know that women occupied an extremely powerful position in Celtic society. The evidence comes from Iron Age tombs, such as those of Reinheim in Germany and Vix in Burgundy – which were very obviously rich female burials belonging to the highest stratum of Celtic aristocracy – and from literary evidence. We know from the writings of classical historians on Britain that powerful Celtic women existed, with political autonomy in their own right: two British queens, Boudica of the Iceni and Cartimandua of the Brigantes, were monarchs who created more fear and havoc among the Roman conquerors than any male British opponent. We know also that women were important in Insular Celtic society. Queen Medb of Connaught for instance was far more powerful than her husband Ailill and the wedding of territorial nature-goddess to mortal king is a commonplace in Irish tradition. In the Irish and Welsh sagas, there is mention of descent being traced through the female line; the Welsh god Mabon (Divine Youth) is referred to in the Mabinogion as son of his mother Modron – not of his father; likewise the Irish divine race, called the Tuatha Dé Danann were the immortal people of the goddess Danu or Anu, and there is parallel mythology associated with the Welsh goddess Don. This Mother-Monarch (or dynasty-founder) association is interesting. Irish literature tells us that sovereignty depended very much upon land-fertility. King Bres in the sagas was deposed not only on account of his meanness but also because, under his rule, the land became barren. In Ireland, as we will see, a number of goddesses combined the functions of fertility and prosperity with the character of a territorial, topographically-defined deity. In this capacity, such a divinity may also be involved with warfare, presumably in protection of the land. We will meet this war-aspect to the Mothers again, together with abundant archaeological evidence for the topographical association.

Some final introductory points may be made concerning fertility symbolism. One is that though the overtly maternal aspects of Celtic worship are the primary concern here, there are a number of associated deities or images whose attributes indicate a link with fecundity, prosperity and well-being, even if procreation is not obviously portrayed.

Thus we will discuss a wide range of Celtic god-forms.
Another is that the preoccupation with fertility is evidenced
in classical and vernacular literature in contexts other than
those directly concerned with the Mother-Goddess cult,
demonstrating the fundamental importance given to such
powers. We know from Pliny that the Druids were
responsible for fertility-ritual; he gives us a graphic
description of the mistletoe-cutting ceremony which took
place on the sixth day of each month and involved bull-
sacrifices and invocations to the gods. Mistletoe thus har-
vested and consumed could make the barren fertile.
Cunliffe points out that the Coligny Calendar with its
evidence for auspicious and inauspicious days, could be
used to calculate the best times for planting and harvesting
crops, slaughtering beasts in winter and sending them out to
graze in summer. Finally, Insular evidence for the great
Celtic festivals of Samain, Beltine, Imbolc and Lugnasad
indicate an association with the various parts of the
seasonal cycle. Samain on the the First of November was
tied up with the rounding up of livestock and the choice of
which would be killed off and which kept for breeding;
Imbolc on the First of February is thought to be linked with
the lactation of ewes; Beltine on the First of May marked the
beginning of open pasturing; Lugnasad was connected with
the harvest in August. Thus, all the main festivals were
linked with seasonal events and essentially with fertility.

## THE MOTHER-GODDESS IN PREHISTORY

The later prehistoric, specifically Celtic, periods in Britain
and Europe have yielded very little overt evidence for the
worship of female fertility deities. Nevertheless there is
indirect evidence during the first millennium BC of fertility
symbolism and veneration of a power concerned with the
seasons and with resulting prosperity or hardship. Indeed,
from the Neolithic onwards – when settled farming became
the norm – it would be surprising if the invocation of such
supernatural powers did not take place. The Neolithic
phase does present very clear evidence of a mother-goddess
in Europe. Although some millennia earlier than the period
with which we are now concerned, it is interesting to glance
briefly at the cult and its manifestations. Gimbutas has
traced the cult of the Mother in Europe from circa 7500 BC
to 3000 BC, a period spanning the later Mesolithic and
earlier Neolithic. In France during the later Neolithic,
schematic depictions of a maternal goddess appear on

cave-walls and in tombs, as in the Valley of Petit-Morin.
Here her prime function appears to be that of protectress of
the dead. There is virtually no evidence from Neolithic
Britain save one depiction – a crudely fashioned figurine
made from a small chalk block and found at Grimes Graves
in Norfolk. The figure comes from a probable ritual deposit
at the end of one of the flint-mine galleries: that a mother-
image is intended is suggested by the gravid belly and heavy
breasts. At the beginning of the Bronze Age, 'statue-
menhirs' – such as those of the Tarn and Aveyron areas of
southern France which depict roughly hewn female figures
with small but definite breasts – are seen by some scholars
as the beginning of the mother-goddess tradition of Celtic
Gaul.

During the Bronze Age proper in western Europe, there is
little indication of a female fertility-cult. But, as Gimbutas
points out, the imagery of water-birds and bull-horns in
Central and East Europe does incorporate implicit fertility-
symbolism. In Late Bronze Age Scandinavia, goddesses
became important; women's items were more commonly
deposited as sepulchral offerings. Such rock-carvings as
that from Slänge, Sweden depict a meeting of the solar god
and earth goddess.

Iron Age evidence for a mother-goddess cult is sporadic

29  Plaque of the Triple Mothers; Cirencester. Photograph: Betty
Naggar. Corinium Museum.

but interesting. To the Hallstatt phase belongs the cult-wagon from the grave-mound at Strettweg near Graz in Austria, probably dating to the seventh or sixth century BC. The emphasis (size and centrality) of the central female figure carved on the wagon (Fig. 13) suggests that she must be divine; she carries a ritual bowl or cauldron and is surrounded by mortal retainers. The importance of mortal females during the later Hallstatt period is indicated by such finds as the sixth century Vix (Châtillon-sur-Seine) barrow-burial, surely that of a Celtic princess. A plank-built chamber contained a dismantled funerary wagon; the lady was buried with a huge bronze Greek *krater* weighing 210 kg and was accompanied by such valuable items as a massive gold diadem worn round her head, an Attic bowl and an Etruscan bronze jug.

As de Vries, Grenier and Szabó have pointed out, the mother-goddess cult, so dominant in Gaul and Britain during the Romano-Celtic period, must have its origin during Celtic prehistory, simply because of its occurrence almost entirely in Celtic territory. The evidence for prominent females in Celtic society is relevant here. The British queens Cartimandua and Boudica, recorded by classical writers must have been part of a tradition of autonomous and influential women. Classical writers say little concerning Celtic goddesses, although Dio (*LXII*, 2) refers to a war-goddess Andraste in Britain. But such writers as Ammianus Marcellinus (*XV, XII*) comment on the valour, indomitability and sheer physical strength of Gaulish women, who were just as formidable in war as their husbands. As remarked in Chapter One, there is little extant anthropomorphic iconography in the Iron Age and very little of this depicts female deities. The female head from the *oppidum* at Entremont in Provence, probably of third or second century BC date, could conceivably be that of a mother-goddess, as may be the first century BC female stone figure from Bourges (Cher). Occasionally, wooden sculptures, probably of pre-Roman date, portray females who may be mother-goddesses. The pre-Roman and Romano-Celtic sanctuary at the Source des Roches de Chamalières (Puy-de-Dôme), a healing thermal shrine has produced a stylised wooden female figure with aureoled head. At Ballachulish in Argyll (Fig. 5), an oak female figurine was found in peat in circumstances suggesting its context within a wattled-wall structure, possibly a shrine. It is undated but maybe first century BC or earlier. The figure is crudely carved, but it is naked with an emphasised pudenda which suggests its sexual/fertility symbolism. Of greatest interest, in terms of iconography, is perhaps the goddess-imagery on the Gundestrup Cauldron. On outer plate (e) and inner plate (B) (after Olmsted 1979) are female busts, the sex indicated by small, distinctive breasts and pigtailed hair. On plate B the goddess is flanked by 'rosette' wheels and the author suggests the interpretation that the goddess is being carried in a wagon. If this were so, a parallel is suggested with such burials as Vix and the Irish literary tradition of the Connaught Queen Medb being driven in her chariot around her camp before battle. In this context, Olmsted also cites the first century BC Danish votive bog-deposits of two Gaulish cult-vehicles at Dejbjerg, dismantled and placed in a mound with a cremation-burial; there was a throne-like construction in the centre of each, clearly non-functional, wagon, and the finds imply that the burial was female. There is a parallel, too, with Tacitus' description of the Teutonic earth-goddess Nerthus who rode in procession through cities. This imagery recalls to mind the Strettweg cult-wagon with its female figure and, also, later Romano-Celtic mother-goddess portrayals in chariots (below, p 92). That pre-Roman territorial goddesses existed in Gaul is evidenced for example at Bibracte, the hillfort predecessor of Autun. The eponymous goddess Bibracte, patroness and spirit of the Iron Age town, continued to be venerated after the abandonment of Mont Beuvray: an inscription records the devotion of a *sevir* of Autun to the goddess, but the cult was not simply transported to the Roman town. A shrine was built on Beuvray itself after the Conquest and was frequented until the fourth century AD.

In addition to the evidence of specific mother-goddess forms during the Iron Age, there are other indications of a reverence for fertility powers. Rock-carvings, like those at Mont Bego in Liguria in southern France and Val Camonica in North Italy, portray numerous inconographic motifs, in the case of the Camunian site extending back as far as the Neolithic. Amongst the motifs and images at Mont Bego during the Iron Age are both ploughs and oxen depicted with solar symbols. In the Bronze Age at Camonica (period III) the stag, fertility and sun are associated; and in the Iron Age (Period IV) the stag-god, an emblem of strength and potency, assumes major importance. Certainly, southern France and North Italy both came under Celtic influence during this period. Of interest in this connection also is the evidence from Spanish rock-carvings where the solar disc is associated with the sexual act and fertility, a composition which may be paralleled on Scandinavian Bronze Age portrayals.

Finally, a potentially significant British occurrence is attested at South Cadbury, where the burial of young domestic animals, especially newborn calves, could be interpreted as fertility sacrifices. Twenty such burials were found in a narrow zone beside the approach to a small shrine. This is but one example of what must have been a common Celtic Iron Age practice of invoking the supernatural by means of appropriate sacrifices, to ensure the continued prosperity of land and livestock.

## THE ICONOGRAPHY OF THE CELTIC MOTHERS

As with so many Celtic cults, physical representation of mother-goddess worship manifests itself in full and mature form only during the period of Roman influence on Celtic lands. In terms of material culture, we possess both written dedications and iconography, generally in stone or clay but more occasionally in metal or bone. This evidence may be used to answer a number of questions: the form of worship; method of physical representation; the type of dedicants and above all the real function of the cult. The Mothers are a homogeneous group and share many iconographical features which establish their essential identity. I shall look first at the different types of representation, attitudes, attributes and associations.

### The Triple Mothers

Triplism as a basic phenomenon of Celtic religion is discussed in detail elsewhere (Chapter Seven). The mother-goddess is perhaps the commonest type of Celtic divinity treated in this way and the triadic form appears to have played an important role in her worship and cult-expression.

The three mothers or *Deae Matres*, as they are frequently called in inscriptions, were known also as *Matronae* , especially in Cisalpine Gaul (North Italy) and Lower Germany. We know more about the cult of the triple mothers than of some other cults of Celtic origin simply because they are often named and bear descriptive surnames which give clues to their identity. By far the majority of these epithets is linked to locality, thus asserting their essentially territorial character. Some are regional, embracing a large area or even a province – like *Gallicae* or *Britannicae*. A dedication from Winchester mentions the Mothers of Italy, Germany, Gaul

30  Plaque of the Triple Mothers; Cirencester. Photograph: Betty
    Naggar. Corinium Museum.

and Britain. A York inscription invokes the African, Italian
and Gaulish Mothers. Others refer to the Mothers of the
Homeland or Overseas. Many, however, tie the Mothers to a
specific locality: the *Nemausicae* only occur at Nîmes and
are really spirits of that city; the *Treverae* were worshipped
solely among the Treveri around Trier. The *Matres Glanicae*
belonged only to Glanum in Provence, worshipped with a
local god Glanis. What is interesting is that topographical
surnames did not occur in Britain, suggesting perhaps
that they were not indigenous but rather were imported
from Gaul. The Rhineland mother-goddesses are
distinguished by the number (and outlandish nature!) of
their epithets. Thus we find dedications *Matronis
Assingenehis*; *Matronis Mahlinehis*; *Aufanibus* and many
others, always expressing locality. These 'land'-names may
refer either to the birthplace of the dedicant or to the
location of the altar. The *Matronae Aufaniae*, local to the
Bonn area, are associated with the *Matres Domesticae* found
in Britain and several dedications and representations are
recorded from Bonn itself. Apart from topographical
surnames, others attest specific roles for the goddesses. The
epithet *Comedovae* at Aix-les-Bains refers to health or
healing. The *Suleviae*, known in Hungary, Rome, Gaul,
Germany and Britain (at Bath, Cirencester and Colchester,
the latter associated with an apsidal shrine) are linked with       79

healing and the sun. The *Iunones* were protectors of women (the Latin epithet being adopted as a surname for the mothers in Treveran territory. At Castleford, Yorkshire, a depiction of three crude female heads, with an inscription to the Nymphs found below the courtyard of an early second century building in the *vicus*, endorses the healing water association alluded to earlier. Again, at Carrawburgh, the shrine of Coventina, a local goddess of springs has produced one depiction of a trio of Nymphs, presumably a version of the deity herself.

31  Plaque of Triple Coventina; Carrawburgh, Northumberland. Copyright: University of Newcastle upon Tyne.

Inscriptions can give us some idea about worshippers. Henig stresses the evidence for wealthy, romanised dedicants in Britain, citing such invocations as that of an *arcarius*, probably a municipal treasury official, at Chichester and the York dedication by Audens, the Ship's Pilot of the Sixth Legion. Certainly corporate worship is attested at London where an inscription refers to the restoration of a shrine by a district, but the majority of dedicants may well have belonged to the peasant classes. That Celts were involved in British dedications is attested by such instances as that of the sculptor Sulinus, son of Brucetus who set up shrines to the *Suleviae* in Bath and Cirencester. It is at first glance surprising that many dedicants were military and therefore male, but women were frequently involved in Gaul and Germany; the Rödingen altar to the Mothers of the Gesationes (a

32 Statue-base dedicated to the *Suleviae*, by Sulinus son of Brucetus,
a sculptor; Bath. Photograph Betty Naggar. Roman Baths Museum.

Rhineland tribe) for instance was dedicated by a man and
woman jointly. Haverfield makes the point that of the many
dedications by soldiers, most were of low rank.

The iconography of the three Mothers gives us valuable
information as to how they were looked upon by their
devotees. The vast majority are seated side by side, fully
draped. But within this framework, there are many
variations, all of which stress the maternal, nourishing and
fertility role of the goddesses. The commonest attributes are
baskets of fruit, *cornuacopiae*, loaves, fish and children. In
some instances the Mothers actually suckle infants and one
breast may be bared, as at Alesia. Swathing bands and
baby-bathing materials are indicated at Vertillum (Côte
d'Or). An Autun group depicts the Mothers with a child,
*patera* and *cornucopiae* respectively. A stone from Trier
depicts the deities, one with swathing band and the other
two with distaffs, as if here the Mothers take on the role of
Fates, spinning out men's lives. This, and the association
with Fortuna or Good Luck, is interesting and understandable in divinities whose role was essentially 81

33   Altar to the *Suleviae*, dedicated by Brucetus; Cirencester. Photograph: Betty Naggar. Corinium Museum.

concerned with well-being and prosperity. The silver 'feather' or 'leaf' plaque from London shows the three Mothers seated on a bench, each with a branch or reed and a *patera*. It is suggested that the former could represent a palm-leaf and therefore a Victory symbol. One or two other features are noteworthy: dogs not infrequently accompany the Mothers, as at Ancaster and Cirencester. A recently-discovered London carving apparently shows four Mothers, but it is possible that the intrusive one may represent a deified empress as a *Dea Nutrix*.

It is quite clear from the attributes of the Mothers that they represent primarily fertility and general prosperity, whether in the directly maternal manner of infant-association or through portrayals of the earth's fecundity. The carefree attitude of the Cirencester relief – where the goddesses sit chatting as if they were human mothers at a coffee morning with children playing and lap-dogs – is exceptional. More frequently they sit rigidly, staring straight in front of them. However, their basic benevolence is clear. Some of the Rhineland groups are interesting in

34   Relief of Triple Mothers with children; Cirencester. Photograph:
Betty Naggar. Corinium Museum.

that, as at Bonn a young woman with long, free-flowing hair
is flanked by two maturer women in large circular bonnets.
This apparent age-difference may symbolise different stages
of womanhood and, by implication, the seasonal
progression. One interesting point concerns the
iconography of triadism itself. Sometimes, as in the Côte
d'Or region, each goddess is identical, with exactly the
same attributes: here the significance of triplism seems to be
intensification – a triple avowal of devotion. In many
instances, as described above, the deities are treated differ-
ently: thus, at Cirencester and Maryport hairstyles or stance
may differ or attributes may vary. At Cirencester, for
instance, the Mothers hold a dog, fish and fruits
respectively, and at Carlisle a knife, fruit and flower are
each held by a different Mother. Here, in addition to
straightforward intensification of the image, fecundity-
symbolism is enhanced by the encompassing of different
aspects of fertility.

### Distribution, Context and Associates of the Triple Mothers

The cult appears to have belonged exclusively to certain
parts of western Europe, specifically within the Celtic
world. The proliferation of topographical surnames in the
Rhineland and in parts of France and their absence from
Britain, argues for Gaul as the original homeland.

The Mothers were worshipped as domestic, private
deities by individuals, as is evidenced in Hungary by
quantities of pipe-clay and lead figurines, and perhaps at
Backworth in Durham where a silver skillet and one of the

gold finger-rings found inside was dedicated to the Mothers. But the monumental character of much of the evidence suggests some element of public worship, in shrines. Even small portable items, like the silver plaque from London, may have been set up on a shelf against the wall of a shrine. There is substantial direct and indirect evidence for mother-goddess shrines. Temples were common in the Rhineland where they were sometimes important religious centres, as at Bonn where the *Matronae Aufaniae* were worshipped. At Pesch a third century shrine was dedicated to the *Vacallinehae* (a topographical name for the Mothers), invoked mainly by soldiers of Legion XXX Ulpia. At Trier, a curious group called the *Xulsigiae*, possibly a type of Mother associated with local springs, but whose name may be linked with the *Suleviae*, were invoked in a small chapel in one of the lesser Lenus-precincts. The association of mother-goddesses with springs and water was important at, for example, Aix-les-Bains and Gréoulx, a thermal shrine in the Durance Valley, where the Mothers were called *Griselicae*. Nemausus of the Nîmes Spring was male but the *Nemausicae* were local Mothers (see Chapter Five).

In Britain temples were associated with forts on Hadrian's Wall, such as Housesteads, where important cult-remains occur, or Castlesteads, where a centurion rebuilt a shrine to the Mothers. There may have been more than one temple in London where an inscription actually refers to the restoration of a temple probably during the third century, and two monumental sculptures survive.

We will examine below the significance of other deities in relation to the mother-goddess cult – whether the Triple Mothers or other versions of the fertility-goddess. Here, it is interesting simply to mention direct associations in epigraphy or iconography between the *Matres* in their distinctive plural form and other god-forms. What one might term direct associations are those where the Mothers are linked on dedications with other cults, or where they actually share imagery on a given item of iconography. Indirect association, where a shrine may yield a number of diverse religious objects, may or may not be significant in that if the Mothers and, say, Mercury are clearly dominant, as at Bonn or Baden, this means something in terms of cult. On the other hand Celtic temples often housed a number of deities who may have little or nothing to do with each other.

The association in the Rhineland between the Mothers and a (presumably) Celtic version of Mercury has been mentioned. Such a link is supported by such iconography as that from Trier, where a fragment of sculpture depicting the Mothers bears also a three-headed god, frequently identified in Gaul with Mercury. At Wellow in south-west Britain, a relief of a now headless group depicts a nude god with Mercury's purse associated with two out of three surviving Mothers. At Cirencester an altar is dedicated to Mercury and the Mothers. This link with Mercury makes sense in the context of his role as commercial/prosperity god and it is a small step from there to see him as adopted by the Celts as a general god of well-being. Indeed, countless Gaulish reliefs depict the god associated with fertility and prosperity-emblems and, at Tongres, Mercury is triple-phallused. We shall see later that he was frequently linked with a Celtic consort, Rosmerta, who is quite clearly herself a type of mother-goddess. In addition to Mercury, the Mothers are on occasion linked to a number of other god-forms. Fortuna is sometimes present herself, as on an inscription at Glanum, to the Mothers *Glanicae* and *Fortuna Redux* or the Mothers themselves assume Fortuna's attributes. Epona herself also a mother-goddess (pp 91–94) is linked to the *Matres* cult, and there are many others, all with an enhancing well-being function.

## Single Mother-Goddess Types

The cult of the *Deae Matres* or Three Mothers is sufficiently distinctive in its plurality to justify separate treatment. There remain other, single goddesses, sometimes with names but more often anonymous, with the same attributes of children, fruit, bread, *cornuacopiae*, dogs, *paterae* and other symbols of human or earthly prosperity. Where single representations are particularly interesting is in their evidence for a personal, individual cult expressed by small relatively cheap votive objects, usually white pipe-clay though occasionally bronze.

Few inscriptions mention single mothers by name. Whilst Ross and Cunliffe would argue that all Celtic goddesses embody a fertility-element, I prefer to classify as Mothers only those portrayals which carry an intrinsic fecundity-association. Thus Celtic goddesses known only from inscriptions, such as Icovellauna at Trier and Metz and Ritona at Trier, who are water-goddesses (see Chapter Five), may or may not be linked to the cult. However, one goddess, Aveta, from a Trier shrine is associated with several pipe-clay depictions of a nursing goddess. Rarely, as at Daglingwoth, Cirencester, the name itself 'Cuda', referring

35  Mother-goddess with three apples; Ashcroft, Cirencester. photograph: Betty Naggar. Corinium Museum.

directly to prosperity and inscribed on the base of a mother-
goddess carving, has essential fertility connotations.

Stone depictions of isolated mother-goddesses usually
take a form similar to the *Matres* in being seated, draped in a
long robe, with *cornucopiae*, *patera* or fruits. At Naix, a
mother has a dog and fruit and is associated with acolytes or
suppliants. At Crozant in Gaul a single mother stands with
three children – the number here is probably significant. A
parallel exists at Cirencester where a single mother bears
three apples. At Trier, outside a chapel in the Altbachtal
religious precinct, a statue of a mother bears a deep fruit-
basket and a dog; the statue had been deliberately decapitated, possibly by fourth century Christians. It is interesting
that at Trier the single mother version seems to have been
chosen rather than the triple form, whilst, for example, at
Cirencester both types co-existed. A particular kind of
depiction is present in the Luxembourg area, around
Dalheim where single mothers frequently sit in stone
*aediculae*, perhaps representing household shrines. A
distinctive type of mother-goddess occurs also in Holland
where two shrines to Nehalennia, at Domburg on the Isle of

86

36 Altar to Nehalennia; Colijnsplaat, Netherlands. Copyright: Rijksmuseum van Oudheden, Leiden.

Walcheren at the mouth of the Rhine, and Colijnsplaat on the East Scheldt Estuary have been identified. The Domburg sanctuary has been known from dedications and sculptures since 1647; the East Scheldt one was discovered in 1970, when fishermen recovered altars from a depth of eighty-five feet. Over 120 altars and sculptures have been recovered since then from the sea. What seems to have happened is that a temple on the banks of the river which, from epigraphic data, had its *floruit* around AD 200, later sank into the sea. The mother-goddess represented here is interesting for several reasons. First we know her name, Nehalennia. Second prolific finds suggest her cult to have been an important one. Third, inscriptions tell us details of her worshippers, for she was a native goddess invoked also by Romans and romanised Gauls. Tradesmen and seafarers dedicated altars to her in her temple out of gratitude for safety at sea and prosperity granted by her. Fourth, her images are remarkably consistent and she sits usually with baskets of fruit and frequently associated with *cornuacopiae*. Most important, however, is the fact that she invariably appears in company with a dog. We have already noted the occurrence of mothers with dogs, but this is normally sporadic. What we have here is essential identification with an animal similar to that of Epona with

87

37 Mother-goddess with palm; Caerwent, Gwent. Copyright: National Museum of Wales. Newport Museum.

her horse (pp 91–94). The symbolism of the dog is important here: if we use the mythology of the Graeco-Roman world, the beast could represent either healing or death, both of which are functions of the mothers. In the context of dogs and healing, the presence of a mother-goddess image at Lydney, Gloucestershire is relevant. The temple here was primarily associated with the healer god Nodens, whose zoomorphic attribute (abundantly represented here) was the dog (Chapters Five and Six). One or two other stone images of single mothers are worth mentioning. The stylised and schematic figure from Caerwent is interesting in its exaggeratedly large head, its grasp of a palm-branch (similar to the mothers on the London silver plaque) and perhaps its aquatic context, being found at the bottom of a well. This last supports the water/thermal spring connections noted for instance at Aix-les-Bains and at Bath. Seemingly the most curious British context for a mother-goddess is that of the anteroom of the Carrawburgh Mithraeum, but this is paralleled at Dieburg and may well represent the popular female alternative to Mithras, suggested for Epona on the Limes.

We may turn now to small personal offerings to the mother-goddess, the most frequent occurrences being those of white pipe-clay, manufactured in Rhineland and Central Gaulish *officina* or factories. These, termed *Deae Nutrices* or nursing goddesses depict a goddess seated sometimes (in the Central Gaulish ones) in a high-backed wicker chair, nursing one or two infants (one in the Rhineland workshops, two in Gaul). They occur frequently in Gaulish shrines as at St Ouen de Thouberville (Eure), at Trier (associated with Aveta) and among the Mediomatrici of Alsace, as at Sarrebourg. At Dhronecken near Trier, a shrine was apparently devoted to this goddess, represented not only by numerous statuettes of a nursing goddess, but by busts of children – presumably envisaged as being especially protected by the deity. At Alesia, a shrine yielded a pipe-clay mother with two infants in an *oppidum* with other, monumental, evidence for a mother-goddess cult. At a 'lararium' at Rézé near Nantes, standing pipe-clay figures with fruits and stamped solar signs are recorded. But their personal nature is shown by their occurrence in graves, as at Ballerstein and Hultenhause and Hassocks, Sussex (though their presence in British graves is rare). The sepulchral context of some pipe-clay mothers is interesting, especially since they sometimes appear with dogs, as at Canterbury, Titelburg, and in the Aveta-shrine in Trier. The dog-association could be connected with the Underworld or, indeed, as suggested, with healing. Some *deae nutrices*, as at Trier, are linked with healing-cult establishments.

One or two other individual cult-objects may finally be examined. The raven-attributes of a bronze seated goddess with *cornucopiae*, from an unprovenanced Gaulish location

38  Left. Pipe-clay mother-goddess and mould; Toulon-sur-Allier, France. Photograph: Miranda Green. Musée des Antiquités Nationales, St Germain-en-Laye. Right. Pipe-clay mother-goddesses; London. Copyright: Museum of London.

may embody death and underworld symbolism. A bronze seated female figure from a probable villa-site at Dawes Heath, Thundersley (Essex), nurses what may be a dog on her left knee. Other British bronzes are known, for example from Culverhole Cave in Gower and Owmby, Lincs. Finally, a unique wooden mother-goddess from Winchester sits holding a key, which could be an otherworld motif, the key to heaven. Keys are uncommon attributes, but an example occurs on an Epona-depiction from Gannat in the Allier area of France.

Associations of isolated mothers are interesting. Leaving aside divine couples as a separate issue (pp 95–98) one or two other direct links from Britain are worth examing here. At Kingscote, Gloucestershire an enthroned female bearing an object (possibly fruit or bread) in her lap, is accompanied both by a devotee pouring a libation onto an altar, and by a horseman god, perhaps a type of Mars (see Chapter Four). This is interesting because there is some suggestion of a war-element in Celtic fertility cults (p 101). Second, in the Cirencester area, single mothers are frequently associated with *Genii cucullati*, hooded dwarves, occurring often as triads in Britain, especially on the Cotswolds and on Hadrian's Wall. At Daglingworth near Cirencester three *cucullati* accompany a mother-goddess: one seems to be offering or receiving something from her. The goddess

39  *Genii cucullati* and mother-goddess (one *genius* offers something to the goddess); Cirencester. Photograph: Betty Naggar. Corinium Museum.

40  *Genii cucullati* and mother-goddess (two *genii* bear swords);
Cirencester. Photograph: Betty Naggar. Corinium Museum.

herself is called 'Cuda'. Another relief from the same place
portrays a seated mother holding a cake or fruit with
sword-bearing *cucullati*, again showing a war/protective
element. A *cucullatus* from Cirencester accompanying a
mother, holds an egg, whilst she carries fruit. This egg-
bearing characteristic is repeated, for example at Wycomb,
Glos, where two triads of *cucullati* hold eggs. Toynbee
definitely links these hooded gods both with fertility and
with death. The former is self-explanatory (the association
with the mothers and with eggs) but she would argue that
death-symbolism is demonstrated by the hooded, shrouded
heads suggestive of the Otherworld and the mystery of
death. Certainly *cucullati* share many characteristics of the
mothers. Even where they do not occur on the same carving,
they have a very similar distribution and they too inhabit
therapeutic spring-sanctuaries – like Bath and Springhead
(Chapter Five).

## Other Deities associated with the Mothers and Fertility

### Epona

Epona is first and foremost a patroness of horses, and thus
will be examined in detail in Chapter Six. However, many
features of this goddess associate her with the fertility and

prosperity role of the mother-goddesses. As is the case with
the mothers, many dedicants were soldiers but, appropriately, usually cavalry. Epona is essentially connected
with horses: her Celtic name is etymologically linked with
the beast, and she invariably appears riding side-saddle
(more rarely astride a horse) or in company with horses
and/or foals. Her inanimate attributes are the same as the
mothers – *cornuacopiae*, fruits and corn. Magnen &
Thevenot describe her as a specialist mother presiding over
Gaul's most important beast. Her association with dog and
birds and with healing springs (as at Allerey, Côte d'Or, and
Luxeuil) demonstrate close kinship with the mothers. At
Thill Châtel a third century soldier invoked Epona, the
mothers and a local *genius* together. A monument at
Jabreilles (Haute-Vienne) has on one surface Epona and a
mare and the Triple Mothers on another. At Santenay Epona
appears with a mare and a suckling foal, in image of
maternity, and Epona sometimes feeds a foal from a *patera* –
showing her function as a nourishing goddess. The Mothers
and horses are linked for instance on a relief from
Armançon (Côte d'Or) where the goddesses sit in a cart
drawn by two horses, perhaps riding round the fields to

41  Stone Epona; Luxembourg (unprovenanced). Photograph: Miranda Green. Musée d'histoire et d'art, Luxembourg.

42   Bronze Epona; Dalheim, Luxembourg. Photograph: Miranda
Green. Musée. . . Luxembourg.

ensure fertility; and this representative type appears again
at Essay (Côte d'Or).

Again, like the mothers, Epona is associated with graves
and death at such cemeteries as La Horgue au Sablon. Of
particular interest is the triple Epona from Hogondange
(Moselle), treated exactly like the *Deae Matres*, and at
Varhély in Dacia a dedication to 'the Eponas' is recorded.
As Thevenot points out the great majority of monuments
show Epona to have been worshipped in rural, domestic
contexts. Linduff has made a recent study of the Epona-cult,
and has a number of interesting arguments concerning its
interpretation. She comments that the Celts used horses,
primarily mares, as work-animals on farms. Linduff is of the
opinion that Epona was specifically concerned with the
craft of horse-breeding and was associated with the qualities of the domestic, pastured beast where the protection
and fertility of the horse itself is clearly emphasised on
iconography, for instance where mares and foals are
depicted. The fact that the Celtic horse-deity was female is
significant. Plant and beast-tending activities may well have
been in the hands of women 'as is the case in most          93

agricultural warrior-groups' (Friedl 1975) so that women may have been seen as great earth-mothers who nourished and protected as well as simply produced. Linduff explains the popularity of the cult among the mounted soldiery of the Celtic provinces in terms of its personal, beneficent nature which, unlike Mithraism, imposed no restrictions and offered protection both for the cavalryman himself and his horse.

### The Celtic 'Venus'

The pipe-clay seated figurines of nursing mothers described above appear to share context and function with another type of clay figure made in the *officina* of Central Gaul and the Rhineland, namely the so-called 'Venus', consisting of nude statuettes resembling the Graeco-Roman goddess of Love. Despite their appearance, it seems as though the figures portray a domestic/protective fertility deity and this is a view supported by a number of scholars. Linkenheld argues that the cult of Venus in monumental form is so rare

43 Pipe-clay 'Venus'; London. Copyright: Museum of London.

44 Pipe-clay 'Venus' with solar symbols; Allier, France. Photograph: Miranda Green. Musée des Antiquités Nationales, St Germain-en-Laye.

in Gaul that the pipe-clay figures cannot represent a true Venus-deity. Certainly their context seems to demonstrate their domestic nature, and they occur in quantities in houses, shrines and graves – as at Verulamium – and at many cemeteries and sacred springs, including Vichy in Gaul and Springhead in Kent. Their water/healing association in Britain – at the Kent shrine, at Bath and possibly the Walbrook Valley reflect their very strong link with thermal sanctuaries in Gaul (Chapter Five). The Gaulish 'Venuses' would appear to have represented a domestic cult favoured by the lower echelons of society, such items being offered by a frequently feminine clientèle, for the restoration of good health and fertility. The goddess was invoked by women to aid them in conception and to protect them in childbirth and against disease. Indeed, the goddess here represented may herself have represented health, abundance and fecundity. The classical Venus herself was originally a deity of the fertile soil and she may well have been the conceptual as well as the physical inspiration for this Celtic cult. The essentially Celtic character is demonstrated not only by context but by, for instance, the alien accompanying images of cosmic bodies and the sun (Fig. 44).

## Divine Couples

Very often a Celtic goddess is portrayed in company with a god of Roman or Celtic origin. It is difficult to establish who is the main deity and who the consort, but we should perhaps recall the Irish vernacular evidence (Chapter One & below, p 101) that the territorial goddess took a mortal sovereign as mate. This may be the origin of the presence of Celtic divine couples, even though, as is the case with Mercury and Rosmerta, she adopts his attributes of *caduceus* and purse. Sometimes a couple may simply represent the masculine and feminine elements in a given cult-concept or image.

Many indigenous couples are recorded, and the combined presence of god and goddess may itself imply divine marriage and therefore consequential fertility. Among the Gaulish tribe of the Aedui an anonymous couple is a dominant iconographical type: the goddess here usually has a *cornucopiae* and *patera* as badges of her prosperity-role, and sometimes the god also carried a *cornucopiae*. Epigraphy gives us a number of couples, some of whom are tied to locality. Thus we have Luxovius and Bricta at Luxeuil; Bormo and Damona; Ucuetis and Bergusia; and Sucellus and Nantosuelta. These last two are enigmatic but

45   Bronze Sucellus; Lyon. Photograph: Miranda Green. Musée . . . St Germain-en-Laye.

46   Silver finger-ring dedicated to Sucellus; York. Illustration & copyright: Miranda Green. Yorkshire Museum.

important: the god, who often appears on his own, is characterised by a long-shafted hammer, and is called 'the Good Striker'. In southern Gaul, he is associated also with the emblems of the woodland/fertility god Silvanus as peasant-protector of harvest and cattle, and in the Moselle area, he seems to have dominion over the local wine-trade and, by implication, the fertility of the vine. The goddess, Nantosuelta, has varied attributes but, in the land of the Mediomatrici of Alsace, she often bears the image of a house on a long pole, emphasising her essentially domestic function. The couple have other attributes such as pots and barrels and this may reflect the wine-protection alluded to just now. The goddess' name 'Winding River' demonstrates water-symbolism which is not unknown to the Mothers, and her repeated association with ravens may suggest underworld symbolism. British representations are rare: possible evidence comes from East Stoke, Notts, and a silver ring to Sucellus comes from York.

Of divine couples, the most interesting for Britain are Mercury and Rosmerta. The phenomenon of Celtic female and Roman male name alluded to in Chapter One occurs here – as if the goddess were the indigenous, territorial deity. Mercury, we have already seen, had associations with the Mothers, and Rosmerta may well be a version of the Celtic fertility goddess. Her name means the 'Good Purveyor', a prosperity-title. She frequently appears with a basket of fruit or Mercury's purse and it is apparent that the trading (hence prosperity) function of the Roman god is here adapted to a Celtic context. The British evidence forms an interesting group: at Bath the couple share a relief with three Genii *cucullati* and a ram – both fertility symbols, and the former at least linking them directly with the Mothers. Three reliefs come from Gloucester, where there must have existed at least one temple dedicated to the couple: the Bon Marché site stone (Fig. 48) is significant in that Rosmerta's head is bigger than Mercury's, as if she were the more important, and the couple are associated with Fortuna who is sometimes linked with the Three Mothers. Rosmerta's bulging bag on another Gloucester stone denotes her prosperity-function, and on a third (Fig. 47) she holds a *patera* over a bucket – perhaps a similar symbol of plenty to the Celtic cauldrons of Irish and Welsh tradition. The relief of Mercury and Rosmerta from Nettleton Shrub is fragmentary but the goddess holds a basket, fruit or cake, and the item is noteworthy in coming from an important temple-complex, perhaps associated with healing (Chapter Five).

47  Tablet depicting Mercury and Rosmerta; he has *caduceus*, cock-
erel and purse; she has double-axe, *patera* and wooden bucket;
Shakespeare Inn, Gloucester. Copyright: Gloucester City
Museum.

## Male Fertility Associates

Several male Romano-Celtic deities possess links with the
Celtic fertility cult. Mercury – or a Celtic god disguised in
the art-form of the Roman god – has been cited already as
having strong and specific associations with the Mothers.
The Celtic Mercury has other aspects connecting him firmly
to an indigenous, territorial divinity similar to the goddesses; thus, like them, he frequently possesses
topographical surnames, for example Arvernus or Visucius
in Gaul. A bronze statuette from Tongres portrays Mercury
with triple phallus, as we have seen. It should be remembered that in Roman religion, too, Mercury had a fertility
function – as evidenced by his animal emblem of the ram –
and it need not surprise us that this was adopted and
developed in a Celtic environment. Mars too had a fertility
role, probably from his original Italian function as an
agricultural and storm-god. He sometimes bears geo-

98

48  Mercury, Rosmerta and Fortuna; Mercury has a winged hat and
    *caduceus*, Rosmerta a second *caduceus* and 'mushroom' coiffure,
    Fortuna a *cornucopiae* and a rudder on a globe; Bon Marché site,
    Gloucester. Photograph: Betty Naggar. Gloucester City Museum.

graphical names – such as Condatis, and was associated
particularly with healing and thermal sanctuaries (Chapters
Four & Five).

Perhaps the most curious associate of the Mothers and
fertility was the Celtic sun-god (Chapter Two), linked in the
Roman period with the sky-god Jupiter. The Rézé 'lararium'
with its standing goddess bearing solar symbols has already
been mentioned. At Clarensac a fragmentary altar is
dedicated . . . . . *et Terrae matri* and bears the wheel-sign of
the Celtic sun-god. At Trier Jupiter and the Mothers are
associated. A curious find from Toutenant in Gaul, which
could possibly have significance, is a bronze statuette of
Jupiter discovered under the roots of an old oak-tree
nicknamed the 'oak of three daughters'.

The association of the Celtic celestial god and the Mothers is interesting. If, as generally conceded, the pipe-clay
figurines of 'Venus' are in reality representative of a domestic fertility cult, then there is a definite and homogeneous
body of evidence to associate the two cults of fecundity and
sky, in that a number of these 'Venus' figures bear solar
signs. The sun-god cult shows other signs of fertility associations, as we have seen in Chapter Two.

*Fertility and the Human Head*

A strange phenomenon in Celtic iconography is the link between the symbolism of the phallus and the human head. Phallic symbolism is common in Mediterranean Europe, and is certainly by no means exclusively Celtic. But the apparent link between the human head and the phallus is interesting, since we know (pp 28–32/216–220) that the Celts venerated the head, and practised head-hunting, frequently also representing their deities by the image of the head on its own. Since the head was regarded as particularly important, it is logical that it was also, on occasions, endowed with potent fertility-properties. Presumably 'phallic' heads, like those from Eype in Dorset and Broadway, Worcs represented local gods; the same may be true of the

49   Stone phallic head; Eype Dorset. Photograph: Miranda Green. Dorset County Museum.

recent find from a small Romano-British settlement at Guiting Power, Glos, which consists of a crude human figure, itself phallic in shape and the head of which forms the glans. The figure is possibly horned, thus (pp 195–199) increasing its potency even further. Head/phallic symbolism is associated in a different but related way at Colchester, where a face-pot bears an applied phallus and goat-horns. Finally, the curious bronzes from Silchester and Icklingham should be mentioned: here heads of bulls rather than humans are presented but with the features replaced by male genitals. Once again horns, head and phallus are linked, this time associated with the bull, a powerful Celtic emblem of strength and virility.

## Irish and Welsh Tradition

The prominence of women and goddesses in Irish tradition is very striking. The territorial, nature/fertility goddess is supreme, and mates with a mortal sovereign to ensure the continued prosperity of Ireland. Triplism is extremely important: the triadic goddesses of Ireland Ériu, Fódla and Banbha personify the land itself. The three Machas were associated with war and fertility, and in one legend Macha is connected also with horses when, on the verge of giving birth to twins, she is forced to run in a race against the horses of Conchobar, King of Ulster. War seems to be an aspect important to fertility-symbolism in Ireland in that the Mórrígan, a trio of war-goddesses, have pronounced sexual characteristics. Like all Irish war-goddesses, they influence the outcome of battle by magical means. The Mórrígan indulge in nerve-racking shape-shifting before bewildered soldiers, changing in an instant from hag to beautiful girl to death-crow. Ériu, Fódla and Banbha are also involved with war and shape-shifting, as is Badb who confronts the Ulster hero Cú Chulainn in battle and unnerves him by changing into 'Badb Catha', a crow, harbinger of death. The Irish fertility goddesses combine features of war, maternity, youth, age, monstrosity, all as part of a fundamental life/death/protection symbolism.

Welsh tradition is not so forthcoming, but we know of a mother-goddess Modron, and it is interesting that Rhiannon in the Mabinogion is linked with horses, especially mares, fertility, sorcery, destructive power and the underworld.

## Conclusion

It is possible to see that the mother-goddesses in the Celtic world had a complex and varied series of roles, and indeed pervaded very many aspects of life. Cunliffe, as we have seen, states that all Celtic female deities were associated with fertility. Life and death, war, maternity, good-luck, prosperity and protection all come within their sphere of responsibility. Maternity and prosperity are overtly indicated by the images themselves and their attributes. Death and the underworld are indicated by the sepulchral context of some mothers and perhaps the animal-symbolism of the dog and the crow. But the dog may also represent healing (as in the classical imagery of Aesculapius) and health was certainly important to the mothers. Water is a life-source, associated also with healing,

101

the underworld and fertility, and thus provides a common element for much of the mothers' activities. But the main image projected is that of the fecundity and well-being of human beings, beasts and the earth. The war-element, so prominent in Ireland, may arise from land-protection, and the sword-bearing *cucullati* from Gloucestershire may symbolise the triumph of fertility over barrenness or disease rather than war itself. Toynbee suggests that the Mothers were goddesses of fertility both in this and the otherworld.

The *Matres* cult is especially interesting because of its evidence for the popularity of a relatively homogeneous and widespread Celtic cult. It grew to full maturity only in the Roman period but it was absolutely foreign to the Roman world, especially in its triadic form. Inscriptions demonstrate that the cult was popular throughout the Roman period and devotees of the mother-goddesses were setting up altars from the time of Gaius (AD 37–41) to that of Gordian (AD 238–244). Style is sometimes interesting: sometimes it is romanised and naturalistic but, as at Nyon and Bath (Fig. 92), it may be schematic and abstract, as if craftsman and patron owed little to Roman tradition (Chapter Seven). A few other points may be made. In nearly all cases the maternal rather than the sexual aspects of the female image are projected – indeed the goddess is invariably clothed – the sexual parts of the body are not emphasised. Instead, the images rely for their symbolic power on accompanying attributes including animals (a powerful fertility/nature symbol in themselves (Chapter Six)) and, sometimes, on the power of triplism or plurality. Perhaps of most interest is that the cult appealed not only to women but to soldiers, merchants and even Roman officials. Essentially maternal characteristics were employed to visualise and worship a deity whose sphere developed from that of simple fertility to protection and well-being in all aspects of life.

# CHAPTER FOUR:
# WAR, DEATH AND THE UNDERWORLD

## Introduction

At first glance it appears curious to link the two concepts of death and war in one chapter. But closer examination of the evidence reveals a number of associations in Celtic religious belief. Caesar makes an interesting comment in this context:

> 'The Druids attach particular importance to the belief that the soul does not perish but passes after death from one body to another; they think that this belief is the most effective way to encourage bravery because it removes the fear of death' (*de Bello Gallico VI*, 14)

The two strands of death and combat have further connections: we know from a number of classical writers that a warrior-élite existed in Gaul and Britain, second in rank only to the tribal king; this highly stratified society is endorsed in the vernacular traditions of Ireland. We will see that from the earlier first millennium BC, a warrior-aristocracy is represented by rich and elaborate graves, attesting not only to the wealth of this class long before the historical Celtic period but to a strong belief in a positive, personal and tangible afterlife where the accoutrements of earthly life will be required and the terrestrial status retained. War and the underworld were closely linked from the Middle Bronze Age where we see evidence of the dedication of weapons and armour to the infernal powers. Repeated cross-references between war on the one hand and chthonicism on the other can be observed.

## WAR AND WAR-GODS

The Celts enjoyed fighting: literary evidence tells us of a warrior-élite, where display of prowess was a prominent feature of life, a world of chariots, individual feats of valour and skill, single combat and splendid weapons. The ready adoption, during the Roman period, of the main Roman war-god Mars, makes sense when seen against this backdrop. The tribe was seen as protected and glorified by

103

the local war-god who personified and led his people to victory. It is in the Roman period in Britain and Gaul that we can identify numerous different facets to a martial cult. But there is evidence that war-gods were worshipped long before in western Europe.

## The Prehistoric War Gods

Depictions of deities in warrior-form may go back to the earlier Bronze Age, exemplified by the statue-menhir from Puech-Real (Tarn) which bears a dagger. We have seen that there existed from the early first millennium BC a warrior-aristocracy, evidenced especially from rich grave-goods, and one may assume the presence of appropriate divinities. At Val Camonica, religious rock-carvings show Bronze Age weapon-types such as halberds and daggers and certain rocks are covered with weapon-carvings; there is an implication that weapons were definitely venerated in the Bronze Age. Towards the end of the Bronze Age the Camunians portrayed battle-scenes between warriors whose ithyphallic character demonstrates fertility/potency symbolism. The Bronze Age rock-carvings of both North Italy and Scandinavia share an association between warriors and sun-symbolism. Scandinavian tradition also reflects weapon-reverence: the great group of carved spears from Uppland 'suggest . . . . delight in, and respect for, the weapon itself' (Gelling 1969, 31).

The hoards of weapons which were buried at least from the Middle Bronze Age, may reflect a religious act of offerings made, perhaps, by soldiers to a god of war. Rapiers from the Cambridgeshire Fens exemplify this tradition, which is reflected also by swords and spears once more frequently found in aquatic contexts. We have to be careful here: as in the succeeding Iron Age, it may be prestige items in general rather than specifically war-equipment that were being offered maybe to local water-gods. Certainly valuable martial accoutrements were deliberately deposited in rivers and lakes during the Iron Age. The Battersea Shield, the Waterloo Helmet and the lake hoards of Neuchâtel and Llyn Cerrig are just a few of numerous examples.

Cults associated specifically with weapons are a feature of Iron Age religion. Weapon-burials, apart from aquatic deposits, are present at the South Cadbury hillfort where, associated with the Iron Age porched shrine, weapon-burials formed a group discrete from the young animal-burials also associated with the shrine. Alcock suggests that

50    Bronze shield, first century AD; from Thames at Battersea, London. Copyright: trustees of the British Museum.

51  Bronze horned helmet, first century BC; from Thames at Waterloo
Bridge, London. Copyright: Trustees of the British Museum.

perhaps both warrior and peasant offerings are represented
here. The Hayling Island sanctuary contained numerous
pieces of cart-fittings, spears and swords; and at the Iron
Age shrine of Gournay-sur-Aronde (Oise), hundreds of
deliberately-damaged weapons are recorded. Caesar (*BG VI*,
17) mentions weapons as part of the booty piled on the
ground dedicated to the god of the winning side in intertribal warfare.

Miniature weapons, probably votive or talismanic items
occur in pre-Roman and Roman contexts, sometimes in
shrines. Worth in Kent and Frilford (Oxon) have produced
Iron Age-type shield-models and a sword and shield
respectively, from pre-Roman strata at temple-sites, suggesting the supremacy of a war-god here. The later Romano-
Celtic shrine at Worth continued the worship of a warrior,
as evidenced by a huge fragmentary statue at a site where
few other cult-objects are present. Shield-models appear
elsewhere at, for example, Breedon-on-the-Hill hillfort,
Leics and Garton Slack. The tradition continues into the
Roman period, when multiple spear-models are particularly
common. At Woodeaton (Oxon) six spears were found,
some ritually bent double at a temple-site yielding
iconographical evidence for the worship of a war-god. The
Romano-Celtic temples of Harlow and Lamyatt Beacon each
produced some half-a-dozen spear-models, the latter associated with brooches depicting horsemen. The Bancroft
Roman Mausoleum site has produced also a circular shrine,
probably late in date, associated with a number of large iron
spear-models and a ritual pig-burial. The presence of multiple spear-models is interesting since it seems to continue

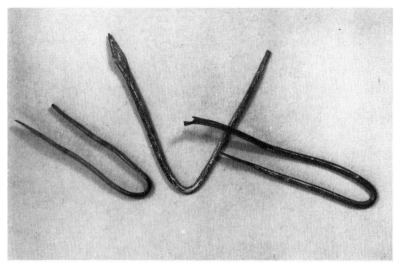

52   Group of ritually-bent bronze spear models; Woodeaton temple,
     Oxon. Photograph: Betty Naggar. Ashmolean Museum, Oxford.

the Iron Age practice of burying warriors with groups of
spears (presumably reflecting their possessions in life)
rather than single examples.

Armour and weapons had important symbolism for the
Celts. Indeed, as Hodder points out, artefacts in general
were not simply functional but were also symbols. The
spear was standard (Gaulish *gaesatae* or spear-warriors
were an important group of fighters (Polybius *II*, 22–2)) and
swords are common burial-finds. Traditionally Celts fought
naked but helmets were sometimes worn, and there is some
evidence for the use of chain mail, as depicted on
sculptures of Celtic warriors. Helmets and shields bore
animal-motifs: Diodorus Siculus (*V*, 30) mentions the
projecting bronze animals attached to shields; and we know
– for example from coins and the Gundestrup Cauldron – of
boar and bird-crests on helmets. The function of the latter
may have been partly to enhance height, and therefore
terror, and partly talismanic: certain birds and boars
(Chapter Six) did possess a war-symbolism. Definitely
apotropaic are the amulets depicted on the Orange Arch
where wheel-symbols appear on cuirasses and helmets, and
the latter are sometimes shown with horns. The wheel-sign
may have been a motif of solar protection (Chapter Two)
and it is apparent (Chapter Six) that horns may have
combined ferocity and fertility/potency symbolism. The
Orange Arch dates to the mid first century BC but an earlier
tradition of solar motifs on weapons is exemplified by the

107

Hallstatt dagger with the wheel-decorated hilt, from Grave 696 at Hallstatt.

Though iconographic evidence for deities during the Celtic Iron Age is comparatively sparse, there are some images of warriors; the difficulty is in deciding whether these are representations of gods or people. Celtic coins portray numerous illustrations of warfare, as one might expect within the milieu of a heroic society. Indeed, as Laing comments, it is impossible to tell whether divine or mortal beings are depicted. Cavalry, infantry and chari-oteers are all represented. The Aeduan chief Dumnorix, who fought Caesar, is probably depicted on an inscribed coin showing a warrior with carnyx, boar-standard and severed head, presumably a battle-trophy. Coins of the Andecavi (around Angers) display the motif of a charioteer under whose horse lies a fallen warrior with shield and spear. The charioteers so prominent in classical and Irish written sources, and represented also in Iron Age graves, are depicted on the coinage: for example, on Remic and Kentish coins a spearman is depicted walking down the chariot-pole, reflecting the feat of bravado remarked upon by Caesar (IV, 33). Warriors are frequently naked, as in the literature, but some wear a cuirass. A special group of riders is noteworthy in that the soldier who brandishes sword or spear in a gesture of ecstasy is usually naked and female. This may represent one of the war-goddesses so prominent in vernacular sources. In this context the portrayal on certain Gaulish and British coins of a horse with a crow or raven perched on its back probably represents the Irish war-goddess Badb Catha who could change her shape to that of a carrion bird. We know, too, of at least one British war-goddess, Andraste of the Iceni, mentioned, for exam-ple, by Dio Cassius (LXII, 2).

Sculpture usually reflects similar ambiguity. The sixth century Hallstatt Hirschlanden warrior is, in Celtic tradi-tion, naked, but with torc, helmet and sword-belt. The sculpture comes from a barrow and may represent the fallen hero. The warrior-images from the southern Gaulish shrine of Entremont (Fig. 11) are probably deities: they sit cross-legged, some wearing mail and sometimes resting one hand on a severed head. One torso bears on the breastplate a severed head symbol, seen as having a dual function of apotropaic power to protect the fighter with an image of victory and at the same time terrifying his enemies with the symbolism of their defeat. Other southern Gaulish warrior-sculptures are recorded, from as early as the fifth century BC at Grézean near Nîmes to the Celto-Roman warrior at Vachères

53 Iron Age chalk figurine of warrior; Garton Slack, Yorkshire.
Photograph: Miranda Green. Great Driffield Museum.

(Vaucluse) where a Celt wears armour showing Roman influence, but with a Celtic torc. At the beginning of the Romano-Celtic phase in Gaul, a cult-stone was set up at Mavilly (Côte d'Or) on which a 'Mars' figure accompanied by a ram-horned snake bears a La Tène III shield. This beast is elsewhere associated with war-imagery; on the Gundestrup Cauldon (plate E) one scene depicts a large 'god' dipping what appears to be a human sacrifice into a vat or bucket. A procession of horsemen and footsoldiers is led by a ram-horned snake. A bronze Mars with two such serpents comes from a British votive hoard (p 193).

Two British occurrences are especially interesting considering the general lack of pre-Roman cult-imagery. The major Iron Age sites of Garton and Wetwang Slack have produced many chalk figurines, some of which at least represent warriors, and a chalk shield is also known. More curious are the five pinewood figures of nude warriors with quartz-pebble eyes, detachable phalli and round shields, set up in a simple boat-model found at Roos Carr, Humberside. Not precisely datable, they are thought to be at least as early as the Iron Age.

## Romano-Celtic War-Cults

When Graeco-Roman historians encountered the Celtic world, the combative character of these people was particularly noted. Caesar shows the warrior to have been a man of rank, above a mere freeman in status, and his special place in Celtic society is endorsed by the heroic tales of the Ulster Cycle. War-princes ride to battle in chariots, collect enemy heads as trophies, display feats of skill and valour and indulge both in constant local battles and in individual fighting between champions. All these practices are supported by the archaeological evidence for splendid weapons, chariots and severed heads (real or sculptured), as characteristically Celtic traditions. With such a pre-occupation with warfare, Celtic war-gods must have existed at the time of Roman influence. Indeed, such deities were observed and commented upon in the sources. But such writers were biased by their own context of named and strictly functional gods and Caesar, for instance (BG VI, 17), speaks of the popularity of Mars among the Gauls and of the consecration of booty to him, sometimes in mounds of precious items with whom no one dared to interfere on pain of death or torture. Caesar cannot himself have encountered the worship of Mars in Gaul. Rather, at some time the Romans superimposed the name of their principal war-god on native warrior-deities and/or the Celts themselves adopted this name. What the Romans may have met in Celtic lands are tribal protector-gods with a war-role. In this connection Lucan's comment on Teutates, who was one of three Celtic gods said to have been encountered by Caesar's army in Gaul, may be relevant. The name 'Teutates' refers to 'tribe' and one of the later Berne Commentaries on Lucan identifies Teutates with Mars. The other commentator identifies Esus with Mars, but even this may have a certain consistency in that 'Esus' may simply mean 'Lord'.

The interest of archaeological evidence for a Romano-Celtic war-god lies in the identification of Roman with Celtic divine forms. In some cases there is straightfoward use of Roman god-names and iconographical form to represent a native god with the same basic role and a Celtic name referring to warfare or victory. We will see, however, that sometimes Mars becomes very strange and unclassical in a Celtic context.

## The Evidence of Inscriptions

In Gaul and Britain the name 'Mars' is linked epigraphically to a vast number and variety of Celtic names. The tribal element alluded to above is supported by dedications to Mars Toutatis, for instance at Barkway (Herts). Again, Teutates appears alone, for example, at Kelvedon, Essex on a pottery graffito on the same site as a late Iron Age pot depicting stamped warriors. But the basically tribal nature of the epithet is demonstrated by the linking of the name with other Roman gods – like Mercury and Apollo: thus, Teutates is a description rather than a name. Other Celtic epithets describe a war/victory or, interestingly, a kingly function for the native Mars. 'Caturix' means 'Master of fighting', 'Camulos' – 'powerful', 'Segomo' – 'victorious', 'Rigisamus' – 'greatest king' and 'Albiorix' – 'King of the world'. Some surnames refer to light or brilliance: thus, 'Belatucadrus' – 'fair shining one' or 'Loucetius' – 'brilliant'. The allusions to 'king' and 'light' are interesting in that such terms are more appropriate to celestial deities (and indeed the Roman Jupiter sometimes bears the description 'Loucetius'). But in the fluid religion of the Celts, nothing can be neatly compartmented and we have seen that the sky-god in his turn possessed a warrior-aspect (Chapter Two). Some names like Loucetius (occurring at Bath and Angers) or Camulos (in Britain and Germany) are scattered in the Celtic world; others appear perhaps only once or twice in a small area. Cocidius, for instance, at Bewcastle (where there was probably a cult-centre) and Belatucadrus, for instance at Carvoran, belong solely to the area of Hadrian's Wall. These two have frequent dedications to the Celtic name alone, suggesting that they pre-existed in their own right before the introduction of Mars to the military zone. Fairless suggests that both gods may have had a tribal aspect and this is hinted at in some of the dedications. Indeed, only three of the twenty-eight Belatucadrus invocations are demonstrably military. This god was worshipped by the lowest ranks of society; the great variations in the spelling of his name imply a low literacy-rate. Cocidius, by contrast, was definitely a soldiers' god, invoked by all echelons of the army, from the ranks to legionary commanders. Many Mars-epithets describe non-warlike aspects of the cult. They may be topographical, like Mars Condatis – god of the watersmeet in the Tyne-Tees area, and the Celtic Mars is often associated with sacred waters. At Bath Mars Loucetius and Nemetona (goddess of the grove) may have been imported from Germany, and the

111

54  Two silver repoussé plaques dedicated to Cocidius; Bewcastle, Cumbria. Copyright: Carlisle Museum.

grove-association is picked up by an epithet Mars Rigonemetis (king of the sacred grove) in Lincolnshire. Healing too was a function of this composite god, according to the epigraphy (Chapter Five). In Gloucestershire, 'Olloudius' refers to a sacred tree; and Cocidius near Ebchester is linked with tree-symbolism, being equated with Vernostonus (alder tree), reinforcing the link between this deity and the woodland god Silvanus. On the evidence of epigraphy alone, Mars seems to have been equated with a local tribal god whose functions embraced leadership of the army in wartime and guardianship of the tribe against disease, famine and evil at all times. The character of the Romano-Celtic Mars, as demonstrated in inscriptions, possibly means that by the Roman period the Celtic war-god did not exist *per se* but was a recognisable aspect of a wider protective role.

*Iconography*

Iconographical evidence for a Romano-Celtic war-god is common, especially in Britain, but it is frequently separate from epigraphy both in terms of physical association and in

112

terms of the role of the god represented. Images are often unnamed and, where there is a name, either 'Mars' is used to describe a very unroman deity or the god appears as a warrior yet with his name implying a peaceful role. Shrines associated with the war-god are notoriously scarce in the Celtic world but Britain has one or two interesting exceptions. Bewcastle, already referred to as a findspot for Cocidius-dedications, may well be the *fanum Cocidi* of later Roman Geographies such as the Ravenna Cosmography: two silver plaques from there are dedicated to Cocidius and represent a stylised Celtic warrior-god. The Woodeaton temple-site has yielded substantial quantities of cult-material, but including several miniature spears and two images of a war-god. One of the most interesting recent discoveries comes from Northumberland and was situated in a remote area near the Yardhope Roman marching-camp. Here a natural rock-cut chamber seems to have been adopted as a shrine; carved on the rock-face is the figure of a warrior, naked but with close-fitting cap, spear and small circular shield. His face is Celtic – with jutting brows and elongated eyes, and he is definitely a native warrior. He could be Cocidius, a major war-god of the Wall area, or an anonymous divinity. It may be that the soldiers of the nearby camp propitiated a native Celtic god already residing in the place before they came.

British 'Mars' images vary from the totally Graeco-Roman to the completely native in style, and it is the latter that are of particular interest since indigenous craftsmen were involved, responding to the wishes of a Celtic clientèle. North Britain – as befitted a predominantly military zone – contains numerous, frequently very schematised, war-figures, some horned, ithyphallic and nude, as at Maryport, Cumbria. The horns denote aggression and both they and the emphasised manhood represent virility; the combination is of similar symbolism to that of the bull. Wales too has occasional warrior-depictions though all iconography here is sparse: a Caernarfon stone bears a fragmentary image of a god with tri-lobed helmet and spear; and a recent find from Tre-owen near Newtown (Powys) consists of a circular mudstone block from a well, associated with third century material, on which is outlined a figure with a wreath, shield and sword, together with a possible dedication to Mars.

One interesting feature of the northern warrior-cult is its association with geese, linked with war in vernacular mythology. At Risingham, a war-god appears on an altar with a goose and a goose likewise accompanies the Ger-

113

55 Naked horned warrior-god with spear and shield; Maryport,
Cumbria. Copyright: Netherhall Collection. By courtesy of the
Hon Curator.

manic Mars Thincsus at Housesteads. I have noted
elsewhere (p 126) that goose-bones are frequently found
with Iron Age warrior-burials and, here, the suggestion is
that, as a fierce, aggressive and alert creature, the goose was
an appropriate theriomorphic attribute for Celtic war-gods.
An odd example of goose-iconography is the Caerwent
dedication to Mars Lenus (Fig. 56) who, peaceful healing
god as he was, nevertheless had this belligerent companion.
Caesar, in fact, mentions the goose as a taboo, non-edible
creature, perhaps therefore sacred.

Southern Britain has also produced stylised Celtic warrior-
depictions: the Stow-on-the-Wold warrior, for instance; the
curious triple Mars from Lower Slaughter, demonstrating the
Celtic predilection for triplism; and the 'Mars' with ram-

56  Statue-base with human and goose-feet, dedicated to Mars Lenus Ocelus Vellaunus Caerwent. Copyright National Museum of Wales. Newport Museum.

57  Stone tablet depicting triple Mars; from Roman well at Lower Slaughter, Glos. Copyright: Gloucester City Museum.

115

horned snakes from Southbroom, Wiltshire. But it is as a horseman that the Celtic war-god is at his most popular in southern Britain. If there was a specific horseman cult-centre, it was among the Catuvellauni of eastern England (Fig. 59) and, at Brigstock, Northants, a sacred precinct yielded several bronze horsemen and may have been dedicated to him. At Martlesham, Suffolk he was called Mars Corotiacus, but otherwise his name is unknown. The site of Kelvedon in Essex is noteworthy in this connection: here, there was a temple with various cult-objects dating both to the pre-Roman and Roman phases. A pot, which could be of later first century BC date, is stamped with horsemen with spiky, stylised hair, hexagonal Celtic shields and curious shepherd's crook-like objects; and associated, also, are sherds portraying footsoldiers apparently bearing standards. The whole scene is reminiscent of the imagery on plate E of the Gundestrup Cauldron showing a procession of horsemen and infantry. The parallel is even closer, since the Gundestrup plate bears also the image of a deity thrusting a man headfirst into a vat, the same activity mentioned by Lucan's commentators as human sacrifices to Teutates. A recent find from Kelvedon is a part of a grey jar with a graffito 'Toutatis'.

Horsemen occur elsewhere in the south; the temple of Lamyatt, Somerset produced horseman-brooches and miniature spears; and Bisley and Kingscote on the Cotswolds each produced stone reliefs of mounted warriors. It is interesting that equestrian warriors are extremely rare images in northern, military Britain. Southern, especially south-eastern Britain does appear to show a genuine preference for the worship of the war-god in this form.

The significance of depicting war-deities on horseback deserves closer examination. In the Roman world Mars is rarely equestrian, and thus the horseman form may refer to a specifically Celtic cult. We will see (Chapter Six) that the horse was a powerful symbol in Celtic religion. We see also from epigraphic evidence that the Celtic Mars could have a celestial role akin to that of such sky-gods as the Romano-Celtic Jupiter. Mars Rigisamus ('greatest king' or 'king of kings') and represented by a dedicatory plaque and crude figurine at West Coker, seems a term more suited to the supreme god than Mars. This role of 'Mars' as a high god is supported by some iconography: for instance, the Corbridge warrior bears the wheel-symbol of the Celtic sky and sun god; and the Celtic, wheel-bearing, Jupiter often appears as a warrior, for instance at Séguret in southern Gaul (Chapter Two). Most significant of all in this context are the 'Jupiter-columns' depicting the sky-god as a warrior-horseman

58  Stone relief of horseman-god; Margidunum, Notts. Photograph:
    Miranda Green. Nottingham University Museum.

fighting evil and death. Thus Celtic warriors on horseback
fall within a tradition of horse and horseman imagery. The
Celtic cult-horse was a solar being and thus was appropriate
to the high gods whose duty it was to protect the living
against the dark forces of the underworld. We have seen that
the Celtic war-god was a protector as well as simply a
warmonger and in my view the symbolism of the horseman
trampling evil is an important aspect of the Celtic Mars. We
may remember the Martlesham statuette to Mars Corotiacus,
where the god rides down a foe, perhaps symbolic of
negative, death forces. Mars as a celestial protector, similar
to Jupiter, is attested throughout the Celtic world. Thevenot
comments that shrines to the god in Gaul are frequently in
mountains (as are those of sky-deities), in addition to the
horseman aspect common to both the Celtic Mars and the
Celtic Jupiter.

117

59  Bronze horseman; Westwood Bridge, Peterborough, Cambs.
Copyright: Peterborough City Council. Peterborough City
Museum.

### The Warrior-Guardian

That the universal protection-guardianship element of Mars
in the Celtic world was his major role is shown by the
frequent occurrence of iconography and epigraphy representing the god in areas like south-west Gaul and the British
West Country, which had only a brief and early military
presence. Gods called 'Mars' were sometimes healers and
*genii* of prosperity and wellbeing and, even if the god is
depicted in the physical guise of a war-god, other peaceful
attributes or names betay this pacifist element. Both healing
and well-being could easily fall within the overall sphere of
guardianship against evil influence of whatever kind.
Where 'Mars' is a topographical spirit, again he is there as a
protector over territory. The cult perhaps reaches its apogee
in the Cotswolds where the god appears as a beneficient
godling of bucolic prosperity. Two altars from Custom
Scrubs serve to demonstrate this (Fig. 14): on one, a *Genius*
wearing tunic, cloak, cap and with double *cornucopiae* and
offering a *patera* over an altar was dedicated by a Celt to

60   Altar depicting Celtic Mars; King's Stanley, Glos. Copyright:
Stroud District Museum.

'Mars Olloudius', the surname meaning 'great tree'. On the
other a figure in the guise of Mars (though called Romulus)
bears a *cornucopiae* in addition to his arms. A number of
Mars-altars comes from the Bisley and King's Stanley area
of Gloucestershire and, though the god usually appears in
full armour, it is doubtful whether he was worshipped by
the peaceful, rural and prosperous Dobunni in his capacity
as a war-god. It should be noted that the Italian Mars
originally had an agricultural role as guardian of fields and
perhaps also as a storm-god, and a parallel symbolism was
developed for the god among these western Britons, even
though his introduction to this country must surely have
been in his normal military guise and role.


The Irish War-Deities

Throughout this chapter allusion has been made in passing
to Irish vernacular tradition and its bearing on evidence for
warfare and war-gods. But we need to examine this in
slightly greater detail since it has interesting similarities to
(and distinctions from) both classical literary evidence and
that from archaeological sources.
   The Ulster Cycle projects an image of a Celtic society very
like that recorded by Caesar and his fellows – a world of       119

aristocratic warriors, boasting, feats of valour, single combat or petty battles and headhunting. But the main supernatural powers concerned with warfare in Ireland are female, and, indeed, women often seem to have been directly and actively involved in war: Medb of Connaught was a war-queen-goddess; Amazonian teachers of the martial arts, like Scathach who taught Cú Chulainn, ran hero-schools for young warriors.

Many Irish war-goddesses are recorded, both in single and triple form: the Mórrígan, Macha and Badb are but the best-known. These deities have complex characteristics and functions, combining the roles of war and destruction with maternal and territorial features (Chapter Three). In this they are not dissimilar to the dual 'Mars' cult in Gaul and Britain just discussed, which embraced war, protection against disease and guardianship of land and prosperity. But Irish war-goddesses had a propensity for death, chaos and destruction. They did not normally themselves engage in battle but inspired terror and panic among contending warriors by magical means. Thus Badb confronted Cú Chulainn on the field of battle wearing a red cloak, with red eyebrows, driving a chariot, intent, by her appearance, on unmanning the young hero. This goddess had the unpleasant habit, too, of metamorphosing into a carrion bird 'Badb Catha' (Battle Raven) gloating over bloodshed. That such goddesses could be spiteful and capricious is demonstrated by another Cú Chulainn incident: preoccupied with fighting, the hero spurned the attentions of a young girl who turned out to be the battle-Fury, the Mórrígan. In revenge she attacked Cú Chulainn in different zoomorphic forms.

## Conclusion

We have looked at war-cults from the earlier first millennium BC to the Roman period, and from Eastern Europe to Ireland. The preoccupation of a Celtic society with warfare is reflected in religious evidence. We have seen that, diverse though the data is, certain common themes recur: the close association between war and death symbolism; the protective and tribal nature of war-deities; and the link with fertility. I suggest the symbolism of war appeared on at least two levels in the Celtic world. First, we have a straightforward warrior-cult or cults but, second, there is also the allegorical aspect concerned with life-death-rebirth and the struggle of light and life and prosperity/fertility against opposing negative forces. It is a dualistic, interdependent cult – as seen by the allegory of the Jupiter-columns and by the warrior/mother features of the Irish divinities. It is thus easy to see the metamorphosis, during the peaceful Romano-Celtic phase, from a true war-role to that of guardian and general protector.


## DEATH AND THE UNDERWORLD

### Literary tradition on the Afterlife

> 'Although Gaul is not a rich country, funerals there are splendid and costly. Everything the dead man is thought to have been fond of is put on the pyre, including even animals. Not long ago slaves and dependants known to have been their master's favourites were buried with them at the end of the funeral' (Caesar VI, 19).

Caesar noted that especial attention was paid to a 'good send-off', and indeed for the higher ranks of society, this kind of attitude is evidenced archaeologically by the early first millennium BC and even before. Lucan remarks that the Celts regarded death merely as a pause in a long life, as a bridge between one life and another and believed that human souls still controlled their bodies in another world after death. Caesar has the same message from observance of Druidic lore. Diodorus Siculus comments that the Celts held the souls of men to be immortal and after a definite number of years men lived a second life when the soul passed to another body.

There are substantial points of contact between the Graeco-Roman literary evidence and that of early Irish written sources on the afterlife. Transmigration of souls, in one form or another, is recorded, but it may be that it was metamorphosis or shape-changing that was thus inter-preted, rather than the Pythagorean theory of true soul-transmigration.

The classical historians' comments on transference of souls and life after death have vernacular support also on the question of rebirth. There is a strong Irish tradition of being born again, perhaps several times: Manannan, 'king of the Land of Promise' was associated with magical powers including, particularly, rebirth. He is interesting because he is associated with the historical seventh century AD Irish king Mongan. Irish evidence on the afterlife is both confused and confusing. One interesting feature is the otherworld feast, which is characteristic of the Heroic Tales. The story of Mac Da Tho's Pig is particularly famous; here Mac Da Tho (in reality a god presiding over the communal otherworld banquet) acts as host to the opposing companies of Ulster and Connaught; a large pig is provided and there ensues the usual squabble over the Champion's portion. We have already seen (Chapter One) that pork figured largely in such feasts and, indeed, that pork joints are frequently found in Iron Age Celtic sepulchral contexts. This chthonic meal may be seen also in late Iron Age 'Belgic' graves where wine and hearth were provided for the dead chief and a guest.

The Irish otherworld is basically a happy one, free from care, disease, old age and ugliness. Abundance, magic, music and birdsong dominate the scene. But it is not as simple as that: the otherworld can change character according to human imagination. Ironically, heroes can still fight, and unpleasant elements are introduced when mortals visit, perhaps explicable in terms of hazards deliberately present to prove the metal of heroes. This leads on to a further point on the fluidity of the Irish otherworld for traditional tales record visits of living humans to the world beyond the grave, usually enticed by supernatural beings. Conla son of Conn was enticed by a young woman to the otherworld; Bran son of Febhal was another mortal hero invited to the chthonic regions. But the otherworld was not always 'Elysian'. Sometimes distinct is the Irish Land of the Dead, a sombre place presided over by the god Donn, reflecting a dark aspect to the afterlife. At the Festival of Samain, it is the sombre images that predominate; the spirits of the dead move freely among the living at that time, considered to be a junction between summer and winter, when the barriers between the natural and supernatural world are temporarily broken down.

## The Evidence of the Grave

The burial of human remains in the ground may be carried out for hygiene, convenience or religious tradition. The accompaniment of such remains by grave-goods other than items of apparel implies a positive ritual concerning death. The objects may be associated with relatively nebulous rites, but the presence of very elaborate and essentially secular items suggests a belief about life after death and, indeed, the kind of life envisaged. Thus the burial of pots, toilet-equipment or martial gear, reflecting a person's earthly activities and needs, may indicate belief in a tangible afterlife. This, as we have seen, is a strong part of Celtic tradition as reflected in written sources. Grave-archaeology supports this belief. In the Late Bronze Age and the Hallstatt Iron Age, graves may be elaborate but, conversely, complex rites or beliefs are not apparent. However, by the later (La Tène) Iron Age, a number of very different customs recur, which we are not able to interpret but which attest to a complexity of sepulchral belief.

*Iron Age Burial Ritual*

As early as the later Bronze Age Urnfield phase in Europe, the very consistent and widespread adoption of the new burial rite of cremation in flat cemeteries – or urnfields – around the close of the second millennium BC suggests major changes in belief about death and the afterlife. In the succeeding Hallstatt phase the cremation rite of the urnfields was superseded by that of inhumation. From this time until, and including, the period of Roman influence, the view of the afterlife can be seen – on the evidence of elaborate, aristocratic, graves – to mirror earthly life; the otherworld was clearly one where earthly status was recognised and prolonged to eternity. The burials of the highest stratum of Celtic society were characterised by enclosure of the body in a plank-lined chamber with, very often, a four-wheeled vehicle; sometimes with even the horse-team itself, and the badge of the warrior – the long Hallstatt iron sword. It is interesting to look in detail at just one of these aristocratic graves. The Höhmichele Barrow, of sixth century BC date, is associated with the hilltop fortified residence of the Heuneberg, situated above the Danube. Inside the barrow were two wooden chambers, one containing a female burial and a wagon, the other a male burial with wagon and harness, laid on a bull-hide and with a woman beside him. With this male were buried his quiver, two bows and fifty iron-tipped arrows; and the barrow contained several other burials. The wealth of the grave is indicated not only by the accompanying weapons, bronze vessels and jewellery, but by the rich textiles – both clothing and tomb-wall drapery – which included true Chinese silk thread. Höhmichele is exceptional, though there are parallels. Less opulent but nonetheless élitist are Hallstatt warrior-graves without chamber or wagon. Such is the burial recorded at Ebberston, Yorks, where the body of a soldier with a Hallstatt C sword and chape was inhumed together with another sword associated with human bones.

123

The interest here is that both swords were deliberately – and evidently ritually – broken into four pieces.

Otherworld rites at this period could be complex and sometimes fairly grim. At Býci Skala in Czechoslovakia areas of a cave were used for funeral pyres, and ritual wagons, vessels, grain and animals were offered to the infernal powers. Forty, mostly female, people were buried here, many with heads, hands and feet missing; nearby the quartered carcases of two horses were deposited. Within a cauldron was a human skull; another skull formed a drinking-cup. This last feature is of particular interest since, as we have seen (Chapter One) human heads were collected as trophies by the Celts, and Graeco-Roman authors, indeed, record the use of the skulls of enemies as valued drinking-vessels.

In the La Tène Iron Age, rites connected with burial and the afterlife continued to reflect beliefs in a tangible otherworld though, as will be discussed, by no means everyone was afforded burial. Whilst far too many localised rites exist within Britain and Europe to describe them all, I will select a few distinctive occurrences which serve to demonstrate the varied character of burial and associated ritual. First I will examine evidence which supports the statements of both classical and later Irish authorities concerning the aristocratic/warrior-élite existing in Celtic society. Perhaps most distinctive are the two-wheeled vehicle-burials. Called variously carts or chariots, they may be connected with literary evidence concerning chariot warfare and parades. Such two-wheeled 'chariot' burials begin in fact early in the La Tène period (from the fifth century BC) in the Rhineland and Marne areas and continue late in such 'fringe' areas as Yorkshire. On the Continent warriors were frequently buried with chariots, but in Britain the late and localised 'Arras Culture' chariot-burials were usually not demonstrably those of soldiers. 'La Gorge-Meillet' is a chariot-burial from one of the main areas of the tradition, the region of the Marne in north-west France. Here two contemporary inhumations were present, the upper one a mature male with a sword, the lower a youth lying on a two-wheeled cart and dressed in a tunic: he was well-equipped for the otherworld, with jewellery, toilet-set, long sword, four spears, food and wine. In Britain, a group of continental Celts established themselves in East Yorkshire in the early fourth century BC and spread elsewhere in eastern England. They brought with them a distinctive material culture (the 'Arras Culture'), manifesting itself in specific burial traditions including chariot-burial, the associated artefacts dating generally to the second and first centuries BC. The vehicles were buried with their owners, sometimes complete, sometimes dismantled but, unlike their continental counterparts, only rarely with weapons. Women as well as men are represented: the 'Lady's Barrow' at Arras contained an extended skeleton, with pig-bones (for the infernal feast), a dismantled chariot, whip and a mirror behind the head. The 'King's Barrow', similarly, contained an extended inhumation but with the horse-team killed and buried with the chariot. Though the exception,

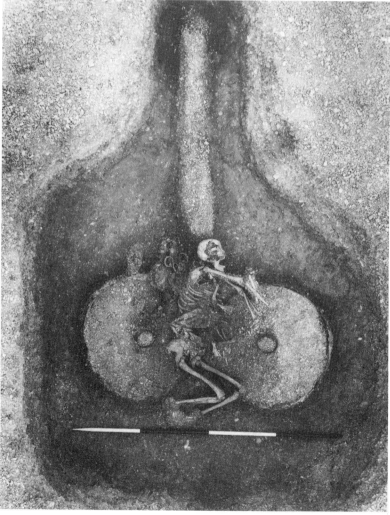

61    Iron Age chariot-burial of young adult female, found with pig-
      remains and work-box, excavated in 1984; Wetwang, Yorkshire.
      Copyright and information John Dent, Archaeology Unit, Hum-
      berside County Council (Dent 1985, 85–92).

warrior-charioteers are represented: the newest finds from Wetwang Slack include two chariots at the centre of each of two adjacent square barrows, the possessions of a man and woman respectively. Both chariots were dismantled before interment and both burials followed a deliberate and ordered ritual: the tyres and chassis were buried first; then the dead person with a side of pork; and then the wheels and (?) chariot-body, pole and yoke. The great interest here is the differentiation in metal in the two graves. At first glance the woman's tomb is the richer in that the main metal was bronze, whilst in the male grave, iron predominates. The woman was buried crouched, with her pork-joint, a mirror, a swan's neck dress-pin and what seems to have been a work-box. The man was undeniably a warrior, with his sword, seven spears and a shield of early La Tène type. These Wetwang burials are probably the richest 'Arras' graves so far, and demonstrate perhaps dynastic burial of chief and chieftainess. The choice of different metals for the different sexes is an enigmatic piece of ritual; whether or not it marks the female as being the more important is impossible to verify. It may be that here the objects were chosen as seemingly appropriate to one sex or the other, with the actual metals reflecting functional constraints.

Relatively wealthy non-chariot burials, recorded both in Britain and, more especially, on the Continent, reflect the veneration accorded to the aristocratic warrior-caste, both male and female. Warriors were often buried with their complete battle-equipment and other items appropriate to this world and the next, such as weapons and the inevitable provision of pork, as at North Grimston, Yorks. In Central and Eastern Europe geese frequently accompanied these soldiers either as food – like the joints of pork – or perhaps (again like the pig) because the goose was a war-symbol (p 113). Geese accompany the Celtic and Germanic war-gods in the Roman period, as we have seen, and the bird has a war-symbolism in Irish sources. Women were often buried with jewellery and amulets: Reinheim was a rich female fourth century BC grave in an oak-lined chamber and containing elaborate gold jewellery, surely that of a Celtic princess. Klein Aspergle (Württemberg) was a very wealthy early La Tène grave containing exotic Mediterranean imports. One feature of interest is the custom, for example in both the Marne and East Yorkshire regions, of burials associated with shrines, as at Écury-le-Repos and at Garton Slack.

Strange and individual rites are sometimes demonstrably

62   Iron Age pit-burial of male (25–35 years old); fifth century BC; Danebury, Hants (Cunliffe 1984, fig 8.1, 3). Photograph: Mike Rouillard. Copyright: B W Cunliffe.

present and these may be indicative of human sacrifice. At Wandlebury, Cambs, the legless body of a child was wrapped in cloth and cast into a pit; at Danebury a specially-dug pit contained three human legs, a lower jaw and part of a trunk. A late La Tène grave at Hoppstädten may equally illustrate human sacrifice, unless perhaps a whole family had died at the same time. Here Caesar's statement concerning 'suttee' (or 'sati') may be endorsed archaeologically. A recent study of Iron Age burial-tradition in central southern England indicates that, taking Danebury as a working sample, only some six per cent of the population were given 'formal' burial and, of these, many may have been the result of human sacrifice (in the case, for example, of burials beneath hillfort-ramparts, interment of part of a body, or single skulls). The skull-burials are interesting in that they invariably represent adult males, perhaps reflecting a practice of burying head-trophies as an apotropaic act, a tradition which links closely with head-

127

63   Iron Age bog-burial of adult male. The man was poleaxed,
     garrotted and his throat cut; 300 BC; Lindow Moss, Cheshire.
     Copyright: Trustees of the British Museum.

collecting customs indicated in the literature. The other
category which may have been singled out for burial, as
demonstrated in this specific case-study, is that of socially
deviant outcasts – such as witches, or the victims of
inauspicious death, suicides, murders and, indeed, victims
of human sacrifice. Most of the burials studied here were
devoid of grave-goods and in this connection it should be
pointed out that comparatively few Iron Age graves in
Britain were so furnished. Perhaps one of the most evocative examples of British human sacrifice is the recent
discovery of a peat-bog burial dating to around 300 BC. The
victim, a young ginger-bearded male, was first poleaxed,
then garotted and his throat cut, the elaboration and the
victim's nakedness suggesting a ritual killing. After death
the man was placed, crouched, in a shallow pool at Lindow
Moss near Wilmslow, Cheshire, possibly to propitiate water
or chthonic deities. That the man was not a peasant is
suggested by manicured finger-nails and by his neatly
clipped moustache, worn in the style of Celtic portrayals in
iconography and in the literature. Ritual bog-burials are
known elsewhere in the Iron Age, for instance in Denmark,
but this is the first British occurrence of a murdered
bog-body.

Another equally evocative find is a Garton Slack burial
which looks very like a punitive/ritual killing: here a youth
and a woman of about thirty were found lying huddled

together, with a wooden stake driven between them pinning their arms together. Below the female pelvis was the body of a premature child expelled from the womb while the mother was unconscious; the couple had apparently been buried alive.

It is the late, immediately pre-Roman 'Belgic' graves that most clearly demonstrate the vivid Celtic belief in the afterlife and in particular the predilection for the funeral feast – a practice lasting well on into early Roman imperial times. A lady of the Augustan period at Wincheringen in the Moselle region was buried in a plank-lined tomb with pottery including wine-amphorae, brooches, mirror, knives, scissors, pig's head and cauldron complete with tripod and chains. She was certainly well-equipped for personal splendour after death and for underworld feasting. In this area, late La Tène warriors' swords were ritually bent to consecrate them and render them fit for the otherworld. Another Moselle tradition exemplified by the Belginum Cemetery near Trier continued the Middle La Tène custom found on the Continent (from Czechoslovakia to France) and also from East Yorkshire, of demarcating burials by enclosure-ditches. Perhaps the spirit of the dead inhabited the tomb for some time after death and the *temenos* served to prevent it from stalking the earth as a malevolent force.

Otherworld feasting seems to have been the main preoccupation of the chieftains of the very late Iron Age. Deep grave-pits in, for instance, Essex, Hertfordshire, Cambridgeshire and Kent, contained quantities of wine in amphorae, drinking vessels, food and fire-dogs for spit-roasting, so that the dead man could enjoy himself in the otherworld or even in the tomb beforehand. As Collis points out burials before the first century BC are rare in south-east Britain when evidence of cremation with sumptuous grave-goods suddenly appears. At Welwyn Garden City a young man wearing a bearskin was cremated and placed in a grave-pit with five wine-jars, Italian vessels of silver and bronze, and glass gaming-pieces. At Welwyn, Herts and Barton, Cambs, for instance, we have abundant evidence for the Celtic hearth of hospitality so commonly referred to in Irish sources. Here twin fire-dogs (as well as drinking equipment) point to provision for a banquet beyond the grave not just for the chief himself but for a guest. This custom of otherworld feasting did not stop when the Romans appeared in Britain. In the late first century AD at Winchester a grave contained remains of a meal consisting of a young pig and poultry. Certainly all this rich sepulchral evidence from southern Britain demonstrates that even after

129

initial Roman contact the Celts believed that the valorous gained rich rewards after death.

### Romano-Celtic Burial Traditions

Very few people were actually brought into Britain from Mediterranean lands during the period of Roman influence. Soldiers, officials and foreign merchants would have made very little statistical impact upon the vast mass of the indigenous population. The same is true (to a lesser extent) in Gaul where Roman influence is somewhat greater. But in general one would expect that something as fundamental as rites and beliefs concerning death and what happened afterwards would remain basically unchanged from Iron Age to Roman times in the Celtic world, the difference being more of representation than of belief. Indeed, Roman and Celt may sometimes have held similar personal beliefs concerning the otherworld. Certainly the idea of the survival of the soul after death was deep-seated among the majority of people in the Roman world; sometimes the spirit was definitely regarded as being at or near the burial-site, which is why food and drink were offered there.

It would be foolish to attempt here a survey of all Romano-Celtic burial practices. However, a glance at some reinforces the pre-Roman tradition of belief in a substantial and positive otherworld existence; and some rites are sufficiently curious to demand attention, especially in Britain. Very few large urban Romano-British cemeteries have been the object of detailed modern study: Lankhills, Winchester is an exception which has produced evidence of some weird and outlandish funerary ritual, some of which may be paralleled elsewhere. The rites are complex and would seem to be the result of essentially Celtic religious practices. Two customs noted here and elsewhere are decapitation, and the presence of hobnailed boots. Seven Lankhills graves contained beheaded bodies, all of later fourth century date and usually of elderly women who had been buried with the head placed by the legs. All of these were associated with elaborate or unusual graves of other people who seem normally to have met a violent end – soldiers for instance. One very curious grave with a decapitated body contained two dogs, one whole, the other dismembered, with the ends of the bent-over backbone tied together. Deliberate ritual governed the decapitation-process itself: it was invariably performed from the front, with great care as to position of severance, and with a knife. Ritual beheading at other British sites reflects similar beliefs and an increased anxiety, especially during the fourth century, that the dead might not reach the otherworld; hence the need for increased ritual to prevent this. At Odell, Bucks, the severed head and neck of a woman was placed deliberately behind the wicker lining of a well. Curbridge in Oxfordshire produced three beheaded burials from a late Roman cemetery, all with the head between the legs. Kenchester and Stanton Harcourt have produced similar evidence. At Orton Longueville, Cambs a second century cemetery produced the remains of an old woman beheaded and with the head placed at the foot of the grave. Alcester produced ten infant-burials of fourth century or later date, and a young girl with the head placed between the legs. Two infant victims of human sacrifice as foundation-offerings at the Springhead (Kent) religious complex were decapitated. It was in Dorset that the rite of beheading took on an especially sinister aspect. The victims were middle-aged or elderly women, the heads severed and placed by the knees or feet, the lower jaws removed, and the burials accompanied by spindle-whorls. This rite seems to have taken place in the later third and fourth centuries. One example from Kimmeridge was particularly complex: here a late third century cist-burial contained an old woman, the head placed by her feet and with the lower mandible removed and with a spindle-whorl placed with the body; on top of the cist a second body had the jaw from the first burial placed by the knees, together with a second spindle-whorl. If we look at this decapitation-rite as a whole, the predominance of elderly women may denote a specific occupation – perhaps witchcraft – where there was an especial need to make sure the body stayed dead and with the head pointing towards the underworld. In the case of Dorset, the lower jaw removal may have been to prevent the spirit not only walking but talking! Were these not so much witches but village-scolds? Whether old ladies or babies, the decapitation-rite must have surely been connected with ease of entry to the otherworld.

The other Winchester-rite echoed elsewhere, as at Ospringe (Kent), Guilden Morden (Cambs) and Bradley Hill (Somerset), is that of placing hobnailed boots in the grave, perhaps because shoes were needed for the journey to the otherworld. These boots or nails were present in a third of the Lankhills graves, and the rite persisted at last until the end of the fourth century. A curious, related, phenomenon is recorded in a shrine at Cambridge where infant-burials were accompanied by shoes that were far too big for them, as if it was felt they would grow in the otherworld.

Other British burial-rites may be noted: the accompaniment of human by animal burials, as at the Bancroft Roman Villa site, at Lankhills, or at Brampton , Norfolk. There, a male inhumation was deliberately overlain by parts of ox-skulls and other bones together with third century pottery. Infant-burials are common as foundation-offerings at, for instance, the Frilford and Springhead temple-sites and, indeed, the presence of burials in the vicinity of shrines suggests the special regard the Celts had for the dead in religious terms. A number of burials in Britain and Gaul stand out in being accompanied by such religious objects as figurines: the pipe-clay 'Venus' figures found at Verulamium and York and elsewhere signify a special attempt to protect the dead in the underworld.

Sometimes the tomb itself denotes the view of the living towards life after death. The Simpelveld (Netherlands) sarcophagus is carved internally with a furnished room, and several tombstones are carved with banquet-scenes. Treveran burial-traditons in the Roman period translate the more basic Iron Age beliefs in a tangible otherworld into elaborate stone monuments showing the deceased enjoying the same life as above ground, a basic idea unchanged from pre-Roman times. In Alsace and elsewhere in eastern Gaul, 'stèles-maisons' proclaim the need for the dead to have a home, and the solar symbolism on many Alsace tombstones denotes perhaps a belief in resurrection. A similar tradition may be reflected in funerary monuments of the Comminges region of Provence. Whatever the differences in elaboration or between Iron Age and Romano-Celtic practices, the essential belief in an afterlife carries through. That there was differential treatment of the dead is demonstrable especially in the earlier periods, where only a minute proportion of people were buried. What we do not know, of course, is whether in the Iron Age everyone was conceived of as enjoying an earthlike afterlife or only the élite. Perhaps the ordinary man, not afforded formal burial, was viewed as having as dreary a life after death as before.

## Pits – Entrances to the Underworld

The custom of digging deep pits or shafts in the ground, where the primary function was apparently religious rather than utilitarian dates back, in Europe, to at least the Middle Bronze Age. In the Graeco-Roman world *bothroi* and *mundi*, pits which linked the underworld to earth, were used in acknowledgement of the dualistic chthonic and celestial powers. It is a fair assumption that 'ritual' pits occurring outside the main sphere of Mediterranean civilisation performed similar roles, though the evidence is far from clear. Shafts at Wilsford and Swanwick date from the later second millennium BC; waterlogged wooden finds at Wilsford have yielded a radiocarbon date of 1380–±90 bc. The Swanwick pit is especially interesting: it is about eight metres deep and at the bottom were remains of a wooden post with traces of human flesh and blood adhering to it. A precisely similar occurrence is recorded much later at Holzhausen, Bavaria, where an Iron Age *viereckshanze* or square religious earthwork contained three shafts, including one with an upright pole and organic remains. Here we have very possible evidence for human sacrifice to appease the underworld gods. At Iron Age Danebury, it has been suggested that ritual was assocated with digging grain-storage pits, in that the gods of the underworld may have been disturbed and required propitiation. Indeed the storage of crops underground implies a certain trust in chthonic powers. Evidence for veneration of plutonic deities manifests itself here, for instance, in special pit-bottom deposits: groups of pots or iron implements, layers of grain and animal-burials. The sheer number and recurring patterns of deposition in these pits suggest complex and ordered religious behaviour. Similar evidence of the appeasement of chthonic gods exists on the Continent. In Aquitaine, deep pits dated to 50–30 BC contain cremations and animal bones including those of toads, suggested as having magical properties. In St Bernard (Vendée) one shaft contained a cypress trunk, antlers and the figurine of a goddess; the presence of a tree is interesting in that, with its tall branches reaching towards the sky and its roots burrowing deep underground, the tree possesses perhaps similar symbolism to the pits themselves which bridge earth and underworld. In this context, certain aspects of tree-iconography are of relevance: at Paris and Trier, for instance, a god, Esus, fells a tree containing birds. It may be that here the Tree of Life is being felled, but with its constant regeneration symbolised by the birds in a life-death-rebirth image.

The great majority of so-called 'ritual pits' belong to the late pre-Roman and Romano-Celtic periods in Britain, and are clustered geographically in the south-eastern (Belgic) areas. Of Ross' 220 lowland examples, I believe about a quarter only to be genuinely ritual in function. Some contained dedications to, or depictions of, deities; some had

special chambers; others contained complete dog-skeletons:
here, the Muntham Court 200 foot pit associated with a
shrine contained numerous dog-burials, and the known
association (Chapter Six) between dog and the underworld
would seem to support their chthonic purpose. In shafts of a
shrine in Cambridge, there were human burials each with a
dog. Most interesting in this present context is the number
of pits associated with human burials. At Newstead in
southern Scotland, several shafts are recorded including
one containing the upright body of a man. Many pits in
central-southern England contain whole or part burials. At
Goadby, Leics a well contained two adults, head down and
covered in stones; someone wanted to make sure these
spirits went down and stayed down! At South Cadbury a
young man was buried in a pit (? as a human sacrifice to

64    Chalk figurine; found in chamber at bottom of pit; Deal, Kent.
      Photograph, copyright and information: Keith Parfitt, Dover
      Archaeological Group.

consecrate, or reconsecrate the hillfort) dug into the rear of the bank. There are numerous such examples from Britain, but a curious continental pit-burial is one from Villeneuve Renneville, where a Gaulish warrior was buried with a domesticated stag, complete with bit.

The final pit I will mention is a recent discovery and is exciting in that within it was an underground 'shrine' associated with a chalk sculpture, perhaps of a chthonic deity. At the bottom of this shaft, found at Deal in Kent, in all some 2,50 metres deep, was an oval chamber containing a complete figurine, composed of a featureless block of dressed chalk from which rises a long slender neck and a head with a well-carved, very Celtic face. This figure may have stood in a niche high up in one wall of the chamber. The presence of footholds in the shaft indicates that access to the shrine was intended but only four or five adults could have sat in the chamber at once and the shrine was perhaps meant for the deity or god and priest alone. Pottery would indicate a first or second century AD date for the structure. One purpose of ritual pits may have been, indeed, as some kind of sanctuary. The idea of sinking shafts into the ground seems to have been primarily for communication with underworld powers who inhabited regions deep below the earth. Human beings and animals were sacrificed to these deities, and they were propitiated also by offerings of food and other items. The Deal find is extraordinary in showing us, perhaps, a glimpse of how such deities were thought of by their Celtic devotees. If the chamber were a store rather than a shrine, then the god may have been present to protect the contents.

## Gods of the Otherworld

We have little idea as to how the Celts actually perceived the gods of the dead; most of our information concerns ritual practices and beliefs about the afterlife itself. However, there is some iconographical and literary evidence. Prehistoric rock-carvings from Val Camonica in North Italy appear to demonstrate that the dead themselves were venerated. In Bronze Age carvings, the dead man is portrayed laid on the ground with his weapons, priest, relatives and a sacrifice. Iron Age Camunian Celts depicted death scenes with four-wheeled wagons bearing funerary urns and processions of worshippers. A totally different tradition is represented by the Iron Age 'Tarasque' of Noves (Bouches-du-Rhône), an immense stone lion-like monster

135

with paws, claws extended to clutch human heads, as if depicting the triumph of death over life. This may date as early as the fourth century BC, and an interesting parallel (though of more dubious date) comes from Linsdorf, Alsace. These and the bronze monster devouring a human body from a Romano-Celtic context in Oxfordshire reflect concepts similar to the essentially Roman Corbridge Lion or the Colchester Sphinx, both of which symbolise the victory of death.

Named Celtic gods of the underworld are rare. Irish vernacular tradition tells us of Donn, the sombre god of the dead from whom men were considered to be descended. This tradition is interesting because of its links with a remark of Caesar's that the Gauls claimed descent from Dis Pater, the Roman Lord of the underworld (*BG* VI, 18). By Dis Pater, Caesar must mean a Celtic equivalent, and the preoccupation with death and the afterlife indicated by some burial-traditions supports the importance the Celts may have attached to otherworld powers. Trying to trace this Gaulish god archaeologically is not easy. Certain inscriptions, especially in southern Germany and the Balkans are dedications to Dis Pater and Aericura (a Gaulish Hecuba), for example at Salzbach near Ettlingen. Some depictions of Sucellus also indicate a funerary aspect: At Unterseebach (Lower Rhine) and at Varhély (Romania) Sucellus has a raven and three-headed dog. The crow or raven is a common funerary symbol, deriving presumably from its carrion habits, and Cerberus was the classical triple-headed dog of Hades. Sucellus' hammer could possibly have a chthonic function: Tertullian (*ad Nationes* 1, 10) states that Dispater had a hammer and was assimilated to the Etruscan god of the dead, Charon; Lambrechts considers the hammer to be possibly a weapon against underworld forces. Reinach considers that the wearing of specifically Gaulish dress by Sucellus on bronzes and stone sculptures, could be seen as appropriate for the divine ancestor of the Gauls. Boucher thinks that Sucellus could have had a chthonic aspect; indeed, she comments that bronzes of the god strongly resemble Jupiter and that, if you substitute his hammer for Jupiter's sceptre, the representation becomes that of Jupiter's serene underworld brother, Dispater. In the infernal world. Dis has the same role as that of Jupiter in the sky. Finally, in this respect, we should mention the role of the Celtic Jupiter (Chapter Two) as fighter, on horseback, for life against death. Sucellus' role may have been similar in that, whilst he has funerary associations, he is also, especially in Gallia Narbonensis, equated with the woodland/vegetation god Silvanus, thus embodying fertility and regeneration in the same way as the Celtic sky-god. No one Celtic god can be tied down to the underworld exclusively, but a number of deities appear to have had a partially funerary or chthonic role. Even the mother-goddesses, as we have seen (Chapter Three) were not dissociated from death. To the Celt, death and the afterlife played an important role in religious beliefs. Druidic teaching and elaborate burial-rites are evidence of this. It is not surprising, then, that many of their gods possessed a chthonic function in addition to their other main spheres of influence.

# CHAPTER FIVE:
# WATER-GODS AND HEALERS

## Introduction

Water held a fascination for the Celts; rivers, lakes, bogs, springs and of course the sea were sources of especial veneration, and naturally so. Water itself was recognised as essential to life and fertility; the constant movement of rivers, springs and the sea must have seemed magical, particularly that of springs which bubbled up from deep underground and were often hot and possessed of medicinal properties. Water could be beneficent as a life-giver, healer and means of travel, but it could also be capricious and destructive: storms could batter crops and, associated with thunder and lightning, strike and destroy; the sea could wreck ships; and then there was death by drowning. Gaul, with its long coast-line, its large and numerous rivers and its many thermal springs, had a particularly strong tradition of water-veneration; but we shall see that other parts of Europe too (including Britain) had their share of aquatic religion.

I deal with water-worship in two main parts: first, water and healing have a very strong and repeated association, yet water-cults could also be independent of this link and existed in their own right with no specific evidence of healing symbolism from at least the mid second millennium BC. There existed also Romano-Celtic healer-deities whose water-affinities were not evident.

## AQUATIC CULTS IN PREHISTORY

Whilst water-gods themselves have left little trace of their presence before the Roman period, there is nonetheless abundant evidence for the veneration of unnamed prehistoric supernatural powers associated with water. First, from the later Bronze Age, especially in Central Europe, we have the persistent tradition, in metalwork, of water-bird symbolism. Second, there was a widespread practice of depositing valuable items, particularly metalwork, in aquatic contexts – a tradition which appears to commence in the Middle Bronze Age and to carry on right up to the Roman period in non-Mediterranean Europe. Third, we have parallel evidence from Scandinavia both of depiction of ships in the religious context of rock-carvings, and of human sacrifices in Danish bogs.

Throughout later European prehistory precious objects were cast into bogs, lakes, rivers and springs. The nature of the objects – undamaged and costly weapons, sheet-metal vessels and coins – argues against rubbish-disposal and points rather to gifts offered in propitiation or appeasement of the powers residing in water. The most striking evidence is that of weapon-offerings, a custom which goes back to the later second millennium BC. The Thames, for instance, received great quantities of fine metalwork during the Bronze Age. In Britain, Middle Bronze Age rapiers are found in contexts which are predominantly riverine, and later Bronze Age swords have a similar distribution. It has been suggested that river-gods were being entreated for water during dry periods. Similar pleas may be represented at the Late Bronze Age settlement at Lichterfelde, Berlin, whose wells may have dried up; here cult-offerings, including small vessels in rows with layers of grass in between may be a request to the god responsible for well-water to continue to provide it in a period of drought. Conversely, it has been argued that the onset of wetter conditions in the late second millennium BC was responsible for increased activity associated with water-religion. Again in the eighth and seventh centuries BC, renewed interest in water-offerings could reflect worsening climatic conditions and consequential appeals to the gods for their alleviation. The interesting thing here is that during the Bronze and Iron Ages it is weapons which are the prime prestige offerings. Rapiers and swords, spears and Iron Age daggers are among the most numerous gifts. Fitzpatrick has suggested that this pattern of weapons in rivers represents a true picture rather than a mere accident of survival since many martial items are early La Tène, from a period when other material culture is relatively a great deal scarcer than in the later periods. What we do not know is the precise function of such deposition. It may be that precious items of armour such as the Battersea Shield (Fig. 50), the Waterloo horned helmet (Fig. 51) and the swords, carnyx and shield from the Witham were chosen as offerings simply because prestige-items *were* mainly military. The Celtic élite, as we have seen was a war-aristocracy, and if the gods were to be seduced by valuable gifts, then martial equipment may have been the most appropriate. La Tène weaponry could have been selected 'because of its ambiguous roles as a symbol both of authority and wealth and of security'. As Hodder remarks artefacts possessed a symbolism over and above and independent of, their utilitarian function.

## Rivers

Rivers were very important offering-places: valuable metal objects were cast into the Thames throughout the Bronze and Iron Ages, not only splendid pieces of armour but also Iron Age coins and brooches are common Thames finds. Hawkes makes the point that in Britain the bulk of Iron Age metalwork finds are riverine whilst in Central Europe, they come mainly from dry hoards or graves. The large amounts of Iron Age ironwork and coins in the Walbrook stream in London are probably religious offerings; and Merrifield believes that the continual deposition of metalwork in the Thames over long periods represents votive offerings to a local deity whose cult *foci* may well have been at regular crossing-places.

In the later Iron Age we have some evidence for specific river-cults, from a combination of archaeological and literary sources. First, but not strictly Celtic, is a reference by Orosius to the Germanic Cimbri and Teutones who, victorious over the Romans at Orange in 105 BC, destroyed and cast into the river all war-booty, because of a new vow. It is surely likely that a pre-existing river-cult was being recognised when on the 1st August 12 BC Drusus established the Cult of Rome and Augustus just outside Lugdunum at the confluence of the Rhône and Saône rivers. Here, a temple and great altar were set up by all the Gauls, the altar bearing an inscription with the names of sixty Gaulish tribes. The ceremony was presided over by the chief priest of the Aedui, and must represent the recognition of native politico-religious ideas. The specific veneration of particular river-spirits is evidenced throughout Roman Gaul and Britain, particularly rivers at their source – Sequana of the source of the Seine (below, pp 150–151) is a case in point. The name of the consort of Sucellus, Nantosuelta, means 'winding-river', and numerous Celtic rivers had their own genius, very often female. Verbeia was probably the goddess of the river Wharfe in north-east England; Lydney (pp 160–161) was sited, perhaps deliberately, overlooking the Severn where Nodens may have commanded the impressive Severn Bore. Many shrines, such as Chedworth on the Coln, overlook rivers. The god Condatis to whom four dedications were made in County

Durham was the god of the watersmeet or confluence. His altars belong to the Roman period but he and gods like him must have existed in their hundreds during the free Celtic period.

## Springs, Lakes and Bogs in Prehistory

The healing symbolism of springs is so powerful that the subject is discussed later in connection with their therapeutic properties (whether real or imagined). I will mention here only one phenomenon which is apparently religious but without an overt healing association. This is the 'Giant's Springs' at Duchcov in Czechoslovakia, a natural spring to which was dedicated in the third or second century BC a huge bronze cauldron containing over 2000 bronze objects, mostly bracelets and brooches. This is interesting especially in view of Fitzpatrick's observation that ritual aquatic deposition as represented by martial equipment seems to have been exclusively male. Here perhaps at Duchcov, where jewellery was the main offering, we may have a cult dominated by women – perhaps a female deity. But this should not be overstressed; men as well as women wore jewellery in the Iron Age.

Lakes and bogs were *foci* of very active prehistoric European ritual, especially in the Celtic world. It is difficult always to separate the two types of context since what is now bog may once have been a lake. In general, in any case, the ideas behind bog/lake deposition may have been similar in function – that of offering items to the gods in such a way that they could not be disturbed, stolen or violated in any way. Celtic lake-deposition is recorded by classical writers: Strabo (*IV*, 1, 3) comments on how a massive gold and silver religious treasure, belonging to the tribe of the Volcae Tectosages in the Toulouse area, was plundered in 106 BC by the Roman general Caepio. This treasure consisted of metal ingots rather than coins which were heaped up some in temple-enclosures and some in a sacred lake. Strabo tells us that treasures like this existed in many parts of Celtica 'and the lakes in particular provided inviolability for their treasures, into which they let down heavy masses of silver and gold'. The Tolosa sanctuary was especially revered and its treasure very large – none dared profane such a place (until 106 BC!). Treasure like this could have been put into lakes primarily because of inaccessibility, but there is no doubt as to the sacrosanctity of the sites over and above convenience. Gregory of Tours mentions an annual three-

141

day festival at Lake Gévaudan in the Cevennes where peasants cast in food, clothes and sacrificed animals. The impossibility of recovery from lakes, bogs or any deep water or the sacral nature of water itself may not have been the only ideas behind such deposition. Over and above this, the idea of casting something away irrevocably may in itself have been a holy act, a commitment of certain items beyond earthly control to that of the divine.

It is worth looking at a few Iron Age lake-deposits in some detail. On the Continent the most important must be La Tène itself, where a huge deposit of metalwork was found in offshore peat in a small bay at the east end of Lake Neuchâtel (the central deposition-date being circa 100 BC). A wooden platform was built from which the offerings were cast into the water, and the lake-god received among other things some 400 brooches, 270 spears, 27 wooden shields and 170 swords. The jetty-like construction resembles a platform at Port on the north-east end of Lake Biel, also in Switzerland, whence again Iron Age offerings were made, mainly swords and spears.

There are two very important Iron Age sacred lakes in Celtic Britain, at Llyn Fawr in South Glamorgan and Llyn Cerrig Bach on Anglesey. Llyn Fawr is the earlier, the date of deposition of the objects lying around 600 BC. Here a hoard was found in a peat-deposit that had once been a natural lake; finds include two sheet-bronze cauldrons, exotic Hallstatt material, harness and vehicle-fittings and such implements as socketed axes and sickles. Savory has suggested that the deposit represents the offering of loot carried off from a rich settlement in the English lowlands but the method of construction of the cauldrons is known only in Wales. Whatever the historical context of deposition, it looks as though the South Wales offering was made on a single occasion, but the cauldrons would have been deposited as antiques several centuries old. The same need not be the case at Llyn Cerrig. The material here ranges in date from the second century BC to the first century AD and deposition could either be the result of repeated offerings over a long timespan or an accumulation of material over some centuries which was then deposited as one act of propitiation. The area of Llyn Cerrig is one full of rocky outcrops and small lakes, an awe-inspiring spot in prehistory. The finds come from the edge of a bog at the foot of an eleven foot high sheer rock cliff which provided a good vantage-point for throwing offerings. In the Iron Age the lake would have extended to beneath the rock platform and the uncorroded condition of the metalwork shows that it sank immediately into water. The offerings are almost exclusively of a military/aristocratic nature: weapons, slave-chains, trumpets, chariots and harness-fittings, but also cauldrons and ironworkers' tools, over 150 objects in all. The deliberate damage done to otherwise perfect objects recalls similar damage to Iron Age metalwork at the Hayling Island temple and at the La Tène sanctuary at Gournay-sur-Aronde (Oise) which contained hundreds of ritually damaged weapons. Savory's argument against the idea of uniform deposition on the grounds of chronological range has the corollary that Llyn Cerrig was a sacred site visited again and again. However, Cunliffe suggests it could be booty from intertribal fighting before the Roman advance, and indeed such material could have been looted from a sacred treasury of the kind recorded by Strabo at Tolosa. Other classical writers mention the ceremonial piling up of war-plunder for the gods; and Llyn Cerrig could represent this. But Cunliffe's idea of one tribe thieving another's sacred objects and devoting them to their own gods seems to me to go against the grain of the very strong universal feelings against violation of religious tradition noted among the Celts by Mediterranean observers. In any case, as Lynch points out, the wealth of the lake's offerings do suggest that it possessed more than local sanctity. Some of the metalwork could have come from as far to the south-east as Somerset and beyond, and the number of chariots represented implies more than local war-offerings. So if looting by Anglesey war-bands is not the answer, it may be that Celtic chieftains travelled some distance to make offerings at a lake-shrine that was holy to all Britons. The Druidic association with Anglesey makes a connection between this nationalistic priesthood and Llyn Cerrig a very attractive theory. Whatever the precise circumstances of the ceremonies involved, the presence here of animal-bones recalls the Cevennes lake-sacrifices alluded to earlier.

A number of Iron Age ironwork deposits has been identified in lakes or bogs in southern England and northern England/southern Scotland. At Blackburn Mill (Berwick) and Carlingwark (Kirkudbrightshire) hoards associated with cauldrons were offered to deities of lochs, at about the time of the Roman Conquest. Indeed, the practice of placing deposits of ironwork in wells, bogs or lakes can be distinguished in two phases – one in the late Iron Age and a later occurrence in the fourth century AD. Such caches of ironwork are thought to be religious simply because iron was perhaps not valuable enough to have been hoarded for any secular reason.

143

As said before, lakes and bogs are not always distinguishable in terms of original prehistoric cult-deposition. But sometimes indisputable bog-offerings may be recognised. The pony-cap and horns from Torrs (Kirkudbright) were from a bog; and the fact that nearly all Irish late prehistoric cauldrons are bog-finds may not be coincidental. We shall see later that metal vessels themselves had significance for water-ritual. Bogs have a special property in being dangerous, in appearing to have lives of their own, and in the consequent inaccessibility of bog-offerings. Underworld gods, sometimes malevolent, dwelt there in places that looked innocuous but were treacherous to the unwary, and these powers had to be appeased. It is therefore not surprising that the great silver cult-bowl from Gundestrup in Jutland (Fig. 9) was deposited as an act of invocation probably immediately prior to the Roman Conquest of Gaul. The cauldron had been dismantled and placed in a dry, flat part of the Raevemose Bog, possibly an object of plunder from the Celtic world and offered by Teutonic tribes on return from a raid or, possibly, the gift to the local bog-deity by the men of the Borremose village near to the site of deposition. Certainly Danish Iron Age peoples had a strong tradition of bog-offerings: pottery, meat, weapons, clothes and vessels were given as well as people, and wagons and carts were also dedicated, as at Dejbjerg and Rappendam. Perhaps the most interesting Iron Age ritual bog-finds are those of human sacrifice. The bulk of these are Danish, perhaps representing the activities of the Teutonic Cimbri who may have come from there; they are thus of peripheral significance to the present study. But the recent discovery of a sacrificed 'bog-body' in Britain whose circumstances closely resemble the Danish finds brings the latter suddenly into sharp and relevant focus. 'Lindow Man' has already been mentioned in connection with death-symbolism (Chapter Four). Here the interest is in his being offered as a sacrifice to the marsh-deity at Lindow Moss in about 300 BC: a young man stripped naked except perhaps for an armband of fur and hair, hit twice on the head, garotted with a sinew rope and his throat cut, then placed face-down in a bog-pool. The mistletoe in his stomach may suggest the Druids were involved. We know (p 27) that mistletoe was involved in their ritual. Some of the Danish bog-bodies of the Iron Age were treated in a strikingly similar manner: Tollund man was hanged with a sinew rope and deposited naked apart from a cap and girdle; Borre Fen man was similarly hanged; Grauballe man had his throat cut. A particularly chilling sacrifice was that of a woman in Juthe

Fen, Jutland; she was pinned down in the peat by wooden crooks driven down over each knee and elbow-joint, and thick branches were clamped across her chest and stomach. The feature of all these sacrifices which impresses one most is the thoroughness with which victims were despatched! Were these people criminals, simple human sacrifices or both? The only clue from written classical commentaries is that the Cimbri, after victory, hanged their conquered enemies in trees with ropes, the latter perhaps recalling the garottes of the bog-bodies.

## Wells

The tradition of endowing wells with supernatural power is at its commonest immediately before the Roman period. The study of wells is problematical first because it is not always easy to be sure for a given example whether religious activity is involved or not; second, there is the problem of distinguishing between wells and dry pits or shafts. Deep shafts may also be wells if they are not too narrow; pits may begin as wells which later dried up. Indeed the religious function of pits and wells is quite similar. In both cases underground forces are at work and communion with the underworld involved. But a well is a different phenomenon in that only here is water-symbolism present. There is little specific evidence for cult-wells before the later Iron Age in Gaul and Britain. On the continent, we have already mentioned the Late Bronze Age Lichterfelde site near Berlin, with its probable well-symbolism. In Britain the most relevant prehistoric well is at Wilsford in Wiltshire; the shaft itself is over 100 feet deep ending in a well, containing wooden buckets and ropes. Its great depth and its proximity to Stonehenge and broad contemporaneity with the final phase of that monument have been held to suggest a ritual purpose. Some Iron Age metalwork hoards occur in wells, as at Thatcham, Berkshire, but most of these are of Roman rather than pre-Roman date (see below). At Montbuoy near Orléans a well contained a crude wooden figure, possibly of Iron Age date; and the well at Kelvedon, Essex, with a ritually-deposited chalk figurine may also be pre-Roman.

## Vessels, Birds and Boats

Prehistoric water-symbolism is not associated only with    145 rivers, lakes, bogs or wells, but may be conveyed also by vessels for holding liquid, and by the depiction of boats and water-fowl.

It has already been noted that cauldrons appear in aquatic, sometimes ritual contexts. The Gundestrup Cauldron, already alluded to, was of impressive size, of solid and gilded silver, fourteen inches high and twenty-eight inches diameter, with a capacity of 130 litres (Fig. 9). Even bigger was the bronze Brå Cauldron also from a Jutland bog, which could hold more than 600 litres. Duchcov, Llyn Fawr, Llyn Cerrig, Blackburn Mill and Carlingwark were all ritual water-deposits associatd with cauldrons and so it is not unreasonable to associate vessels with water-

65    Votive deposit of ironwork within two cauldrons, one inverted over the other; late Iron Age/early Roman; from bog at Blackburn Mill, S Scotland. Copyright: National Museums of Scotland.

66    Votive bog-deposit of ironwork within cauldron; late Iron Age/ early Roman; Carlingwark Loch, S Scotland. Copyright: National Museums of Scotland.

symbolism. As early as the Late Bronze Age cult-wagons carrying vessels, sometimes drawn by water-birds, must reflect water-magic, perhaps appeals to the gods for water in drought, or a magical attempt to move water away in times of flooding. The seventh-sixth century BC vessel from Orăstie (Czechoslovakia) is just such an example: it was mounted on wheels and 'drawn' by sets of water-birds. The function of ritual cauldrons is problematic: in vernacular Irish and Welsh tradition the cauldron symbolised plenty; the Dagda, for instance, possessed an inexhaustable magic cauldron of abundance, rejuvenation and inspiration. In Welsh tradition – as in the Tale of Branwen in the Second Branch of the Mabinogion – cauldrons have magical powers of regeneration, like water itself, and so are a reflection of life, prosperity and fertility. But there may also be a more sinister side to cauldrons or other vessels. Strabo (IV, 1, 13) describes the practice of the Cimbri who sacrificed prisoners of war by slitting their throats over cauldrons; such sacrificial vessels were regarded as holy and the Teutonic tribe sent Augustus their most sacred cauldron. Possibly related to this is the scene on plate E of the Gundestrup Cauldron showing a god dangling a human sacrifice over a bucket. A Berne commentator on Lucan describes a sacrifice to the Celtic Teutates where a man is drowned in a vessel of water. So cauldrons and other water-containers could, like water itself, possess the dual roles of life and death.

We saw that prehistoric vessels were sometimes mounted on cult-wagons drawn by water-birds. This leads on to the very persistent symbolism of water-birds from the later Bronze Age in Europe. Their precise significance in prehistoric religion is obscure but that fertility was a factor in the symbolism is suggested by the presence of horns on some depictions. In the later Bronze Age, ducks or swans frequently appear on Urnfield metalwork, constantly associated with sun-symbols; ducks flank wheel-suns on sheet-bronze vessels; and sometimes the image turns into a duck-prowed boat carrying the sun. At Hajduböszörmény in Hungary a bronze *situla* is ornamented with suns and duck-boats. The symbolism may be something to do with the ability of such birds as swans and ducks both to swim and fly. There may well be a cyclical image of sky and sun, rainwater and underworld. The water-bird/sun association continues into the Hallstatt and La Tène periods, and occurs, for instance, on Iron Age torcs from the Marne area. At the beginning of the Romano-Celtic period the duck is linked with an anthropomorphic goddess, Sequana of the source of the Seine near Dijon, within the context of a therapeutic thermal site. The goddess, fully draped in Roman fashion, stands in a boat whose prow is a duck's head with a fruit or cake in its beak, perhaps a fertility-

147

symbol, which is seen again on a bronze duck-figurine from the Milber Down Iron Age hillfort.

The link of boat and water-bird is interesting; just as aquatic birds and solar symbols are associated in the Bronze Age, so on Scandinavian rock-carvings ships and sun-signs recur together constantly. Any attempt at detailed interpretation of rock-carving imagery must be regarded as highly speculative, but once again sun and water appear together, an association which recurs in a healing context in the Romano-Celtic period (infra).

Apart from the aquatic bird connection, boats feature prominently in later prehistoric European religion. Scandinavia, an area which was not itself Celtic but had some Celtic and proto-Celtic influence, has produced the most evidence. The tiny gold-leaf boat-models from Nors Thy in Denmark have a parallel at the Celtic oppidum of the Dürrnberg in Austria. A number of full-size boats display complicated aquatic ritual in Danish contexts. In the third century BC a boat containing a hoard of over 300 swords, spears and shields was deliberately sunk in a peat-bog at Hjortspring on the Danish island of Als. The boat, filled with war-booty and sacrificed beasts was dragged out into a bog; and in Schleswig Holstein, the ritual was repeated at Nydam in the fourth century AD. Boat-imagery appears nearer home too: the Caergwrle Bowl from North Wales dating to around 1000 BC is, in fact, a boat-model. Made of Kimmeridge Shale, it is decorated with inlaid tin and gold leaf to represent shields, oars, waves and boat-ribs; again it evidently comes from an aquatic/bog deposit. From the Humber Estuary at Roos Carr, Holderness comes a curious Iron Age find of a simple wooden boat-model containing five warriors with shields; and at Broighter in County Derry in Northern Ireland a first century BC hoard of gold jewellery, a bowl and boat-model complete with mast and oars may denote some kind of boat/water ritual on the western edge of the Celtic world.

## WATER AND HEALING

Water-ritual in Bronze and Iron Age Europe was the subject of intense activity, as we have seen, and there is no doubt that supernatural powers – whether or not as specific as fully-formed deities – were acknowledged and venerated both by means of appropriate imagery and of votive deposition in aquatic contexts. By the Romano-Celtic period, and indeed, in the century or so before, water-cults were

67  Aerial view of the site of Coventina's Well; Carrawburgh. The
actual well is on the extreme right of the picture. Copyright:
University of Newcastle upon Tyne.

becoming more formalised and recognisable as identifiable
religious entities. In North Britain, the Romano-British
goddesss Coventina presided over a natural spring and well
at Carrawburgh; she is named and is depicted as a single or
a triple water-nymph, reclining on water-lilies and pouring
water from a vessel; and she had a temple built in her
honour. Verbeia was the cult-spirit of the river Wharfe in
Teesdale; the name 'Latis' occurs in North Britain and
means 'goddess of the Pool'; and the name of a
Cambridgeshire god Abandinus at Godmanchester may
possibly suggest a water-association. The small shrine at
Ratham Mill, Funtington (Sussex) was next to a brook and
the innermost of three concentric squares could have
contained a pool or well. In all its Roman phases the Celtic
cult-centre at Ivy Chimneys, Essex had, as its focal point, an
artificial pond. There is evidence of Irish water-cults in the
vernacular sources. The Dagda, an important Irish father-
god, was linked to the land by being married to a
topographical goddess Boann of the river Boyne. There is an
interesting water-legend concerning Boann, who was
engulfed by one Nechtan when she challenged the power of
his sacred spring. The union of the Dagda and Boann is one
example of the many instances of marriage between a tribal
god and a nature-goddess who nourished the earth and
could easily personify a spring or river as a life-source. The
Dagda himself, as a fertility-figure, possessed a magic
cauldron with powers of rejuvenation; the significance of
such vessels, noted above, is enhanced by the association of

149

many goddesses with vats of pure water. Water as a fertility symbol was thus of fundamental significance, and this power of regeneration caused the florescence of a great Celtic cult of healing – the main role of sacred water just before and during the Romano-Celtic period in Gaul and Britain.

## The Healing Cult of Sacred Springs

All water, with its properties of movement, cleansing and life-giving, has an air of mystery. But perhaps the most curious observable phenomenon was that of springs, sometimes hot, sometimes with mineral, curative properties, which bubble out of the ground from deep under the earth. Gaul was especially rich in sacred springs which were sometimes mineralised, with true therapeutic powers. But equally, healing-cults grew up around springs whose only qualities were the presence of gas and warmth or simply as a source of fresh, clear water. The thermal properties of Gaulish springs were recognised long before the Celtic period, but the great healing sanctuaries did not grow up until the end of the first millennium BC. One of the most important sites was at *Fontes Sequanae*, the source of the Seine in a valley north-west of Dijon. Here by the early Roman period the goddess Sequana presided over an important spring-site, though its only merit was as a source of clean water. During the Roman period there was an extensive religious complex centred on a pool and spring; there were two temples and a colonnaded precinct. The deity is represented by a bronze figure of a goddess, in a duck-prowed boat, with her arms outstretched as if to welcome pilgrims to her sanctuary. But Roman influence only monumentalised a pre-existing cult-site; in 1963 a rich deposit of nearly 200 wooden votives was found in waterlogged deposits during the excavation of the Romano-Celtic structures which they appear to pre-date. The fears and diseases of the Celtic population are evocatively illustrated by the mass of votive limbs, heads and internal organs which were modelled in oak or beech and offered to the goddess (Fig. 68). Such afflictions as blindness, arthritis, goitre and hernias are clearly represented; and the depiction of breasts and genitals may indicate milk-deficiency on the one hand (with serious implications for infant malnutrition) and infertility on the other. As early as the first century BC, pilgrims were making the journey to the healing springs and offering models of themselves or their diseases, either as a

68  Iron Age wooden head; from healing shrine at Source de la Seine sanctuary, near Dijon, France. Copyright: Musée Archéologique de Dijon.

reminder to the goddess as to what required treatment or so as to transfer magically their ills from themselves to the model. In any case reciprocity was important if a cure was desired. Many of the complete figures are crudely formed as simple blocks, but the head is carefully depicted: perhaps recognition is important, or perhaps the eye-problems suggested by the closed eyes on many images, caused the head to receive special attention. Certainly by the first century AD when the buildings were put up, there may have been an organised healing ritual, where prayers to the goddess were followed by sleep in dormitories (perhaps the colonnaded precinct) while a cure was awaited. The real interest in this site lies in its evidence for pre-Roman cult-activity. The stone votives which are coeval with the temple-structure show Roman influence, but there is none of this in the wooden figures which have a vibrant and original style of their own, apparently "designed to meet the needs and mitigate the fears of a simple, not very wealthy local population" (Sandars 1984, 148).

An essentially similar and synchronous healing spring-site was the 'Source des Roches de Chamalières', south of Clermont Ferrand, where a deposit of more than 2000 wooden votives lay over three feet deep in the area of two

151

small mineral-water springs. Coins suggest that the shrine was in use for only about a hundred years or so after Caesar's conquest (first century BC to first century AD). There were no structures, simply a sacred pool and an enclosing wall in a marsh valley. The votives were quite possibly set up around the spring itself, perhaps to a nameless goddess depicted here; there were real curative properties in the water and the votives suggest that people sought relief especially from eye-troubles.

Several healing spring-shrines in Gaul, though formalised and monumentalised in the Romano-Celtic period, have their origin in the free Celtic era. Les Fontaines Salées (Yonne) possessed medicinal springs apparently utilised from the early Iron Age: during the first century AD a sacred circular enclosure had in the centre a paved pool and round it the remains of an earlier oval structure. Mavilly (Côte d'Or) was a therapeutic site probably based on a spring which yielded a figure of Mars with a Celtic ram-horned snake and a late La Tène shield. Both here and at Vichy (which may have replaced the nearby site at Chamalières) eye-troubles seem to have been the main affliction, but at Vichy a bronze figure holding a drinking-cup displays a hideous spinal malformation suggesting that the mineral waters were drunk by the afflicted individual.

By the Roman period several Celtic healing springs had named deities: Nemausus presided over the healing fountain at Nîmes, whose shrine predated the Roman structures. Glanum had a local healer-god Glanis and a spring dedicated to health. The hammer-god Sucellus presided over springs at Beire-le-Châtel (Côte d'Or) and at Antigney-la-Ville. We have seen that a type of healing Mars (whom we shall meet again) was worshipped at Mavilly, and he appears too at Vichy, and at a spring-site at Antre Lake in the Jura. The most important spring-water god in Gaul was the Celtic Apollo. His healing role is so important as to merit detailed discussion below and his connection with springs is seen for example at Ste Sabine (Côte d'Or) which was dedicated to Apollo Belenus and has yielded several horse-figurines. Another important site was Hochscheid in the Moselle Basin, a healing shrine dedicated to Apollo and a Celtic consort Sirona. In the second century AD a sanctuary was built around a spring whose waters fed a small cistern; cult-statues of the divine couple are associated with figurines, coins and other offerings: it was a wealthy shrine for so remote a region, and it has been suggested that a rich villa-owner may have patronised the cult.

Epona is another Celtic goddess associated with such Gaulish thermal sites as Allerey (Côte d'Or). She is a horse-goddess, and we have seen that the Celtic Apollo is associated with this animal, probably as a solar symbol. Apollo was a god of light and of the sun as well as healing – his Celtic name Belenus ('bright, brilliant') illustrates this – and we shall see below that water and solar symbolism are closely linked in healing cults. The horse/sun association with springs is carried further at, for example, Luxeuil, a spring-shrine presided over by the eponymous topographial Luxovius (the name meaning 'light') and his consort Bricta. Here Epona was worshipped together with a Celtic Jupiter-horseman from a Jupiter-column, bearing a solar wheel.

Before we leave continental European spring-sites, one comparatively unknown area – that of the Alps of southern France, Switzerland and North Italy – is of great interest. As early as the Bronze Age, people were dedicating votives to a deity of the mineral spring at St Moritz in Engaden. Numerous sacred springs were venerated during the Iron Age and Roman periods. An example is a sanctuary close to sulphur springs at Calalzo 'Làgole' in the Piave Valley. The especial interest lies in the inscriptions both in local Venetic and Latin which tell us of the presence of a cult centred around a Venetic healer-god called 'Sainat(is) Trumusiat(is)', which lasted from the third century BC to the fourth century AD, and in which only men took part. The sulphurous water was drunk from ladles which were then smashed after use and deposited as offerings. Bonfires for feasting and sacrifice are evidence of cult-activity on the site.

## British Spring Sanctuaries and Cult-Wells

There is far less overt evidence for shrines associated with therapeutic springs in Britain than in Gaul, but such cult-sites did exist. One of the most important was the internationally-patronised temple of Sulis at Bath, which we will look at presently. But other, more local spring-sites are also worth discussing. A goddess 'Arnemetia' is implied in Derbyshire by the Roman name for Buxton – 'Aquae Arnemetiae' ('the waters of the goddess who lived at the sacred grove') – the curative springs here, close together at the valley-bottom, yield two kinds of water. The association of groves and springs suggested here is supported by an observation of Lucan (*III*, 411–412) on a forest sanctuary near Marseille which had 'dark springs running there'. In the Roman period the Celtic northern British goddess

153

Coventina presided over a spring enclosed by a rough wall and forming a small pool into which coins, jewellery and figurines were thrown as offerings (Fig. 67). The presence of pins as votives is suggested as having associations with childbirth, and the goddess herself, depicted as a nymph (Fig. 31), may have helped women at this critical time in their lives. Several stone altars, including depictions of the goddess herself, were cast into the pool, perhaps at a time of attack; the presence of a human skull is a more enigmatic find. We do not know the name of the presiding deity of Springhead in Kent, but here, on the concourse of three springs, a temple-complex was built in the first century AD and was later embellished and developed. The votive offerings are varied, and include a bronze thumb – indicative of a healing cult – a bone *genius cucullatus* (a Celtic godling of fertility) and a pipe-clay 'Venus' figurine, both the latter being common occurrences on therapeutic aquatic sites.

The hot springs beside the river Avon at Bath gush out at the rate of a quarter million gallons a day, and must have been visited and venerated as a cult-centre before the

69   Altar to Sulis Minerva, dedicated by Sulinus; Bath. Photograph: Betty Naggar. Roman Baths Museum.

Romans built a massive shrine at *Aquae Sulis*. Sulis was the Celtic goddess of the spring and her name has solar connotations. In Romano-Celtic dedications she is frequently equated with a Roman goddess Minerva, but Sulis' name is invariably put first, indicating that she is the dominant partner in the Celto-Roman equation. Roman engineers converted the spring into a great ornamental pool, enclosing it in an impressive building associated with a Graeco-Roman style temple and a huge bath-suite. The temple itself may be as early as Neronian or early Flavian. Into the spring and reservoir which formed the central focus of the sanctuary were thrown vast numbers of coins and other votive objects, including numerous lead *defixiones* or curses invoking the goddess for revenge against ills done to the devotee. The coins are especially interesting since there is evidence both for some type-selection and also for ritual damage or 'killing' to consecrate the coin-offerings and to render them unusable by thieves. Some votive offerings specifically imply healing invocations; the ivory carving of breasts, for instance. Apart from Sulis herself, mentioned on many dedications and depicted by the huge gilded bronze head hacked at some time from the cult-statue (Fig. 70), mother-goddesses called the *Suleviae* were worshipped, along with Mercury and his Celtic consort Rosmerta, Mars Loucetius and Nemetona (A Treveran couple) and the *Genii cucullati* (already noted at Springhead).

Ritual associated with wells was noted above as being an especial feature particularly of southern Britain in the later Iron Age, the tradition, indeed, going back much further. Sacred wells persist throughout the Roman period and there is some British evidence for a healing association. We have already looked at Coventina's Well at Carrawburgh which was a spring and well-sanctuary associated with the Roman fort of Brocolitia. Here the votive pins and dog-figurine suggest a healing role for the goddess. Two other well-sites possess clear therapeutic symbolism: that at Caerwent was associated with a temple containing a bronze snake and the skull of a dog, both animals connected with the Graeco-Roman healer Aesculapius. Of the several wells known at Caerwent, one contained a mother-goddess (a frequent associate of sacred water-sites); another contained five dog-skulls. The 200 foot well at Muntham Court, Sussex contained numerous dog-skeletons, associated with a first century shrine containing a votive clay leg, itself indicative of a healing-cult.

Many of the 'ritual' wells enumerated by Ross need have no more than a secular function, but some evidence delib-

70  Gilded bronze head of Sulis Minerva; Bath. Copyright: Baths
Museums Service. Roman Baths Museum.

erate and organised activity and deposition. Where healing
is not clearly a factor, it is difficult to know whether the
underground or water properties are uppermost; in any case
the two are linked. A glance at one or two of the most
curious wells illustrates the kind of cult-activity that was
going on. Several have material of a definitely ritual nature:
the religious site at Kelvedon, Essex included a well (filled
in the second century AD) within which was a chalk

156

71  *Genii cucullati* and worshipper from well; Lower Slaughter, Glos.
On pediment are birds and rosette. Photograph: Betty Naggar.
Gloucester City Museum.

figurine set in a niche, a circumstance remarkably similar to
the find in a dry pit at Deal in Kent (Fig. 64), of another chalk
image again in an underground niche. The Lower Slaughter
well in Gloucestershire contained eight altars deliberately
thrown in during the fourth century AD, only a short time
after the well was dug; two of the altars depicted *cucullati* –
recurrent inhabitants of water-shrines as we have seen. A
number of wells contain human skeletons or skulls:
Coventina's Well contained a skull; and this is repeated at
Caves Inn (Warws.). At the Roman site of Goadby (Leics), a
well contained two human beings buried head down and
covered with stones. Perhaps the most curious cult-well is
that at Jordan Hill, Weymouth, a dry well associated with a
Romano-Celtic temple. At the bottom were a stone cist, two
pots, and ironwork including weapons; above were ashes,
charcoal and pairs of tiles within each of which were a
bird-skeleton and a coin. These layers were repeated sixteen
times, interrupted halfway up by a cist-deposit identical to
that at the base. The birds represented were all carrion-
eaters or birds of prey, suggesting chthonic symbolism.

157

## The Sanctuary of Lenus at Trier
## and the Healing Cult of Mars

In Gaul, and to an extent in Britain, the Roman war-god Mars became transformed to become a peaceful healer. This is not so curious as it seems; there is logic in the development and adaptation of a warrior-deity who was originally a protector of territory, to a new role in a civilian context as a fighter against disease. Mars at Mavilly and a local Mars 'Vorocius' at Vichy were associated with spring-shrines, particularly perhaps with eye-troubles: one relief from Mavilly shows a divinity with dog and raven and a devotee with his hands over his eyes. Mars Mullo at Allonnes near Mans (Sarthe) also cured eye-disease; here votives of pilgrims display such afflictions. It is possible that the presence of Mars Loucetius (the name having light-associations) at Bath may have a link with clarity of vision, and we will see a parallel symbolism with Apollo (infra). People with eye-problems also came to Mars Nodens at Lydney in Gloucestershire, whose cult is examined below.

On the Continent, the most impressive Mars-healer cult was that of Lenus Mars centred on Trier. He was worshipped almost exclusively among the Treveri of the Moselle area, but he appears also at Caerwent and at Chedworth (Glos) on a small crude altar from a shrine possibly associated with a water-cult focused on the river Coln which it overlooks. The main cult-centre of Lenus Mars – the Celtic name usually comes first – as is always the case with Sulis (supra) – was situated in a small steep wooded valley of a stream on the left bank of the Moselle opposite the Roman city of Trier. The site was probably already sacred in the Iron Age; certainly an early and much humbler precinct preceded the main second century temple, which was a massive structure displaying strong Graeco-Roman architectural influence, a huge altar and probably a theatre for cult-ceremonial. Inscriptions denote the presence of high-ranking priests, and the sanctuary was rich in offerings from pilgrims seeking to be cured. Lenus was sometimes worshipped as 'Iovantucarus', indicating special protection for the young. Apollo appears in this same capacity, as Maponus – 'divine Youth' – in North Britain. At Trier, there are many cult-portrayals of children, often bearing gifts of birds to the god. Genii cucullati occur here, as on healing sites in Britain, and figurines of several other deities indicate that people invoked their own personal patron-saint as well as the major god of the shrine. The spring

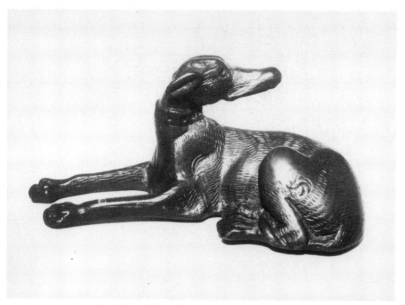

72   Bronze deerhound; Lydney, Glos. Copyright: City of Bristol
     Museum & Art Gallery (BRSMG. F4392).

above the precinct, which had a longlasting reputation for
its healing properties, was canalised to supply a small set of
baths. Lenus was worshipped in the Treveran countryside
as well as in the tribal capital. At Pommern the god had a
large sanctuary with an *abaton* or dormitory for curative
sleep. That Lenus sometimes answered the prayers of the
faithful is indicated by an inscription thanking the god for
curing a terrible illness. Interestingly, in this context, the
great 'villa' complex at Chedworth has recently been re-
interpreted as a large healing shrine The presence of baths,
dining-room and a range of rooms linked by a corridor are
not inconsistent with this suggestion, and it may be
significant that an altar to Lenus comes from here.

### The Sanctuary of Nodens at Lydney

A British healing god equated with Mars (and others) had a
sanctuary at Lydney overlooking the Severn in Gloucestershire. The god's name was Nodens which is etymologically
linked with the Irish legendary figure Nuada Argat-lam (or
Silver Arm). The sanctuary was impressive, with a large
hostel or guest-house, baths and a long building which
could have been a dormitory or *abaton* for the pilgrims'
sacred sleep. It was a wealthy shrine furnished with mosa-

159

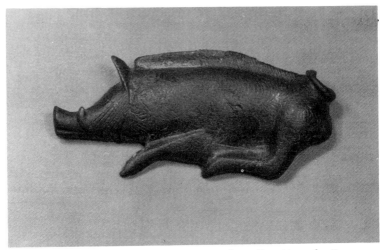

73  Bronze plaque of dying boar; Muntham Court temple, Sussex.
Copyright: Worthing Museum.

ics, and it was probablly built in the later third century AD,
refurbished in the following century. The symbolism here is
complex and interesting: dedications to Nodens alone or
equated with Mars and Silvanus respectively are recorded;
there are no images of the god in human form, but a number
of dog-figurines (Fig. 72) suggest healing to have been a major
function; this is supported by cult-objects including a
votive arm and oculists' stamps. Further imagery at the site
associates the cult both with marine and solar symbolism: a
diadem depicts a sun-god driving a quadriga with tritons
and anchors; the cella-mosaic displays a sea-scene, and a
bronze relief portrays a sea-god. This last has links with a
Chesterholm inscription from North Britain identifying
Nodens with Neptune. At Lydney the water-association
could reflect the Severn Bore; but the sun-imagery is more
significant in that solar and healing symbolism is closely
connected, as we will see later. The link with Silvanus, the
Roman woodland and hunter-god, is interesting. Other
British sites display a link between hunting and healing
symbolism: Apollo was an archer and healer in Graeco-
Roman mythology; and at Nettleton Shrub in Wiltshire,
Apollo is called by the Celtic epithet Cunomaglus (Hound-
Lord). Muntham Court, Sussex provides similar evidence:
we have already noted the deep well containing dog-
skeletons, and the votive clay leg from the circular shrine.
The site produced also a plaque of a slain boar (Fig. 73),
which may represent hunting-imagery. In the late Roman
well found under Southwark Cathedral in London, a group of

160

sculptures included that of a hunter-god with bow, quiver, stag and dog. The well-association here need not necessarily be significant in that the sculptures may originally have been temple-furniture. Hunting and healing are curious associates; the obvious link is with dogs which are common to both concepts. It may be that the image of the 'divine hunt' is relevant with its associations with death and regeneration. Certainly Silvanus had a fertility-role as a woodland and vegetation spirit from whose forest-realm arose the hunting symbolism; and a fertility-image is present at Lydney in the form of a seated mother-goddess with *cornucopiae*.

## The Celtic Healer Apollo

An important healer-god, or maybe a number of local curative deities, existed throughout Gaul in independent Celtic times, with cults centred upon the numerous thermal springs. At the time of the Roman conquest these native healers were assimilated to the Mediterranean Apollo, because he himself possessed a healing function. Dedications to the Gaulish Apollo are far more numerous than is warranted by the status of his Roman counterpart. In addition there are a few very prominent Celtic epithets attached to Apollo's name, some of which occur frequently on their own and it is rare that Apollo is mentioned on dedications without the Celtic identity being present. A point of particular interest is the association between Celtic healing water-cults and sun and light, whilst the Graeco-Roman Apollo possessed also this dual sphere of activity. We shall examine this in more detail later, but first it is worth looking at some of the main manifestations of the Celtic Apollo and sacred springs.

One god was Apollo Grannus who had a cult-centre at Grand in the Vosges and another at Aix-la-Chapelle which was called *Aquae Granni*. Significantly Grannus is named Phoebus on an inscription from Trier, implying an important solar aspect. Grannus was not confined to one or more specific sites; he occurs associated with medicinal waters in Brittany, North-East Gaul and far away in the Danube Basin where an early third century temple at Brigetio in Hungary was dedicated to Apollo Grannus and Sirona, the latter being a female consort of the Celtic Apollo especially in the Moselle and Mainz areas. Her parallel role of fertility goddess is indicated by a portrayal of Sirona at Sainte-Fontaine with fruit and corn; at Hochscheid Sirona

161

appears with a snake and a bowl of eggs, respective emblems of healing and fertility. Grannus is one of the few Celtic gods to be referred to in Graeco-Roman literature where Dio Cassius remarks that the Emperor Caracalla could not find a cure at the shrines of either Grannus, Aesculapius or Sarapis. One of the most interesting inscriptions is one from the temple at Grand which suggests the rite of incubation – or healing sleep – following prayers and a vision of the god. This practice links the cult with the major healing cults of the classical world, such as that of Aesculapius.

Belenus is the commonest Celtic healer associated with Apollo and he again is discussed in literary sources. Ausonius, a Bordeaux poet writing the the later fourth century AD mentions sanctuaries to Belenus in Aquitaine and speaks of one Phoebicius who had been a temple-priest of the cult. The name Belenus has light-imagery, and the sun-bright link is shown also by Phoebicius' name – presumably an adopted one. Belenus was particularly popular in southern and central Gaul, North Italy (Aquileia) and Noricum; Tertullian attests the Austrian (Norican) branch of the cult, and Herodian mentions Belenus in Aquileia.

A Gaulish deity intimately associated with thermal springs and sometimes identified with Apollo is Bormo, Bormanus or Borvo. The name means seething, bubbling or boiling spring water. Borvo, like Belenus, appears more often by himself than linked with Apollo, emphasising the essentially Celtic nature of the cult. He was popular in the Loire and Rhône Valleys, Provence, the Alps and even Galicia in north-west Spain. Important cult-sites existed at Aix-les-Bains and Bourbonne-les-Bains. At Aix, the springs near the city-centre contained bronzes not of Apollo but Hercules, and the idea here may be the invocation of the Graeco-Roman 'strong-man' as a combattant against disease. Among the Lingones Apollo's consort was Damona, and at Bourbonne-Lancy an inscription associates her with healing sleep or incubation, looked at above in connection with Grannus. Another consort was Bormana, who appears with Bormanus at Die (Drôme) but by herself at St Vulbas, a curative spring site, implying less than total dependence upon the male deity for her existence.

We meet Damona again at Alesia where she is present as the consort of Apollo Moritasgus, the Celtic god of thermal waters associated with the *oppidum* of Mont Auxois. Moritasgus – his name meaning masses of sea-water – had a great healing shrine with baths, porticoes perhaps for curative sleep, and a polygonal shrine. As at the source of the Seine site (*supra*) the numerous votives display a lack of concern for high standards of artistic realism – the workmanship was not as important as the idea of reciprocity – a diseased organ in exchange for a healthy one – or of reminding the deity what part to heal. Limbs, innards, breasts and genitals were offered for cure, and once again eye-troubles were prominent. Indeed, the finding of surgeons' tools for cataract suggests the presence of priest-doctors on the site. We have seen already that eye-disease must have been rife in Gaul; in Britain too there were eye problems – we have already looked at Lydney – and Wroxeter has produced recent evocative evidence in the form of a pair of gold model eyes, and more than thirty-five representations of eyes cut from wall-plaster.

There is less evidence from Britain for a Celtic water-healer identified with Apollo; indeed the only likely site is the temple at Nettleton Shrub, Wiltshire. Here there is no direct evidence of a healing cult except for a long hall which by comparison with others, could have been a dormitory for pilgrims. A shrine existed here soon after AD 69 but it was not developed as a major cult-centre until later, reaching its apogee in the mid third century when a large polygonal shrine, hall, hostel, shops and priest's house show the importance of the site. The main god here seems to have been Apollo Cunomaglus ('Hound-Lord') to whom an altar

74   Altar to Apollo Cunomaglus; Nettleton Shrub temple, Wiltshire.
Copyright: City of Bristol Museum & Art Gallery (BRSMG. F4392).

was dedicated, and a bronze plaque was inscribed to Apollo by one Decimus; a ring-intaglio also represents the god. Other cult-material indicates the presence of Silvanus and Diana, implying with Cunomaglus the worship of a hunter-deity. We have already noted a hunting-healing link, and it may be that Apollo was a healer at Nettleton. The site is associated with a river, and such finds as spatula-probes, tweezers and seventy-five pins, may suggest a curative role.

## Healing Waters and the Sun

We have seen the apparent association between solar and healing water-symbolism with, for instance, Mars Loucetius, and indeed the solar name of Sulis, at Bath; and again at Lydney. In Gaul, the link seems to be through the Celtic Apollo, who is called Belenus or Grannus Phoebus, and it looks as though the native healer, like the classical Apollo, possessed dual healing and solar roles. This should not surprise us, since the sun – a life-force –, fertility and healing are naturally associated in the concept of regeneration and, in addition, many curative springs were warm. But light/healing symbolism may have a different connection if we consider the eye-problems evidenced at so many Celtic therapeutic water-sites. The case of the god Vindonnus at Essarois (Côte d'Or) illustrates this link between a god of clear light and a curer of eye-disease. 'Vindonnus' means clear, light or white, and he is depicted as a radiate, solar god. He is associated with water, and to him were dedicated wooden limbs and internal organs, but significantly too, several bronze eye-models.

The link between sun and water goes beyond that contained in the names of healer-gods. At several thermal sites in Gaul votive horses are known, as at Sainte-Sabine (Côte d'Or) dedicated to Belenus, and the horse is a well-known sun-image as early as the later Bronze Age. Epona, the Celtic horse-goddess, is frequently associated with thermal waters, as at Allerey and Saulon-la-Chapelle, where she appears nude like a nymph. The Celtic solar/sky god, assimilated to Jupiter, is also so linked; Celtic sun-wheel signs appear as votives at thermal shrines such as Bourbonne-les-Bains, and were cast into such Gaulish rivers as the Seine, Oise, Loire and Marne. The *Acts of St Vincent* contain an account of a martyr commenting upon pagan cults in Aquitaine in the early fourth century AD. Here there was a custom where a flaming wheel was rolled down to a river, hit the water and was then reassembled in the temple of the god; the image here is that of the Gaulish sun-god sending down his solar sign to earth and recovering it for the sky. Clearly we have a cyclical image of sun, rain and consequent fertility. The divine horseman-aspect of the Celtic sky-god cult is also relevant in that many Jupiter-columns are associated with water, as at Beaune. At the thermal spring-establishment at Luxeuil, a native god Lux-ovius (again a light-name) was worshipped, but present also were images of a sun-wheel-bearing horseman and the Celtic spring-goddess Sirona. Here sun, light and water-symbolism display very strong mutual affinity.

## The Goddesses

We have seen that several Celtic healer-gods had consorts associated with curative spring-sites. That these goddesses had some autonomy is indicated by their frequent presence alone, and by their occurrence with more than one male associate. Thus Damona appears with Moritasgus and Bormo, and Sirona is equally polyandrous. Sirona's images show her to have a fertility-role, and we have seen how close the concepts of healing and regeneration seemed to be. Many other Celtic water-goddesses are known: Icovellauna presided over the nymphaeum at Sablon in the Moselle Basin, a thermal spring-site; the root 'Ico' can mean water. Lenus was sometimes associated with a goddess Ancamna at Trier, and at the same place Ritona was a goddess of fords. We have seen that many British water-goddesses were worshipped – Coventina, Arnemetia and, above all, Sulis. But the fertility-aspect of healing water-symbolism is demonstrated above all by the mother-goddesses. Pipe-clay 'Venus' figures (Chapter Three) are found at sites such as Springhead and Vichy, and the Walbrook stream in London. At St Ouen de Thouberville (Eure) 'Venuses' were offered at a shrine with a circular pond. The Caerwent seated mother was placed down a well; and a mother-goddess was wor-shipped at Lydney. The *Matres* were invoked at Bath also, and they occur again and again at Gaulish curative shrines. The *Matres Comedovae* (the surname is associated with health) were worshipped at the springs of Aix-les-Bains, and the *Griselicae* were venerated at Gréoulx in southern Gaul. At Glanum nearby the healing-spring god Glanis was associated on a dedication with the *Glanicae* – again these were local mothers; the *Matres Nemausicae* shared the Nîmes water-shrine with Nemausus. Mothers were wor-shipped at a spring-site at Armançon (Côte d'Or), and there     165 are many other instances. Nehalennia, the mother-goddess of Domburg and Colijnsplaat, was linked with the sea. Her role is not otherwise clear but she is invariably accompanied by a dog, which is suggestive of healing. She was essentially a goddess of traders and seamen and certainly would have been regarded as a protectress against the peril of sea-voyages.

## The Significance of Water

Water, like the sun, is a regenerative force. Some mineral springs had true medicinal qualities, but others were simply a pure-water-source. Water could heal in a number of ways – by immersion, washing, application and drinking. The numerous baths at thermal sites, the deposition of votive limbs in water, and the evidence for drinking all point to the efficacy of different kinds of contact. Healing and ritual cleansing went hand in hand.

One curious phenomenon possibly connected with water-contact and healing is the association of heads with water, spring and well-cults. Several votives at the Seine site were of heads; skulls were found at Coventina's Well, and at Caves Inn. Merrifield notes skull-deposition in a first century London well, and the human skulls in the Walbrook must surely have a ritual explanation. We know from classical authors and from archaeology that the head – pars pro toto – was of fundamental importance in Celtic religion, and this stress on water-association may be connected with the healing or regeneration of individuals represented simply by heads. If, as some scholars believe, the head-image has a death-symbolism, here we may have the concept of resurrection in the underworld, and the transference of regeneration from this world to the next.

# CHAPTER SIX: ANIMALS AND ANIMISM

## Introduction

Long before the appearance of the Celts in Europe there is evidence for human reverence of beasts. We noted in Chapter One that the essence of Celtic religion was the recognition of the supernatural in all aspects of nature – in trees, water, mountains and the sun. Accordingly, sanctuaries were frequently associated with natural features. It was natural, also, for the wild animals surrounding man in a rural society to be revered as well as tended or hunted. Admiration and respect for such feral qualities as strength, speed, courage, virility, ferocity and cunning can be traced back at least as far as the Upper Palaeolithic when man depicted images of beasts in rock-carvings and cave-paintings.

In later prehistoric Europe, beasts were commonly depicted especially in metalwork, and this tradition continued into the Iron Age. In La Tène art, both human and animal forms were integral and subordinate to the overall design. Unlike metalwork, rock-carvings such as those at Val Camonica depicting multifarious scenes involving humans, beasts (stags, oxen) and inanimate objects were specifically concerned with the image *per se* and, occurring as they do in remote forest locations, must have had a primarily religious purpose.

In the Celtic world of Europe, apart from the very specific category of rock-carvings alluded to above, the evidence for the sanctity of animals takes the form either of ritual deposits (including sacrificial remains) or of iconography. We should not make too much of the sacrificial role of animals: animal-sacrifice is common to a great many religions past and present and, of itself, need imply no specific reverence for, or attribution of supernatural powers to, animals themselves. Indeed, classical authors make little mention of animal sacrifice because they did not find it a phenomenon peculiar to the Celts, and were familiar with it themselves. Nevertheless, since we have independent evidence for sacred beasts, one or two instances of ritual deposits of animal-bones are of interest. The sites of Aulnay-aux-Planches (Marne) of tenth century BC date and the third century Libeniče (Czechoslovakia) share certain features, though widely separated in space and time. Both consisted of elongated rectangular earthworks about 300 feet long and both contained both human and animal burials, perhaps offerings to appease the gods of that particular area of ground. In Britain, at Danebury, the first stage of occupation (1000–500 BC) took place on the hilltop and was defined by large pits containing a number of animal-burials. In one, the bodies of two dogs accompanied a selective collection of twenty bones representing cattle, sheep, pig, red deer and roe deer, vole and frog/toad. Once in position, chalk blocks were laid over the carcases and a massive timber post or tree-trunk was erected centrally in the hole. The tradition continued at Danebury: in the next phase of occupation, after 400 BC, pit-deposits contained grain, pots, iron implements and animal remains, the latter including a number of horse-mandibles. These examples of late prehistoric settlements are interesting not in their illustration of the widespread practice of animal-deposition, but in their implications for the importance of the method of offering. In the case of the continental sites, there is a similarity in tradition as far apart as France and Eastern Europe, and the integration of human and animal remains. At Danebury, the types of beast and the selection are important.

Turning to Celtic iconography, there is evidence before the coming of Rome that beasts played a significant part in Celtic symbolism. Though, in most cases of La Tène art, design takes precedence over naturalism, animals are very often present as part of that design. By the eve of the conquest, in Celtic Europe, beasts occur in iconography in their own right, exemplified by the late La Tène hoard from Neuvy-en-Sullias (Loiret) buried at the time of the conquest and situated opposite the Celtic shrine of Fleury, on the banks of the Loire. Such beasts as horse and boar are common on Celtic coinage, and they often remain recognisable as entities even where the remainder of the design is abstract. Both before and during the period of Roman influence, Celtic artists were good at depicting animals. The diversity in iconography (reflected indeed in insular vernacular sources) is perhaps due partly to the wide range of economies present in Celtic society. Hunting and its associated forest animals must have been ubiquitous (though it may have been an upper class pursuit), but semi-nomadic pastoralism through to sedentary agriculture were practised and thus cattle, horses and sheep were as familiar and important as the wild boar, stag and hare.

Zoomorphism in symbolic imagery may take a number of

forms: animals may occur alone, in company with anthropomorphic divinities, or a humanoid image may possess animal parts. We need to ask why animals were depicted. Gods accompanied by beasts are common both to the Celtic and Mediterranean worlds: Mercury, for instance, is often portrayed with a goat or ram as symbol of fertility; or, again, with a cockerel, reflecting in its greeting of the new day, Mercury's role as herald; and, finally, with a tortoise – a reference to Mercury's mythological invention of the lyre using a tortoise-shell. Thus in the Graeco-Roman world, animals extend and enhance the symbolism, power or mythology of the anthropomorphic deity. Where animals are associated with Celtic gods they may have a similar function. Beasts were chosen who in some way appropriately reflected the cult symbolised. But there is some evidence that they sometimes assumed greater significance. The wild animals accompanying Gaulish hunter-gods are 'fresh from the scarcely cleared forests of Gaul', and there can be no doubt as to the indigeneous character of Artio's bear, Sirona's serpent or Cernunnos' stag. Some Celtic deities, like Epona and Nehalennia, depend for their identity upon their animal-attributes and never occur without them, but the Roman Mercury, for instance, often appears alone and relies on his own artefactual emblems to classify himself. The frequency of occurrence of beasts alone in Celtic iconography endorses this view, as if the beast could represent a deity without a human image always being necessary. But the immediacy of association

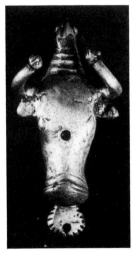

75  Bronze bull/eagle head bucket-mount; Thealby, Lincs; late Iron Age/early Roman. Copyright: Scunthorpe Museum.

between the human and animal image of the divine is shown above all by the composite 'monster' gods which are human but with horns, antlers, hooves or animal ears. Thus Cernunnos is both man and beast.

The intimate link between Celtic god and beast should not persuade us that the Celts worshipped animal-gods, for this would be a simplistic view of the animistic element in Celtic religion. But just as the supernatural in natural features (or true animism) was acknowledged, so animals possessed a sanctity and a divine element. The relationship of human to animal images may be explained partly in the phenomenon of metamorphosis which plays such a prominent role in the Celtic vernacular tradition. As Powell comments, the zoomorphic aspect of Celtic deities of both sexes 'would seem to have been an expression of the powers of shape-shifting rather than a purely archaic concept of the supernatural in animal form' (1958, 123). Anthropomorphic deities were too old a concept to argue for their replacement of the older zoomorphic forms. Most of our evidence for shape-shifting comes from the early Irish sources. Even animals as animals can be endowed with human qualities: the great Bull of Cooley had the power to reason and understand as a human being. The divine bulls of the Ulster Cycle in fact reached their present shape after a series of metamorphoses, and were originally divine swineherds. In Celtic mythology the gods could transform themselves into beasts at will. The Mórrígan, for example, constantly shifts shape from human hag to young girl and, again, to crow; and we will meet further examples of such changes below. This phenomenon is not easy to detect archaeologically, but there are one or two instances in which the iconography is suggestive. The Euffigneix late Iron Age stone pillar shows an anthropomorphic being with a boar suprimposed on his torso; at Nages in southern Gaul, galloping horses alternate with human heads. Indeed, deities with horns, hooves or animal-ears could be interpreted as shape-changers; it is equally possible that such items as the composite bronze bucket-mounts from Thealby, Lincs and the river Ribble with their bull, eagle and human heads could represent the shape-shifting process. A point of great interest which emerges from a general look at beasts in Celtic religion is the relatively greater dominance of the zoomorphic aspect in the case of female divinites. This is seen, for example, in such deities as Epona and Nehalennia, and in the animal companions of the Mothers (Chapter Three). If the acknowledgement of the supernatural in animals is essentially similar in Celtic religion to that recognised in natural features, then we may see here a link with the territorial and fecundity aspects of female deities.

## CULTS ASSOCIATED WITH DOMESTICATED ANIMALS

Of the many domesticated animals with a sacred significance for the Celts, three stand out, namely the horse, dog and bull*. Of these, the first two are distinctive in that there are anthropomorphic god-forms which are dependant upon the animal for their identity and never appear without them: Epona and her horse and Nehalennia with her dog.

### Horses, Horsemen and Epona

Evidence for horses as cult-animals may be traced back as far as the Bronze Age. Scandinavian Bronze Age rock-art depicts horses associated with boats and solar wheels; and the famous 'chariot' from Trundholm, broken and buried in a fen, perhaps during a rainy, sunless time, depicts the solar disc drawn by horses. The horse and sun-disc are important motifs in Urnfield Europe, and this association is continued during the Iron age, where the two images recur repeatedly in Iron Age coinage. By the Hallstatt Iron Age, horses were used for riding as well as traction and the archaeological evidence for Hallstatt warriors, with their horse-trappings and long slashing swords, demonstrates the horse's importance in warfare. The aristocratic prestige-value of the horse is clearly indicated by the four-wheeled funerary wagons drawn by horses. Thus, at Bỳči Skála Cave (Czechoslovakia) – an important cult-centre – funeral pyres with wagon-fittings, human and animal burials and quartered horses attest equine ritual. The reverence for horses carried on into the La Tène period. That horses were regarded as especially precious is illustrated by the Gaulish chief Vercingetorix who, at the siege of Alesia by Rome, sent away his horses for their protection. The Iron Age chariot-warrior was a man of rank and such prestige was due largely to his horse, a fact reflected in burials containing vehicles and their horses. In the Arras Culture site known as King's Barrow, a grave-pit with extended inhumation contained two chariot-wheels, harness and two horses, a practice echoed at Mildenhall, Suffolk and Fordington near

---

* The indigenous wild aurochs was extinct in Britain by 500 BC (Stuart 1982, 141).

Dorchester. Moreover, ritual horse-killing was prevalent in parts of Europe from southern Russian to Scandinavia during the first five centuries AD and can be traced in Russia back to the second millennium BC. There is other Iron Age evidence for ritual or religion associated with horses: at South Cadbury, horse and cattle skulls carefully buried right way up in pits were associated with an Iron Age shrine. Far away at Mouriès, a Celto-Ligurian sanctuary in southern France, rock engravings of horses may be dated perhaps as early as the third century BC. Again, at the coeval shrine of Roquepertuse, a lintel is decorated with a frieze of stylised horse-head profiles.

The importance of the horse in Gaulish society is demonstrated by its continued dominance in religion. It possessed economic, military, prestige, cultural and food-symbolism, and as such occurs in association with many Celtic divinities, as well as frequently appearing by itself. The Gaulish Apollo, a sun and healer deity, appears with horses; at Mauvières (Indre), Apollo is called by the Celtic surname of 'Atepomarus' or 'great horseman'. At Bolards (Côte d'Or) a bronze horse was dedicated to Segomo, an epithet applied to Mars among the Sequani; Mars Mullo, a mule-god, appears especially in western Gaul. At Sougères-en-Pulsaye (Yonne) near Entrains, a shrine contained images of a Celtic Mars and horses. The horse's association with a number of gods shows that it was an independent emblem, probably of strength and fertility as well as in its multifarious significance to the Gauls alluded to earlier. Unassociated horse-images are ubiquitous in Gaul and Britain. At Assche-Kalkoven in Belgium a hoard of pipe-clay horse-figurines, some bearing cosmic signs, probably came originally from a temple. Horses turn up in Britain as isolated finds, as at Northmavine in Shetland, or as shrine-furniture, as at Wroxeter, where a temple may have been dedicated to a deity primarily associated with horses. A small bronze horse from Coventina's Well and a clay one at Springhead, Kent perhaps reflect the water/healing role suggested in Gaul at Bolards and Sainte-Sabine. The numerous horse-figurines in Britain and Gaul need not detain us further, but the British evidence for ritual associated with horses is worth noting. At Newstead, a second century AD 'votive' pit contained horse-skulls in association with those of oxen and humans; the suggestion of some kind of horse-cult here is supported by the presence of a pipe-clay horse-figurine. At Bourton Grounds, Bucks, a basilical building close to a Romano-Celtic shrine, had horses buried under the threshold as (?) foundation-offerings; and at Bekesbourne, Kent a ritual pit contained complete pots and below them a flat stone on which a circle of horse-teeth had been arranged.

I have alluded above to certain instances where the horse is associated with a deity, notably Apollo and Mars in Gaul. Allied to the latter is a very distinctive link between animal and god – the image of a Celtic horseman. There is pre-Roman evidence for this depiction: that it goes back at least to the seventh century BC is demonstrated by Hallstatt Iron Age material, illustrated by a bucket-lid from Kleinklein (Austria) which is decorated in repoussé with stylised horsemen riding around the rim. Horsemen figure on the contemporary cult-wagon from Strettweg (Fig. 13), where they surround the central goddess. There is pre-Roman evidence too from the high mountain of St Michael de Valbonne, where a Romano-Celtic sanctuary was preceded by a sacred place marked with a 'menhir' carved with a horseman and five human heads. A mounted god is evidenced in Romano-Celtic contexts in Gaul, as at Bolards, where pipe-clay horsemen accompany isolated horses, but the cult of Celtic horsemen seems to have found especial popularity in Britain, localised to the eastern tribes of the Catuvellauni and Coritani, and connected with a local Mars-cult (Chapter Four, pp 116–117). The theme of the Celtic horseman seems to be that of conqueror; this is clearly seen at Martlesham, where a bronze figurine of a horseman rides down a foe, and at Stragglethorpe, Lincs, where on a stone relief a horseman spears a 'serpent' beneath him. The imagery is closely paralleled by the Jupiter-columns of eastern Gaul (pp 61–65) where a sky-horseman rides down a serpentine monster, apparently representative of a dualistic life-death symbolism.

The other main divine horse-associate is Epona. Like Apollo Atepomarus, her Celtic name is eponymous with horses and she was the Celtic horse-deity *par excellence*. Epona is interesting partly because her identity is dependant upon the presence of her horse-emblem. She appears on nearly three hundred stone monuments in Gaul, favoured particularly in the east; and she generally appears side-saddle, astride or between two horses or foals. Since one major function of the goddess was that of a mother, she is fully discussed in Chapter Three (pp 91–94). Here we need only say that the horse-association seems to have been important in the concept of horse-breeding and the protection of cavalrymen. Epona is distinctive among Celtic deities in being mentioned by classical writers, including Juvenal and Minucius Felix, who allude to her as presider over stables. That she was much more than that is indicated

76  Bronze figurine of Epona; Wiltshire (unprovenanced). Copyright: Trustees of the British Museum.

by her iconography and her context (see Chapter Three), but the horse-symbolism is essential and very varied. The mare-and-foal imagery is strong, and at Chorey (Côte d'Or), the presence of mare and foal alone may represent the Epona-cult without the goddess herself in anthropomorphic form.

As with so many Celtic deities, Epona is represented in Britain only by a scattering of images. One of these, however, is a pre-Roman coin showing a female equestrian being on a very strange-looking horse. The most interesting is a bronze figure from an unprovenanced location in Wiltshire. Here the goddess sits flanked by two small but adult ponies, one of either sex. The goddess holds a yoke and a *patera* overflowing with corn rests on her lap; the ponies are eating corn. The beasts, it is suggested, are deliberately portrayed small in relation to the goddess, according to the convention of depicting mortal creatures as smaller than divine.

Horses, quite clearly, had a very special significance for the Celts. They were revered for themselves in terms of fertility, sexual vigour (there is evidence for this in vernacular tradition), warfare, prestige and for economic use. Several deities are associated with the horse, and one in particular owed her identity, as divine protectress of mortal horses, to the imagery of the beast itself. The Celts did not worship the horse *per se*, but its secular importance endowed it with reverence, sanctity and with the supernatural attention of the gods.

## Dogs and Nehalennia

This animal is ubiquitous among Celtic cult-representations: it appears by itself in art; its bones occur as ritual deposits; it is associated with a variety of deities; and, as with Epona, there are anthropomorphic divinities to whom it is an essential companion.

In Mediterranean religion, the dog possessed three primary symbolic functions: healing, hunting and death. Aesculapius, the great Graeco-Roman healer-god, has a dog, as does Diana the huntress, and the death-link is illustrated by the mythological Cerberus. Interestingly, these three roles are reflected in Celtic religion. The Gaulish healing goddess Sequana of the Seine received offerings in the form of images of people with dogs. The Mothers at Ancaster and Cirencester are associated with dogs, as is Epona on occasions. We have seen (Chapter Three) that the Mothers possessed both healing and death/underworld associations and here the dog may represent either or both. In Gaul, Sucellus the hammer-god sometimes has a dog; in the Nîmes area the god appears with a dog and snake, and both these beasts possess the joint healing/death association. The classical underworld image is perhaps reflected at Varhély, Dacia, where Sucellus is accompanied by a triple-headed dog, though in a Celtic context triplism has a separate, very powerful symbolism.

Healing, death and hunting may all be associated in Celtic religion; the earth's role as container for death and rebirth (and therefore, spiritual healing) may be involved; hunting had a symbolic link with death, and the divine hunt is common to Mediterranean and Celtic mythology. In Britain, Diana occurs with her hound at both Cirencester and London, but Apollo Cunomaglus appears at Nettleton Shrub, and we know that, elsewhere in Celtic contexts, Apollo is a healer (Chapter Five). The hunter/healer association is demonstrated elsewhere in Britain (above, p 160). The most important British healing dog-cult is that of Nodens at Lydney. Here we have the interesting phenomenon of a late and sophisticated sanctuary, complete with dormitory, dedicated to a British god Nodens to whom inscriptions are known, but represented iconographically not as a human image but solely by his canine attribute (Fig. 72), which occurs in nine instances. That a

175

healing sanctuary is present is indicated, among other things, by oculists' stamps. But it is interesting that hunting may also be represented by dedications to Silvanus Nodens.

The Gaulish goddess Nehalennia mirrors the cult of Epona in that her identity is based entirely upon her companionship of a specific beast, the dog. Nehalennia's cult (see Chapter Three) was based in Holland, where evidence for two sanctuaries exists. Her name appears on dedications, and her image occurs on over a hundred altars, and always the dog is there. Nehalennia's other attributes indicate her essential prosperity-symbolism, but with the dog perhaps as a healing or underworld emblem.

The chthonic function of dog-imagery may be reflected in the numerous British ritual deposits containing dog-skeletons. At Ivy Chimneys (Essex), a religious site, a ditch contained the skeletons of a horse, an ovicaprid and a row of dog-teeth 'set as though in a necklace'. In the Upchurch Marshes, Kent a deposit of seven puppies, one with an adult bitch, was found buried in urns. At the Elephant & Castle, London, two dogs were placed in a wooden box with second century pottery and buried in a shallow pit. Several deep wells or pits with dog-deposits are recorded; Muntham Court and Caerwent have already been mentioned, and there are many others: an illustration is the find at Staines, at a small Roman site near a bridge, of a well dug in the second century AD, in which were cast sixteen dogs and a complete samian bowl. There is, all in all, abundant evidence for the association of dogs with underworld symbolism and ritual.

It is natural that an animal that must have been a common domestic associate of man should have a cult-role to play: hunting-dogs must have been admired for their killing-instinct and physical speed and power. All dogs may have impressed their human companions by their ability to heal themselves with their saliva; and their carrion-instincts may, like those of the rat, have betokened death-symbolism both to Mediterranean and Celtic peoples.

## Bulls

That a reverence for the strength, ferocity and virility of the bull on the one hand, and of the power and agricultural importance of the ox on the other was felt by the Celts and proto-Celts in Europe, is indicated by the repeated use of the animal as a decorative motif as early as the Bronze Age. At Mont Bego, in southern France, a holy mountain was decorated with carvings in which the ox plays a dominant part. Late Urnfield Central European bronze vessels were frequently ornamented with bull-horns; and Hallstatt-period clay bull-horns on stands are illustrated by an example from Sopron, Hungary, of seventh century BC date. At Býči Skála Cave, a bronze bull of sixth century date was found in a pit in the important cult-centre associated with local ironworkings. In the La Tène Iron Age, bull-decorated vessels became increasingly common: the Rynkeby and Brå cauldrons from Denmark were so ornamented, and Megaw would see the tradition deriving, via the Mediterranean world, ultimately from the east in the eighth century BC. According to Hawkes, the bull or ox-head decorations on bucket-mounts, which extend from the Iron Age into the Roman period, were not merely ornamental, but possessed a supernatural, symbolic meaning. The same tradition is reflected on bull-terminal iron fire-dogs in 'Belgic' graves. That fertility symbolism was the primary stimulus is suggested by, for example, the Felmersham (Bedfordshire) find of a bucket decorated with a pair of bull and cow-mountings. One interesting feature of Iron Age bulls is that they often have knob-ended horns. The reason for this is obscure, but some fire-dogs – as at Barton, Cambs – have the feature, and late Iron Age bull-images from, for example Ham Hill, Somerset and the figurine from the Lexden Tumulus near Colchester, have knob-horns. In my view, it could be a ritualising feature, a mark to distinguish sanctity from secularity.

Bull-symbolism is as common in Gaul and Britain during the Romano-Celtic period as before. Its cult-significance on

77  Left. Bronze bull-head bucket-mounts; Holyhead, Anglesey.
Copyright: National Museum of Wales. Right. Bronze bull-mount;
Welshpool, Powys. Copyright: National Museum of Wales.          177

the immediately pre-Roman Gundestrup Cauldron is demonstrated by its appearance several times, including a huge example on the base-plate, apparently a bull-sacrifice. The most famous Gaulish bull is that carved on the complex Tiberian Paris monument, dedicated by sailors. On one relief a bull stands in front of a tree, with three cranes perched on its back; and similar imagery occurs at Trier. MacCana would see this as displaying a specific aspect of Celtic mythology. Bull-iconography is common in Gaul and Britain but, unlike the horse or dog, the beast is rarely associated closely with anthropomorphic representations. An exception is a Reims relief where, as at Gundestrup, the animal is associated with Cernunnos and a stag. Bull-heads figure on the complex monument from Saintes, in company with Cernunnos and a mother-goddess. Of unassociated bull-images little needs to be said except to remark on their quantity. A few examples are noteworthy: the huge size of the Martigny-en-Valais bronze bull suggests its divinity. The Thealby and Ribble bucket-mounts with their complex bull/eagle/human heads could suggest the shape-shifting tradition so common to vernacular literature. One or two British figurines exaggerate the fertility-symbolism of the creature: at Silchester, Icklingham and South Ferriby bronze bull-heads combine phallic symbolism with bull-features.

Ritual deposits associated with cattle demonstrate their sacrificial and cult importance. As early as the later Bronze Age, the ritual enclosure of Aulnay-aux-Planches (Marne) produced an ox-skull associated with human sacrifices. At Iron Age South Cadbury, there is abundant evidence for cattle ritual; newborn calves occurred on one side of the approach to a shrine: cattle-skulls were set carefully upright in pits – 'in fact they gave every impression of having been deliberately buried as part of some ritual'. In addition, outside a porched shrine was the burial of an adult cow. Within the Romano-Celtic period in Britain, ritual associated with offerings of bulls, oxen or cows, manifests itself in numerous instances. Several shrines had associated cattle burials, including Brigstock, Caerwent, Verulamium, Muntham Court and Wroxeter. At the curious subterranean shrine at Cambridge, there was elaborate animal-ritual involving burials of a complete horse and bull and hunting dogs, all carefully arranged; this was going on in the late second or early third century AD.

The precise significance of bull-symbolism in the Celtic world is obscure. But the frequency of its iconographic occurrence as an isolated image, and the abundant evidence for ritual and sacrifice suggests that it possessed a sanctity for its own sake. We know from Pliny that white bulls were sacrificed in the Druidic ceremonial of the mistletoe-cutting. We will see later that bull-horns were a highly potent symbol adopted by anthropomorphic deities, the horns on the animal itself having attracted reverence from great antiquity. The Celtic fascination with this domesti-cated, though savagely powerful, animal is indicated by bull-names: the site-name of Tarbes and the tribe of the Taurini are illustrations of topographical and tribal identification with a revered creature; 'Deiotarus' in Galatia means 'divine bull'. It should be remembered that cattle-ranching was important in some parts of the Celtic world, notably Ireland: here it is interesting that much of the early Irish vernacular tradition is concerned with magico-divine bulls. In the Cattle Raid of Cooley, the climax of the tale is the conflict of two great and supernatural bulls, originally divine swineherds and still retaining the powers of human thought even after a series of zoomorphic metamorphoses. Bulls were associated also with the selection of kings in Ireland. The *tarbfhess* was a bull-feast or bull-sleep, where a bull was killed, the flesh eaten by a man who then went to sleep; four Druids intoned incantations over him, and the sleeper saw in his dreams the person destined to rule. It is even possible that this scenario is represented on the base-plate of the Gundestrup Cauldon where a huge bull lies waiting for the slaughterer's knife.

Two final and cautionary points should be made concerning bull-symbolism. First, whilst it is clear that the bull itself represents powers of strength, fierceness and virility, very often, if the head alone is portrayed, we have no means of telling whether pugnacious bull or docile ox is depicted. The latter may have its own symbolism as an agricultural animal and it is clear that plough-teams repre-sented at Val Camonica and Mont Bego must depict this aspect of cattle-ritual. Second, the bull is by no means exclusive to the Celtic world, in terms of religion. Whilst I would argue that it may attain more importance as a cult-beast, it must be remembered that in the Graeco-Roman world the bull was Jupiter's emblem, and that in a Mediterranean context bull-sacrifices were very common.

## THE WILD ANIMALS

### Boars

Of wild forest beasts endowed with supernatural qualities

by the Celts, the boar and stag are the most important by far. Strabo tells us that the Celts ate, especially, fresh and salt pork. According to the Greek geographer, pigs ran wild and were noted for their height, pugnacity and speed; it was dangerous both for wolves and human strangers to approach them. The culinary/ritual role played by pigs in the Celtic world is emphasised in archaeology, classical and Irish literature. A number of La Tène burials attest the presence of the 'champion's joint of pork' mentioned in vernacular and Graeco-Roman writings (see Chapters One & Four). In Britain, in the Arras Culture graves of King's Barrow and at Garton Slack, chariot-inhumations with pigs' heads are recorded and, in the Marne area, the hilltop burial of 'La Gorge–Meillet' was that of a young warrior with sword, food-offerings, wine-vessels and a pork-joint. Pork was significant as a food appropriate for feasts both in this and the otherworld: it was a hospitality-symbol, and there is abundant Irish mythology woven round boars and pigs. Shape-shifting often involved pigs, and magico-divine pigs were involved in ritual hunts where the invincibility of the beast was stressed; Irish pigs were powerful and destructive, leading men to death and the underworld. Nor is the pig neglected in Welsh tradition, where supernatural beasts such as the boar and his companions transformed from people, in the Tale of Cwlhwch and Olwen (in parallel with the Odyssey-story of Circe and Odysseus' men). In Irish legend pork was an otherworld food which, like the New Testament loaves and fishes, was renewed each day. That certain Celtic sacred sites were concerned especially with pig-ritual is suggested at Hayling Island where pig-bones and sheep-bones formed the bulk of animal-bones present.

Iconographically the boar/wild pig is prominent, both before and during the Romano-Celtic period. On Iron Age coinage, boars are supraregional motifs; the tribe of the Aulerci Eburovices of Evreux struck coins with the boar-symbol on the neck of a human head; Armorican coins have a human head with a boar-image in their hair. This imagery corresponds closely with that on an immediately pre-Roman stone from Euffigneix (Marne) where a stylised, monolithic human figure wearing a torc, has a boar-image with raised dorsal crest superimposed on his torso. On the Gundestrup Cauldron, a boar attends Cernunnos; again a number of Iron Age boar-figurines, usually with ferociously raised dorsal bristles, are scattered throughout the Celtic world from Britain to eastern Europe. A tiny bronze boar was associated with an early Iron Age swan's neck pin at

Woodendean, Sussex; the first century BC Neuvy-en-Sullias hoard of bronze figures included three nearly life-size boars; a second century BC boar-figurine comes from Báta in Hungary and at Sopron in the same area, a whole boar-skeleton was found packed into a separate stone grave. The most easterly boar recorded is the first century BC bronze from Luncani, Romania. The ferocity of the wild boar made the image popular as a battle-ensign or talisman. On the Gundestrup Cauldron a large boar-crest adorns the helmet of a horseman in a military procession; and there is other evidence of this. The Iron Age shield from the river Witham was decorated with an elongated boar-image, and Tacitus mentions the 'Celtic' tribe of the Aestii wearing boar-amulets as battle-protection.

Boars remained as popular a cult-beast during the Romano-Celtic period in Gaul and Britain. Boar-gods such as Mercury Moccus among the Lingones and Arduinna, boar-goddess of the Ardennes, attest the function of the boar as an important attribute, and now for the first time in the Roman phase, it is identified with named deities. Stone boars appear in a shrine at Forêt d'Halatte; and the bronze dying boar-plaque from the Muntham Court shrine (Fig. 73) may suggest a hunting-cult. Of great interest is the three-horned boar from the Avrigney area of Bourgogne, where the attributes of a common cult-animal, the triple-horned bull (below, p 190), have been transferred to an alien beast. In Britain, cult deposits of the Roman period suggest ritual associated with pigs or boars: at Chelmsford, a young boar was buried possibly as a foundation-offering and a similar occurrence is attested at the Hockwold temple where the cella's four column-bases each had a pit with pig and bird-bones at the base. Boar-tusks were buried with antlers and over a hundred pots in the Ashill (Norfolk) ritual shaft.

It can be seen from the above that boars were important symbols of food, hunting and battle for the Celts. Like the bull, there was no one predominant boar-god, and the beast must, rather, have been regarded as possessing supernatural powers independent of any anthropomorphic deity. An interesting point emerging from the iconography is the emphasis – not on the tusks, as might be expected – but on the dorsal bristles which could be raised in battle or at rest (Fig. 1). Clearly the choice was deliberately made among Celtic craftsmen both to stress the ferocity of this beast, so popular as a personal amulet or talisman, and to enhance the impact of the image in the artistic design.

## The Stag

As a symbol, the stag is of considerable antiquity in the Celtic or proto-Celtic world. For hunters, the stag with its tree-like antlers represented the spirit of the forest; its agility, speed and sexual vigour were admired, and there was mystery in the autumn shedding and regrowth of the antlers in the spring, which could easily symbolise seasonal death and rebirth. The seventh century BC cult wagon from Strettweg (Fig. 13) depicts what may be a ritual hunt, with central goddess, horsemen and footsoldiers and two stags. The sixth century BC gold bowl from Altstetten (Zürich) portrays a schematic doe and stag. On later prehistoric rock-carvings of Scandinavia and Val Camonica the stag is prominent, associated very frequently with solar symbolism. At Paspardo the solar rayed symbol takes the form of antlers. Here in North Italy the stag, as an appropriate forest beast, takes precedence over oxen and horses are almost totally absent. Camunian stag and sun-symbolism reached its apogee during the first millennium BC; and in the fourth century, we have an anthropomorphic stag-figure with whom we become increasingly familiar during the later Iron Age and Romano-Celtic period. Stag-symbolism is prominent on the Gundestrup Cauldron where the stag-horned god Cernunnos is associated with a stag and where on another plate, a god grasps a stag in each hand.

In-the-round stag-figures are not common in pre-Roman contexts, but a handsome bronze occurs in the conquest-period cache at Neuvy-en-Sullias (Loiret). At Balzars, Liechtenstein, a bronze stag, boar and soldiers date from the third to first centuries BC, and a first century BC bronze stag comes from Saalfelden. In Britain, the Iron Age hillfort at Milber Down, Devon produced a stag-figurine. Stags are important in Romano-Celtic iconography; first and fore-

78   Bronze, late Iron Age, stag; Milber Down Hillfort, Devon. Copyright: Torquay Museum.

most, the beast occurs as a companion of the stag-antlered
Cernunnos (*infra*) but it appears also alone, or associated
with other images. On a Reims stone, Cernunnos is associated with a stag and bull 'drinking' from a stream of coins;
and a Luxembourg stone depicts a stag 'vomiting' coins.
Here simple prosperity-symbolism takes precedence over
any hunting-imagery. But elsewhere, forest and hunt are
paramount. The stag is associated with the North British
god Cocidius as a hunter, for example at Risingham, and
Silvanus Callirius ('woodland king', a native epithet) at
Colchester was associated with a stag at a shrine and
dedicated by a coppersmith. On a Chedworth relief a hunter
is accompanied by his hound, a stag and hare. The relief of

79   Bronze stag, found in pit in vicinity of rectangular temple;
     Colchester. Copyright: Colchester & Essex Museum.

80   Bronze plaque to Silvanus Callirius, dedicated by a coppersmith,
     found in pit with stag (no 90 above). Copyright: Colchester &
     Essex Museum.

stag and three trees at Castlecary in Scotland reinforces the
forest-imagery. At the mountain-shrine of Le Donon
(Vosges) a god with an animal-pelt hung with fruits is
depicted on a relief accompanied by a stag on whose antlers

183

he rests his hand in an attitude of benediction. Here, forest/hunting and prosperity-symbolism come together in a dualistic, interdependent relationship. the divine hunter hunts the stag but has also an intimate symbolic bond with it and through this link comes prosperity and well-being for the land.

The stag played an important role in Irish tradition: like the boar, it enticed heroes to the realms of the gods in the excitement of the chase; the stag was involved in divine shape-changing; divine bulls metamorphosed into stags and Irish goddesses like the Mórrígan changed into deer at will. There is evidence for British ritual activity associated with stags and demonstrated by archaeology: most interesting is a deposit recently found at Wasperton (Warws) where face-down in a pit was placed a stone inscribed *feliciter*; on the upper surface below a layer of burnt material were placed two sets of unburnt antlers with bits of skull attached, arranged to form a square, in the centre of which a fire had been lit.

In summary, the stag plays a dual role in Celtic symbolism. It epitomised the vastnesses of the Gaulish and British woodlands, and its image was reproduced in reverence by its hunters. But it also possessed a strong prosperity/fertility cult-value, this last reflected not only in its association with Cernunnos – lord of beasts and fecundity – but perhaps also in the curious antler phallic amulets known, for instance, in southern Britain, where the choice of antler for relief-carving of male genitalia may not simply be fortuitous.

## Other Beasts: Bear and Hare

Evidence for these hunted animals is sparse but interesting. A bear-goddess called eponymously 'Artio' is recorded in the Berne area of Switzerland, where she appears in bronze with bowls of fruit, one of which she offers to a bear confronting her. She is a goddess of plenty and she may have the dual function of protectress of bears against hunters and of humans against bears! Elsewhere, dedications to Artio were made in a remote valley near Bollendorf. Mercury Artaios is evidenced at Beaucroissant (Isère), but otherwise bears are represented as small figurines, perhaps talismans. Several jet bears occur in North Britain: a York bear-pendant was found in a fourth century AD burial; and at Malton a child was buried with a tiny jet bear-amulet too small to have been a toy.

81   Jet bear-amulet; Bootle, Lancs. Copyright: Sheffield Museum.

The hare has the distinction of being mentioned in classical sources as a sacrifice to the British war-goddess Andraste. Apart from associations with hunters, as at Chedworth, hares may be associated with some interesting evidence for ritual. Hare-bones appear in pits, for example at Ewell, Surrey, and at the Thistleton Dyer shrine a bronze hare was found in a pit; at Ipswich is recorded the curious phenomenon of two pits each with a small piece of hare-fur. Most interesting in its complexity is the ritual deposit at Winterbourne Kingston, Dorset where an eighty-five foot deep shaft contained brooches, coins, bones, a Purbeck marble vase and a bronze hare; nearby was a ritual structure demarcated by eight burnt tiles in the centre of which were a knife and a small conical sarsen.

## Snakes and Amphibians

The 'Monstrous' phenomenon of ram-horned snakes is examined below. Normal snakes would appear to possess the same healing and chthonic associations as in the Mediterranean world. The snake-limbed monster of the Jupiter-columns (Chapter Two) is chthonic, and its appearance with Sucellus may contain similar symbolism. Its paramount role was as a beneficent and health-giving beast. Indigenous healing deities such as Sirona at Hochscheid in the Rhineland, and Borvo and Damona at Bourbonne-les-Bains, had the serpent as their emblem, and it may be as a healer (as at Trier) that Mars is represented with a goddess and snakes at Mavilly. But a war-aspect to the reptile is evidenced in Irish tradition, where the mighty Conall Cernach confronts a snake who guards the fort of an enemy. But even here, protection is the snake's main role, 185 and seen in this context, the snake would seem to have an interlinked role as protector against sickness, war and the terrors of death.

Frogs and/or toads are rare but two instances of ritual associated with them may point to their use for magical purposes. In the primary phase at Danebury a pit contained a widely selected set of only twenty bones representing at least seven species, including frog or toad. Far away in Aquitaine, votive pits, of late first century BC date, are recorded, containing cremations including particularly toad-bones, suggesting that these were other than ordinary burials.

## Birds

The ability of birds to leave earth and fly through the heavens makes them a very natural object of cult-significance in many ancient religions. They were important in this context in both Mediterranean and Celtic Europe, and there is evidence that the tradition of sacred birds goes far back into prehistory. In Roman religion, certain birds are associated with particular deities, normally because they are appropriate to that god: Jupiter's bird was the eagle; the cockerel belonged to Mercury; the peacock to Juno.

### Water Birds

In north-west Europe, birds appear in religious imagery from the time of the Urnfield period (circa 1300 BC onwards). In fact, a very specific cult appears to be represented at this time by the repeated presence of associated water-bird and solar motifs which carry on right through to the Iron Age in Europe (above, p 42). Aquatic birds – swans and ducks – and also marsh/wading birds are prominent in Celtic ritual, both in Romano-Celtic iconography and in the early Irish literature. Most famous in a Gaulish context is Sequana, goddess of the Seine-source, whose sanctuary was near Dijon (Chapter Five). She appears as a bronze statuette standing in a duck-prowed boat, a sacred cake in its mouth. Other Celtic water-birds are known: a bronze swan and duck occur at Vaison in southern Gaul, and a curious figurine from Rotherley Down, consisting of a duck with a human head on its back, may be an instance of shape-shifting or metamorphosis in process. Of the several British occurrences, the bronze duck from Milber Down, Devon is most interesting in that it comes from an Iron Age hillfort together with a stag and raven, and, like Sequana's duck-boat, it bears a pellet or cake in its beak. In Irish literature aquatic birds, especially swans, are prominent and swan-legends abound. Deities appear in the form of swans, and the supernatural element is frequently shown by the presence of gold or silver neck-chains. To take just one story as an example, in the Dream of Angus (possibly as early as the eighth century AD) a girl called Caer and her followers became swans on the feast of Samain. The Ulster Cycle hero Cú Chulainn, too, was involved with chain-bearing water-birds with magico-supernatural powers.

## Geese and Cranes

Marsh and wading birds are commoner in the vernacular insular tradition than in Celtic iconography. The prehistoric evidence is sparse, but the great free-standing stone bird perched on the portico of the pre-Roman southern Gaulish shrine of Roquepertuse may represent a goose. Megaw has pointed out the predominance of goose-bones in Iron Age warriors' graves in eastern Czechoslovakia. Certainly the goose is associated with war-gods in Romano-Celtic contexts (above, p 113). Geese are aggressive, and a war/protection role is a fairly obvious one. The same cannot be said of the crane, which is important in Irish literature and occurs rarely but significantly in iconography. On the Tiberian Paris monument, one stone bears a depiction inscribed to Tarvostrigaranus ('the bull with three cranes'); on it is the image of a tree and a large bull with three marsh birds perched on its back and head. A very similar relief comes from Trier where a god paralleled by the 'Esus' portrayal elsewhere on the Paris monument, hacks at a tree in whose foliage appear a bull's head and three cranes. This is probably some referral to a complexity of Celtic mythology, which we can never fully grasp. But certainly cranes figure prominently in Irish legend, identified particularly with certain kinds of unpleasant women. In Britain, crane-representations are rare, but at Biddenham (Beds) an altar carved with a crane was associated with a human body in a ritual shaft.

## Ravens and Crows

Apart from the water-fowl, carrion birds are most promi-nent in Celtic religion. As consumers of dead things, it is natural that they should possess death and underworld symbolism. In the Mabinogion, ravens are beneficent otherworld creatures associated with Rhiannon, but their magico-divine function in Irish legend is usually concerned with war and destruction. War-goddesses like Badb and the Mórrígan constantly change to ravens or crows, and the Irish raven-goddesses were able to foretell disastrous battle-outcomes. In relationships with the Ulster Cycle hero Cú Chulainn, ravens were generally malevolent otherworld birds. Their prognostic qualities are further demonstrated by their Druidical use in Irish augury. Iconographically, ravens occur in La Tène art, and may there possess a war/death symbolism. Several Gaulish deities appear with birds which may be ravens, and their association with Nantosuelta (consort of Sucellus) may signify chthonicism. Ravens appear frequently as small bronzes in British contexts and at Willingham, Cambs and Felmingham, Norfolk they occur in hoards associated with the Celtic sky-god (Chapter Two) and where they may represent the underworld aspect of his cult.

### Other Birds

Of these the most important are eagles. Their vast wing-span and powerful, high flight epitomize the huge span of the sky and, as Jupiter's bird, their appearance in Romano-Celtic contexts may be due to Roman influence. But they appear in so many instances alone in Britain – more than half-a-dozen at the shrine of Woodeaton, Oxon – that they may possess sky-symbolism not necessarily linked with Jupiter only. A bird of prey is represented at the pre-Roman Provençal shrine of Roquepertuse where a huge curved beak holds two human heads. Similar imagery occurs in Britain where a bucket-ornament from the Ribble (Lancs) is composed of a bull, human and eagle head; and this is partially repeated at Thealby, Lincs (Fig. 75) where two mounts depict eagles' heads surmounting those of bulls.

The problem with bird-imagery is that it is frequently difficult to tell which species is represented. Unidentifiable birds occur in a great deal of Celtic iconography, and it may be that sometimes bird-symbolism is of itself the important element. Many Gaulish deities appear with birds, and Thevenot suggests that they may be oracular. Several times, divinities appear with birds on their heads or shoulders; at Alesia, a god stands with an oak, birds in the branches, and a three-headed dog. Certain deities liked birds as offerings: young people healed by Lenus at Trier are depicted holding birds, and votive birds (probably doves) were offered in the thermal shrines of Côte d'Or.

82   Bronze eagle; Woodeaton, oxon. Photograph: Betty Naggar.
Ashmolean Museum, Oxford.

Whatever the precise significance of Celtic bird-symbolism, it is fair to say that the qualities of free flight and the ability to escape from the earth were seen as attributes suitable to zoomorphic companions of the gods. Birds were regarded, too, as prophetic, as having links with the otherworld, and as representative of the spirit when freed from the body. But they possessed also a multifarious symbolism ranging from war, destruction and death to rebirth, healing, light and the sun.

## ZOOMORPHIC MONSTERS

Two main types of monster are known in the Celtic world: the first is where an animal has something added, the second where a deity is depicted as a human image but with either antlers, bull, goat or ram-horns. The first group contains, notably, the triple-horned bull and ram-horned snake. The second may be divided into stag-horned portrayals – the so-called 'Cernunnos' form – and miscellaneous horned beings. In the case of the bull and snake, it could be argued that these are variants of the     189

83   Bronze three-horned bull; Cirencester. Photograph: Betty Naggar.
Corinium Museum.

normal beast and should be grouped with them, but I feel
that there is an argument for treating all mutations as a
specific iconographical phenomenon. I must emphasise that
monstrous images in the present period and context would
appear to have been an entirely Celtic quirk, resulting from
the very intimate association between animals and men and
between zoomorphic and anthropomorphic divine representation. However, as is well-known, monsters are not
unknown in classical mythology: the multi-headed Hydra,
hundred-handed giant and three-headed Cerberus demonstrate this.

## The Triple-horned Bull and the Ram-Horned Snake

The triple-horned bull is an interesting iconographical
phenomenon: it occurs normally in bronze, though stone
examples appear at the shrine of Beire-le-Châtel (Côte d'Or),
and a pipe-clay figurine comes from a child's grave at
Colchester. It is essentially Gaulish, being a popular cult-
beast among the Lingones and Sequani, and central and
eastern tribes in general. About thirty-five Gaulish bulls are
recorded and only six in British contexts. Of the latter three
are particularly interesting: the sepulchral context of the
Colchester figurine is noteworthy; and the silvered bronze

84   Pipe-clay three-horned bull, from child's grave; Colchester.
Copyright: Colchester & Essex Museum.

85   Silver-washed three-horned bull, with figures of deities on its
back, from mid fourth century AD shrine; Maiden Castle, Dorset.
Copyright: Dorset Natural History & Archaeology Society, County
Museum, Dorchester, Dorset.

bull from Maiden Castle not only comes from a shrine but
bears the remains of three humanoid female figures on its
back. This is reminiscent of the Parisian relief of
Tarvostrigaranus, and it is possible that we have here an
example of transmogrification – the cranes and women
involved in shape-shifting. The third notable British three-
horned bull, from Willingham, is remarkable in its associ-                   191

ation, on a ceremonial bronze sceptre-terminal, with divine images associated with the Celtic sky-god (eagle, wheel and chthonic monster (see Chapter Two)). The triple-horned bull-image is unequivocally sacral; it is an unnatural image; it occurs in temples, and at Auxy (Seine et Loire) a figurine bears a basal dedication to the emperor. The tripling of the horn may have several purposes: triplism was important (see Chapter Seven) both for 'threeness' itself as a powerful sacred number, and for simple intensification. Horns were potent Celtic fertility symbols and thus the multiplication of the essence of a creature, its power, vigour and virility, is a natural way of increasing the symbolism. The beast is interesting because, like the normal two-horned variety, it most often appears alone and is not necessarily associated with any one anthropomorphic divine form. The animal may or may not represent a god itself but it is pulled out of normality and its potency is vastly augmented by its third horn.

The ram-horned snake also has had something added, but here the addition takes the form of an element alien to the serpent-host. Again intensification and augmenting of symbolism appears to have been the intention. Once more the monster is primarily Gaulish, about fifteen instances being known, mainly in the north-east, but only a scattering occurs in Britain. The context of some of the depictions is extremely interesting and diverse: on the Gundestrup Cauldron, the snake appears on one plate as the companion of the stag-horned Cernunnos, and on another at the head of a military procession. The Cernunnos association is a recurrent one: at Cirencester, the god's legs are replaced by snakes who rear up their heads next to two purses on either side of the god. At Sommerécourt (Haute Marne), Cernunnos accompanies a goddess who feeds a ram-horned snake from a basket on her knee, and the god himself also has a snake of his own. This theme is repeated at Crêt Chatelard (Loire) where a (lost) wooden sculpture from a Celtic oppidum depicted a squatting deity (in the attitude of Cernunnos) with a ram-horned snake sliding down his arm and with its head in a basket. The repeated prosperity-symbolism shown in the reliefs is significant: a bronze from Curgy (Seine et Loire) combines several Celtic images in curious intensity; a three-headed god sits cross-legged; he has a torc, antlers and a ram-horned snake entwined round his body. Celtic versions of Mars and Mercury also have this beast as a companion: at Beauvais and Néris the snake's presence would appear to transform Mercury into a Celtic deity; at Mavilly, Mars and a goddess are linked with the

86   Stone plaque of Cernunnos and two ram-horned snakes; Cirencester. Photograph: C J Bowler. Copyright: Corinium Museum.

snake. At Southbroom (Wiltshire) one of the hoard of
bronze figurines depicts a Celtic Mars grasping a ram-
horned snake in each hand, in the manner of the Cirencester
Cernunnos. The monster does occur in other contexts or
indeed alone: at Blain perhaps significantly, the beast
accompanies a horned god. Perhaps the most interesting of
all is the apparent presence of the snake in a pre-Roman
context, at Val Camonica, where a rock-carving depicts a
standing stag-horned deity with two torcs, accompanied by
a ram-horned snake and a small ithyphallic acolyte or
devotee.                                                   193

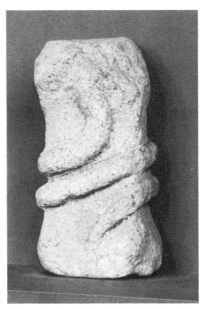

87   Stone altar with ram-horned snake; Lypiatt Park, Glos. Copyright:
Stroud District Museum.

The context and associations of the ram-horned snake
demonstrate its role as a symbol of prosperity and plenty: it
often appears with the antlered Cernunnos, himself a
fertility-image (*infra*), with purses and baskets of food. Its
appearance alone, as at Carlisle and Trier and its sporadic
association with such deities as Celtic versions of Mercury
and Mars suggest that it was not simply a companion but
had a sacred symbolism of its own. We have seen that the
snake's associates suggest prosperity-symbolism; if we
examine the iconography of the monster itself, the same
implications are present. The ram was a fertility-image in
the Mediterranean world: the snake is more complicated; in
Graeco-Roman symbolism it was linked with health and
healing, but also with chthonicism and with death – the
earthbound character of the serpent makes this symbolism
natural. Curiously, as we have noted with the Mothers
(Chapter Three) death, the underworld and fertility are
closely linked, presumably partly because of the
regenerative power of burial and of spring after winter, and
germination of seeds. One particularly significant British
find is that from Lypiatt Park (Glos) where a ram-horned
snake curls round a small altar on the *focus* of which is a
worn wheel-sign, associating the serpent with the sky and
sun-god. This is especially important since there may be
links with the Jupiter-columns, where negative forces are
represented by a snake-limbed creature. What the Celts

194

seem to have done with the ram-horned snake is to conflate and combine the sacred symbols of fertility, healing and the underworld: the monstrous serpent is especially potent because of the multiplicity of images present, and it appears with a number of different deities to enhance their well-being role. Where it appears on its own, the symbolism is just as vital – perhaps a comparison might be made with images of Christ on the cross and the cross alone.

## Cernunnos and the Horned Gods

A different monstrous zoomorphic manifestation occurring in Celtic iconography is that where otherwise anthropomorphic images bear animal-attributes; these are most commonly horns, but occasionally ears and feet may be replaced by animal versions. Two main types may be identified: the first is a comparatively homogeneous group consisting of a cross-legged human figure usually, but not invariably, male with stag-antlers on his head. On a Paris relief – part of the Tiberian Sailors' Pillar – an antlered god with a torc hanging from each antler and stags' ears, bears the name Cernunnos which, as it simply means 'horned one', may be used conveniently to describe all similar beings in Gaul and Britain. The image is once again pri-marily Gaulish, with over thirty examples. Cernunnos is interesting partly because of his homogeneity, but partly because of the pre-Roman evidence which, though sparse, suggests that this divine form was familiar at least from the fourth century BC when a Camunian artist in North Italy carved the image of an antlered deity with torc, ram-horned snake and ithyphallic devotee. The people of Val Camonica were very probably Celtic and we know from their cult-carvings on remote rocks in the forest that the stag was important to them. That they should conceive of an antlered god is no surprise. In Gaul itself, the god manifests himself perhaps as early as the third century BC: a bronze from Bouray shows a god sitting cross-legged, with the hooves of a stag. An antlered god is known in Romania at the first century BC Dacian fort of Popeşti. But it is on the Gun-destrup Cauldron that Cernunnos is perhaps at his most splendid: this great cult-bowl, possibly belonging originally to a Gaulish priesthood, depicts on one plate Cernunnos as lord of animals, with his stag, ram-horned serpent, boar, bull and other beasts. The intimate relationship between himself and the stag is shown by the identical, stylised treatment of both sets of antlers. Stone monuments of the

88    Iron Age silver coin with head of Cernunnos and wheel-symbol;
Petersfield, Hants. Copyright: National Museum of Wales.

Romano-Celtic period reinforce the imagery of the
Cauldron: a relief from Reims shows Cernunnos with a sack
of coins; beneath are a bull and stag; on the pediment above
the god's head is a rat. At Sommerécourt, a sculptured god
with holes for the insertion of real or metal antlers sits
cross-legged with a goddess and ram-horned snakes. At
Vendoeuvres (Indre) Cernunnos is flanked by two young
men standing on snakes; the god holds a purse and both
men grasp his antlers. At Turbelsloch near Differdange
(Luxembourg) a young god holds a brimming *cornucopiae*;
he is associated with a bull and stag vomiting money onto a
table. Of greatest interest is the bronze from Curgy (Seine et
Loire), usually referred to as being from Autun, where a
bearded, three-headed deity sits cross-legged and feeds two
ram-horned snakes encircling his body from fruit piled in
his lap; there are holes in the main head for separate antlers.

British evidence for Cernunnos is very scarce, and it is
obvious that he was an imported deity: a recent find of a
Celtic silver coin, dating to around AD 20, at Petersfield,
Hants constitutes the only pre-Roman trace of the god; he is
here depicted with a Celtic solar wheel symbol between his
antlers, echoing perhaps the imagery of the Gundestrup
Cauldron where the wheel-god is also portrayed. The most
important British relief is that from Cirencester (Fig. 86) –
that home of so many Gaulish deities – where Cernunnos,
with antlers and purses filled with coins, sits grasping two
ram-horned snakes which actually replace the god's legs.
As we have seen, the Cernunnos iconography is varied

196

and complex, but three features stand out very strongly. The first is the very close association with the stag itself which appears with Cernunnos on several monuments. The second is the frequency of the ram-horned snake as a companion, and the intimacy of the relationship is shown at Cirencester where god and snakes merge. Third, the overall symbolism is distinctively that of prosperity and well-being: Cernunnos is lord of nature, of beasts, fruit, corn and even plenty as symbolised by money. The underworld aspect to the snake and perhaps the Cernunnos-cult is suggested by the rat – a burrowing, carrion-feeding and therefore chthonic beast – on the Reims relief. The main feature of the iconography is the close link between man/god and beast. The stag-symbolism is very potent in that often stag and stag-god are present together; it is tempting to see here an example of Celtic shape-shifting, Cernunnos changing at will from beast to man-form.

By contrast to Cernunnos, non-antlered horned beings (usually with bull-horns but sometimes with those of ram or goat) are a particular feature of British iconography, though common in later prehistory to a great deal of non-Mediterranean Europe. Horned creatures, not necessarily human, appear as early as the Urnfield period of the later Bronze Age: Bronze Age Danish art is full of horned, sometimes phallic figures. Horned birds draw cult-wagons in Central Europe and a horned swan appears on a bronze bowl from Biesenbrow. Horned male heads are prominent in La Tène metalwork and an early Iron Age horned

89   Horned stone head; Carvoran, Northumberland. Copyright: University of Newcastle upon Tyne.

janiform stone figure is known at Holzerlingen. On the great arch at Orange, helmets with bull-horns are depicted, and an identical helmet is worn by a warrior on one Gundestrup Cauldron plate. In the Romano-Celtic period, horned gods do occur in Gaul; a deity from Blain near Nantes associated with a ram and serpent bears huge horns. But it is North Britain, the home of the powerful Brigantian confederation of tribes, that was a centre for horned representations. There is a scatter of depictions from southern Britain; a pre-Roman bronze bucket-mount from Boughton Aluph (Kent) depicts a human head with large bull-horns. A small bronze mask from Athelney (Somerset) shows a bull-horned human face and female horned figures appear at Icklingham, Suffolk and at Richborough; there are other examples, too, notably two horned Mercury-heads from Wandsworth and Uley respectively. At Wall, Staffordshire, sandstone reliefs associated with a shrine depict crudely incised heads adorned with horns. These occurrences form a link with the great panoply of horned reliefs from northern Britain, throughout the non-romanised and essentially military zone. Here, as in Bronze Age Denmark, the horned figure is often ithyphallic (Fig. 55). That one single deity is not represented is clear from the diversity of horned images; horns appear on depictions of gods who otherwise resemble Mercury, a warrior, hunter or featureless being, perhaps represented by a head alone. Maryport, Cumbria has produced a large group of naked, roughly incised warrior-figures with horns, shield and spear, often ithyphallic. At High Rochester, there is bull and stag iconography, and it is not surprising that horns also feature prominently.

Horns seem to have been given to certain gods at certain times to increase the power of their symbolism. At Uley only one of several Mercury-images is horned. Horns are manifestly primarily a fertility image; this is supported by the stressed masculinity on some depictions. But horns – especially those of a bull – represent power in general, strength, aggression and ferocity and, as such, are natural associates of warriors or armour. In general, the Celts appear to have used horns to increase the symbolism of whatever role the god himself already possessed, or to add the potency of fecundity and strength. It is interesting that at Maryport, stronghold of horned beings, even a little pipe-clay figurine of 'Venus' bears horns.

With horns and antlers, we have the ultimate in close association between the human and animal form. The Celts deliberately chose to endow human/god images with an animal attribute. The very intimate link between animals and religion was apparently due to the same phenomenon which made nature, fertility and prosperity representations so important – a basic identification between religion, the supernatural and natural phenomena. The strength of this human-god-animal connection is seen most clearly and unequivocally in the presence of horns. Whether or not horned images represent shape-changing, it is true to say that the Celts were not totally bound by the human image in their views of their gods.

# CHAPTER SEVEN: SYMBOLISM AND IMAGERY IN CELTIC CULT EXPRESSION

## Introduction

This final chapter is concerned not so much with the nature of the Celtic gods themselves as with some of the distinctive methods by which Celtic artists symbolised and portrayed cult-material. The character of Celtic sacral art was touched upon in Chapter One and we here examine the specific traditions which develop this theme. Imagery gives clues as to how the gods were envisaged and worshipped. In addition, an examination of the possible purposes underlying the use of varying art-styles reveals a level of sophistication on the part of both craftsman and patron which belies the common definition of much of Gaulish and British indigenous cult-portrayal as 'primitive' and 'incompetent'.

Celtic sacral depiction, whether of human, animal or inanimate subjects, frequently exhibits features which transform 'real' imagery (that is copied from life) into something deliberately less life-like. This was achieved in a number of ways, but all have the dual effect of removing the image from the world of reality and – in some instances at least – of augmenting its power as a symbol. This Celtic iconographic tradition (which must of necessity be studied mainly from Romano-Celtic data) may display a high degree of stylistic abstraction or schematism (Fig. 90). Very often an abbreviated 'shorthand' method of representation is employed not only in stonework (though such is the commonest medium) but also occasionally in metal. The bulk of such iconography is religious in theme. It is here argued that the summary dimissal of these depictions, by 'modern' criteria, as being of inferior workmansip is quite inapplicable: they must rather be examined on their own terms of function and context. Schematised representation was, indeed, a conscious and successful form of image-making. The Graeco-Roman ideal of mimesis was frequently rejected, not because Celtic artists were unable to produce faithful copies but because rigidity was, on the one hand, unnecessary within the context of cult imagery and, on the other, was perhaps viewed as inappropriate for the divine. The same tradition which produced schematised images of deities in

human or animal form, saw no reason not to break the rigid
Graeco-Roman framework of realism in other ways. Of these
the most important appear to be emphasis achieved either
by multiplication/addition or by exaggeration of one
element or, at its most extreme, by the representation of
*pars pro toto*. Enhancement by addition may either be a
straightforward multiplication of the whole or part of the
image, or it may involve the introduction of a new, alien
element or attribute to form a composite depiction.
Triplication of Celtic mother-goddesses is an example of the
former and ram-horns added to a depiction of a serpent of
the latter. As well as by plurality, emphasis may be created
by the exaggeration of an otherwise normal part of an image.
This is exemplified most clearly in cases where the head has
been enlarged out of proportion (culminating in the representation of the head alone). Conversely, other less
important parts of the body may be shrunken to create more
(or less) emphasis.

It is apparent that there are elements common to the
different aspects of emphasis outlined above. Most
important is the conversion of a 'normal' human or animal
image to something which is overtly supernatural on
account of its deliberate departure from the realistic, a
practice which has nothing to do with style or artistic
expertise but rather with deliberate choice of content. It is
advantageous here to stand back from the evidence and look
conceptually at the phenomenon of plurality and exagger-

90    Plaque of *Genii cucullati*; Cirencester. Photograph: C J Bowler.
      Copyright: Corinium Museum.

201

ation. Both forms of manifestation may be treated together since both appear to serve the same purpose of enhancing the potency of the symbol and of 'hammering home the point' both perhaps to the divinity honoured and to the worshipping devotee. In this chapter we will be examining the reasons for over-emphasis and, in that context, we shall raise the question of the role of symbolism in Celtic iconography, an issue equally relevant to the phenomenon of schematism. The final type of portrayal we will look at is a related phenomenon, that of miniaturisation. Though the manufacture of model objects was not Celtic in origin, the practice seems nevertheless to have been adopted *par excellence* for Celtic religious purposes. It will be argued that – notwithstanding arguments concerning convenience and cost – there is a specific symbolism associated with the offering of perfect miniature replicas of everyday tools and weapons to supernatural powers.

## The Role of Symbolism

The issue upon which success or failure of image-making must be judged consists both of the sculptor's or craftsman's intention and of the function of the created image. The production of a religious representation may serve several different purposes, not necessarily all mutually exclusive. If a stone carving which portrays a deity is placed in a temple, shrine or *locus consecratus*, it may possess a function separate from one which comes from a domestic context or a grave. A temple-depiction may be the cult-image: this means that, originally at least, the god would be considered as dwelling within that image. Alternatively, the carving may be seen not as housing the god specifically but may have been set up in order to demonstrate reverence and honour to the god by symbolic physical representation in much the same way as the erection of a statue may commemorate a revered human individual. More prosaically, an image may be created and established in a shrine as a focus of worship, to channel the attention of the devotee and to stimulate thoughts about the divine. All these functions may be true especially of the larger, more monumental, representations. If, however, we turn to small objects (usually of metal), two categories may be recognised: first liturgical material associated with cult-practice or ritual and, second, personal items. The first group occurs generally in temples or buried in caches (presumably originally in shrines or sacred places) and may be regarded as the sacral property of priests or religious officials. The second group may be viewed as generally belonging to individuals, and examples of these occur in shrines as offerings, in houses or in sepulchral contexts. The function of ritual material is more or less self-evident: it may be assumed that a ceremonial sceptre or priest's mask and headdress bearing divine images is itself imbued with sanctity or that holy power is invested in the object by means of the divine portrayal. The interpretation of personal items is more complicated. Symbolism of the divine must in all instances be present to a greater or lesser extent; small bronze or clay figurines must have been purchased and dedicated to the deity represented. But whilst some would have been dedicated 'officially' and placed in roadside, urban or domestic shrines, others, such as amulets, might remain in secular contexts and be regarded rather more vaguely, as good-luck symbols or talismans rather than as possessing any genuine sanctity as a result of deliberate consecration.

Finally, in arguments concerning the function of symbolism or a symbolic object, it is necessary to clarify the responsibilities involved in the production of cult-images as visual expressions of belief. In each instance, two distinct individuals were generally involved (perhaps more if epigraphic dedications are present), namely the initiator and the executor – the patron and potential purchaser and dedicant on the one hand, and the craftsman on the other. I would argue that both are key figures in determining the type of image produced for both patron and stonemason/craftsman need to be in tune with the form of image required. A patron would be unlikely to commission/purchase a cult-image whose iconography he did not understand. Likewise, a craftsman would need to be *au fait* with the style required of him. This means that symbolic content would have been a careful matter of conscious choice by people who were fully aware of what means would best be employed in endowing a cult-object with the greatest possible potency.

## Style and Schematism in Celtic Iconography

Study of stone (and to a lesser extent) of bronze iconography of any Romano-Celtic province reveals a striking diversity of stylistic treatment in the imagery expressed. Whilst many religious depictions in the pagan Celtic world made during the Roman occupation display

203

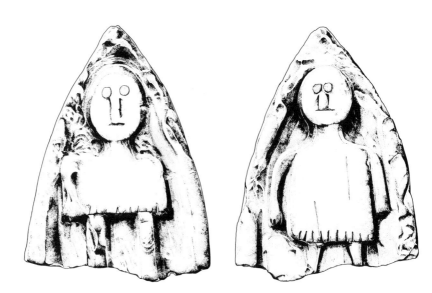

91   Chalk or limestone janiform figure from shrine; Ivy Chimneys,
     Witham, Essex. Illustrator: Margaret Tremayne; copyright HBMC
     English Heritage.

classical realism, this is balanced by a significant
proportion of cult-images which owe little to Graeco-Roman
artistic traditions of verism or naturalism. Some portrayals
indeed, exemplified by the chalk figurine from Deal, Kent or
the Ivy Chimneys carving, give the impression of minimum
attention to the accuracy of the human or animal form, often
being little more than a sketched outline, apparently of
much the same standard of artistic expertise – to a modern
art-historian's eye at least – as a child's drawing.

Stylisation, schematism or abstraction appear to be Celtic
traits. However, whilst there may be some correlation
between the ethnic origins of the deities represented and the
art-form in which they are depicted, this is by no means the
norm. The Emberton Mercury-relief (Fig. 98) is identifiable as
Mercury because of the attributes of wings and *caduceus*
but the style of representation is entirely Celtic. Conversely,
the depiction of a specifically Celtic divine concept such as
the *Matres* from Cirencester may on occasions possess a
high degree of realism, indicating a faithful attempt at
naturalistic depiction of the female human body. Detailed
examination of a cross-section of Romano-British iconography appears to reveal (in terms of art-treatment) not two
but three main categories of image. The naturalistic and the
highly schematised iconography represent opposite ends of
the spectrum of style. But there may be distinguished also a
medial category which poses greater interpretative prob-

204

lems. This group consists of iconography displaying *apparent* (the italics are crucial) attempts at, but incompletely successful production of, the realistic human or animal figure. This category is exemplified by the badly-proportioned Mars-Romulus relief from Custom Scrubs (Fig. 14) and the horseman from Stragglethorpe, Lincs.

Schematism must be assessed within the context not of art for art's sake but of religion. To interpret expertise or the lack of it merely from a present-day art-analyst's point of view is to argue from an entirely false premise, for the Celts' lack of realism may be deliberate, with obscurity and the use of shorthand depiction serving almost as a divine 'code' with the specific purpose of relating the image directly to the supernatural. At the very least, even if not always deliberate, the medial category of semiveristic portrayals may represent the lack of necessity to treat mimetically the human image of a deity. In order to understand this, it is useful to look at the principles of classical and Celtic art.

A fundamental factor in assessing the excellence or otherwise, in artistic terms, of schematised Celtic religious representations, is the recognition and acknowledgement of the existence of specific ethnic artistic traditions. Critics of 'crude' Celtic iconography appear to judge entirely from the classical standpoint that realism or mimesis equal excellence. This can be appreciated by examining some of the basic differences between the standards and traditions of Celtic and classical representative art.

In the classical world, the artist's main function was to please or impress both gods and men; his was an imitative rather than an interpretative role. The aim was to portray man at his idealised best, indistinguishable from the gods represented by him in man's likeness. The naturalism of Greek art in the Classical period was motivated and stimulated largely by the wish to depict human beings (whether gods or men) as real, close-to-life and thus more comprehensible to the beholder. The Greeks were obsessed with the true nature of appearance; indeed the imitation of nature, 'mimesis', was introduced by the Greeks, who escaped from 'conceptual' images and became true to life. In the heyday of Classical Greece art was a curious and uneasy blend of idealism and realism '. . . idealised mortal is near-divine, self-sufficient and above ordinary passions' (Boardman 1973, 120). But by the fourth century BC a new trend can be observed: features became softer and more relaxed and emotion, where appropriate, crept in. If we look at Roman Republican portraiture, we are confronted with stark realism or verism, derived in part from Etruscan influence. The

Roman attitude to artistic excellence is interesting in that the degree of realism achieved is termed *successus*. Pollitt points out that Vitruvius disapproved of the fantastic wall-paintings of his day because they represented things which could not exist in nature.

Celtic art sprang from totally different roots and intentions from those of the Graeco-Roman world. Unless the schematic cult-images of the Celto-Roman world are assessed within this different tradition, criticisms may be made which are both irrelevant and inappropriate. I would argue that, in the light of observations made below, such comments as '. . . one wonders whether all are by the same incompetent hand' (Rhodes 1964, 32ff) or 'some of the carvings from the Cotswolds . . . are very simple' (Henig 1984, 62) are perhaps themselves both simplistic and meaningless.

Celtic figural representation reflects general Celtic artistic tradition which, in the main, was an abstract, symbolic tradition. The art of 'barbarian' Europe was 'symbolic and enumerative, presenting a series of representational clues which can be mentally assembled'. It is interesting that critics of Celtic iconography within the Roman period speak with scorn of the crude images present and at the same time postulate the death of true Celtic art under Roman influence. It may rather be that Celtic tradition is quite logically manifesting itself traditionally but in response to the stimulus of the Roman emphasis on the human or animal image of the supernatural. Prehistoric Celtic art (which predates the period of classical influence) was essentially decorative; patterns and the embellishment of surfaces were of prime importance.

### Schematism: Function and Reason

In examining the stimulus behind abstraction in Celtic humano-divine representation, It has been argued that insular Celtic art differed markedly from the Graeco-Roman tradition in not being man-dominated. Certainly there was no need for a predominantly rural and farming-oriented society to be preoccupied with the realistic. Even where human depiction was present, there may well have been deliberate attempts by craftsmen at de-humanising. Celtic sculptors (and presumably their patrons) did not identify their gods in terms of human perfection, which would very possibly have been largely irrelevant to Celtic notions of divinity, rooted in natural phenomena and sensed rather than envisaged and directly perceived. It is possible to argue deliberate choice on the part of Celtic artists who were producing stylised figures, not lack of ability and artistic skills. Anati believes that the most schematic of the Val Camonica rock-carvings (which date from the Neolithic to the Iron Age) are those with a religious theme. The avoidance of the realistic human element did not mean that Celtic art was necessarily crude (in the pejorative sense), primitive or inferior, but merely different, stimulated by principles other than mimesis. This may be paralleled in other prehistoric symbolism. In the Neolithic Vinča culture of Yugoslavia for instance, schematism in art was demonstrably deliberate: the artist produced something aimed not at aesthetic effects but purely at the symbolic and conceptual. This prehistoric schematism or formalised reduction should not be ascribed to technical ineptitude but to skilled craftsmanship conforming to matured traditions, concepts and beliefs. In old Europe in the seventh and sixth millennia BC abstract and naturalistic forms appear side by side at one and the same time.

Celtic craftsmen may have used *schemata* (i.e. limited or limiting forms) where geometry rather than nature was the inspiration. it may be that Celtic art was especially susceptible to *schemata* or 'minimum clues of expression'. If one abandons the Graeco-Roman criterion for artistic success – realism – the definition of an artist is not one who merely copies lifelike forms as slavishly as possible, but one who acknowledges a theme by means of a physical expression which cannot be achieved by realism. Representation in art does not have to be naturalistic in order to be good; artistic value depends on the presence of a formal element not identical to the form found in nature. One would not equate photography with art simply because it copies faithfully, and that is the highest realism possible. Indeed, the Celtic artist displays a sophisticated genius in his ability to look at a model – perhaps a human figure – and reduce the representational essentials to the stark and manageable few, enough for recognition but no more (Fig. 90). Thus, economy of detail captured the essence of a figure or face with the minimum of physical expression. For an image to be successful, it may need to be no more than a mere scratching so long as it retains the 'efficacious nature of the prototype'. The Ivy Chimneys figure (Fig. 91) is very stylised and deceptively simple, but it is evocative and was carved with some care.

In judging the success or failure of Celtic figurative art, one returns again and again to function and to the realisation that such art is predominantly religious. The form of representation must be assessed in terms of the purpose and requirements of a particular society. In a sacral context, the choice of a particular style of representation may have significance. Allusion has already been made to the non-recognition of a human ideal in deity-depiction and, where gods are portrayed in human form, the stick-like, shorthand, 'careless' method of depiction – seen for instance on the Farley Heath sceptre-binding (Fig. 22) – may be deliberate, due partly to the wider field of general Celtic art-tradition, but also to conscious obscurity, enigmatism and ambiguity. Religious representations may not necessarily be intended as works of art and should not be so judged. Form and exactness may not have been relevant. There may have been no belief that a schematised figure was an accurate reflection of the object represented. Abstraction and schematism can arguably play as important a role in art as naturalism. The geometric pattern of the *Genii cucullati* from Cirencester (Fig. 90) must surely be inspired by something other than a feeble attempt at three cloaked and hooded figures. Here the positive and negative elements of the carving may both be important: the figures themselves and the spaces between them seem carefully and sensitively balanced, as if both abstract pattern and the human image are inextricably blended in terms of intended symbolism, and the essential detail of threeness and hoodedness are very apparent. Veiled, obscure interpretation and ambiguity will be further examined below. I turn now to emphasis – the other, related, theme of this chapter.

## Emphasis: Triplism

Multiplication of the cult-image is perhaps the commonest form of visual emphasis and in Britain, as in Gaul, the most usual form taken is that of triplication. The representation of deities in threes is not specific to any one god-form, but occurs some of the time in depicting particular divinities. Certain forms – such as the *Tres Matres* are defined by their triple form; but single mother-goddesses occur also. *Genii cucullati* are traditionally represented in triplicate in Britain, although in German contexts they appear not as three dwarves but as single giants. Other British examples of triplication include the triple Mars from Lower Slaughter (Fig. 57) and the triple *genius* from Symonds Hall Farm (Glos). In Gaul a triple-faced form was common among the Remi of the north-east where eleven such images are recorded and where even coinage depicts this form. The occasional British three-headed image is exemplified by a carving from Wroxeter, the three-faced head from Bradenstoke, Hants

92   Schist plaque of Triple Mothers; Bath. Photograph: Betty Naggar.
     Roman Baths Museum.

and the triple head from Corleck, Cavan. Rather different
manifestations of the same basic phenomenon include
triplication of horns on bull-figurines, common in eastern
Gaul (Chapter Six); the triple phallus on a Gaulish Mercury
and the three horns on a boar-figurine are further examples
of the ubiquity of triplication in various forms. In the vast
majority of instances where triplism is present, it is evident
that the number '3' is important and so is likely to have
possessed powerful symbolism for the Celtic people. The
archaeological evidence is supported by early Welsh and
Irish literary tradition where triads are prominent. But it is   209

93  Triple vase; Chester. Copyright: Grosvenor Museum, Chester.

demonstrable that triplism is not the whole story; multiplication is significant in itself. This is displayed both by the occurrence of double or Janus-heads, like those from London and Iron Age Holzerlingen, and by the occasional instance of quadruplism. This last evidence is tenuous: it is arguable that the Wroxeter carving may represent either three or four heads, and the quadruple mother-goddess carving from London may, in fact, represent the *Tres Matres* and the Empress Julia Domna (either the living woman herself or the deified version of the deceased empress).

In examining the practice of plurality in iconography, we may identify two related elements – the use of the number '3' and the presence of more than one image. The two ideas are not mutually exclusive but do exhibit certain differences of outlook or stimulus. We have to consider whether '3' possessed power over and above the conceptualisation of a deity with three facets to his/her cult. The *Tres Matres*, for instance, could be interpreted as symbolic of life, death and rebirth, associated with the seasonal cycle of the earth's fertility. Alternatively, the triple aspect may be linked with childhood, adulthood and old age; or the fecundity of people, beasts and crops – we can only speculate as to the possible different symbolism of each of the three images. There may be more to it than that: whilst some representations of the *Matres* are slightly different one from the other, as at Ashcroft, Cirencester, and in the Rhineland, or may bear such different attributes as children, bread, fruit or dogs, other triple depictions, such

94   Three-faced stone head in non-local granite; first century BC –
     first century AD; (?) Sutherland, N Scotland. Copyright: National
     Museums of Scotland.

as the Lower Slaughter triple Mars (Fig. 57), are identical
with each other. Most important, however, is that, of all
multiplication, by far the commonest factor is '3'.

*Emphasis: Exaggeration by Enlargement*

Exaggeration in symbolism is found as far back as the Upper
Palaeolithic, where we may cite the Gravettian 'Venus'
figures; here facial details are disregarded and the
concentration is entirely on the imagery of fecundity and
prosperity. Exaggeration is frequent too in the Bronze Age
rock-art of Scandinavia, southern France and North Italy,
where the image is schematised but where important
attributes such as horns on cattle, weapons and the hands of
men are over-emphasised.

   In the Romano-Celtic world this most frequently manifests itself in the over-emphasis of the human head, as in the
squatting wheel-god from Churcham, Glos, the Epona from
Albaina in Iberia or the cross-legged bronze figure from
Bouray in northern Gaul. In beasts, the stress may instead be
on the horns of bulls and goats, the antlers of stags or, in the
case of boar-figurines, the dorsal bristles may be depicted
larger than normal. Exaggerated horns occur on a number of
Iron Age and Roman bronze bull-head bucket-escutcheons
and on a recently-discovered bronze goat from south-west
Scotland. The bronze stag-figurine from the temple-pit at
Colchester which produced plaques dedicated to Silvanus
Callirius has very prominent antlers (Fig. 79). The boar-
statuettes from Hounslow (Fig. 15), the Lexden Tumulus
and the temple-site at Muntham Court (Fig. 73) all have
exaggerated dorsal spines.                                    211

If we look first at the animal-emphasis, it is apparent that certain aspects have been stressed because of the potent symbolism already latent in that part of the body. The bristle-exaggeration of the boar and the antlers and horns on deer, goats and cattle appear to represent fertility and strength, and as such were obvious features to exaggerate. In the case of the human head, we know that it had special significance for the Celts (*infra*) and, apart from other considerations, the head is the main means of identifying a man or god and so more care may have been taken over the depiction and emphasis of this crucial part of the body in iconography (Fig. 95).

Over-emphasis in Celtic portrayal is interesting in a number of ways. First, negatively, the fertility-bias of Celtic religion does not generally manifest itself in the exaggeration of the sexual/generative parts of the human body. The meaning of the over-emphasis of a human or animal-attribute and the message it was intended to convey to god or devotees have several aspects of which the first is seemingly an acknowledgement or recognition-element. The patron commissioning the sculpture or bronze figure or the craftsman carrying out the manufacture is admitting the power residing in head or horns. To proceed further, the

95   Sheet bronze relief of ithyphallic deity; Woodeaton, Oxon. Photograph: Betty Naggar. Ashmolean Museum, Oxford.

96   Incised figure of deity; Cirencester. Photograph: Betty Naggar.
     Corinium Museum.

role of exaggeration may be multiple – it may offer special
reverence to or propitiation of a particular divinity by
means of 'flattery' or stress of its power by making the
essential part of its body stand out. It may instead (or in
addition) remind the worshipper or spectator that the
potency of the god is linked to a specific body-part and
emanates thence. To my mind an important function of
exaggeration is the transmutation from the mundane to the
sublime. A convincing parallel may be seen in
miniaturisation (p 220–223) where model tools and weapons were deliberately produced for sacral purposes. The
same, inversely, may be true of exaggeration. To create an
image of a beast with extra-large horns was to remove it
from the real world to that of the supranatural. A
phenomenon related to exaggeration is the addition of extra,
often alien, attributes and the consequent representation of
a composite being. It is demonstrable that once again the
onlooker is being taken from the realism of earth and life to
the 'unreal' world of the divine, where nature may be contra-
dicted. The ram-horned snake exemplifies such hybridity;
the symbolism of both ram and snake are combined to form
an image of particular and duplicated potency, rather in the
manner of attaching horns to a human being. The association
of ram-horned and snake-body on one animal renders the
image otherwordly and augments the fertility-symbolism by
doubling it as surely as if either snake or ram were repeated –
as happens on the *Matres* sculptures.

213

97    Lead relief of horned god; Chesters, Northumberland. Photo-
      graph: Miranda Green. Chesters Museum.

The other major composite manifestation, that of horns
added to anthropomorphic depictions, is imagery of a very
similar nature. We have seen (Chapter Six) that in Celtic
cult-iconography beasts were common and acceptable
images of the divine (resembling, indeed, their role in
Egyptian religion); this was not the case in the classical
world. In the Romano-Celtic phase a compromise seems to
have been reached in that we have depictions of deities in
human form but with horns added. The purpose of this
association was presumably to combine the symbolic
potency of both types of portrayal. Both man and beast
elements were important and both were represented. The
sanctity of the iconography appears to have been increased
by the presence of composite and unreal imagery, and the
association of anthropomorphism and theriomorphism
meant that the maximum possible power was vested in the
image. The devotee was perhaps visualising his god as an
ambiguous mixture of man and beast. In the case of

214

98  Stone relief of Mercury, from well; Emberton, Bucks. Copyright: Buckinghamshire County Museum.

Cernunnos, who is often represented with a stag as well as being antlered himself, one sees the adoption of the animal-attribute perhaps to symbolise the very close and indeed essential rapport between beast and deity.

It is apparent that there are elements common to all the aspects of over-emphasis outlined above. Most important seems to have been the conversion of a 'normal' human or animal image to something which, on account of its departure from the realistic, is overtly supernatural or supranatural. For the Celtic suppliant, it was sometimes insufficient to create the image of a god in straightforward human form; it had perhaps to be triplicated, a creature with horns, with a huge head, or a bull with an extra horn. In the case of the three-horned boar, the addition of all three horns is an alien presence, combining the symbolism of the natural ferocity of the boar with the triple horns of a bull whose horned power has itself thus been increased. In all instances of multiplication, addition and exaggeration here examined, the significant act seems to be that of       215 augmentation by visual means. Although by no means always relevant, the lack of an epigraphic tradition in the Celtic world may be a factor. If the devotee was unaccustomed to invoke his god in writing and to inscribe his commitment and devotion, he might have done it visually or iconographically. In this way the worshipper could inform the god that he was aware of his power and, at the same time, he could remind himself and other visitors to shrines of this fact. If it were believed that the god actually resided in the image, then tripling, for instance, of that image would maybe multiply its potency by that factor.

## Shrinkage: *Pars pro toto* and Miniaturisation

### *Heads*

The over-emphasis of the head on divine images has been alluded to above. The frequent occurrence of head-representation alone or of 'severed' heads is, I believe, part of the same concept in its most extreme form. A number of scholars, argue for the presence of a Celtic head-cult, taking as their evidence not only the existence of Celtic head-depictions in stone or metal but also the emphasis given to head-ritual attested both archaeologically by actual skull-collection and by the testimony of Graeco-Roman and Irish literary sources (Chapter One). There is no doubt that the head was considered the most important part of the human body – the emphasis on head-hunting demonstrates this – and the stress on the head in Celtic art is incontestable. Yet I believe it is a mistake to think in terms of a specific head-cult. The significance of the head to the Celts rather means that, as the crucial part, it could on occasions represent the whole. Thus a number of deities could sometimes be depicted by the head alone.

The human head played an important role in continental pre-Roman Celtic art. The Pfalzfeld carved stone pillar of fifth or fourth century BC date (Fig. 4) bears human heads on each of the four sides near the base; a stone head from Mšecké Žehrovice (Czech) found just outside a *viereckshanze* was perhaps set up in a shrine as a cult-image by a third or second century devotee. The carved piles of heads and the column decorated with incised heads at Entremont (Fig. 10) may represent something different. The pre-Roman Provençal shrines are unique in presenting abundant and recurring evidence for head-ritual in the form of real skulls (echoing very exactly Graeco-Roman literary sources) and here the

99 Stone head from shrine; Caerwent, Gwent. Copyright: National Museum of Wales, Newport Museum.

100 Bronze plaque (one of two), showing opposed human faces; late first century BC/first century AD; Tal-y-Llyn, Powys. Copyright: National Museum of Wales.

217

sculptures may themselves represent trophies of conquered enemies rather than gods. Likewise, the carved heads beneath the claws of the 'Tarasque of Noves' from the same region may represent the triumph of death over human life.

Iron Age continental metalwork abounds in stylised or naturalistic head-symbolism. The Waldalgesheim wine-flagon bears a realistic human face but, by contrast, the head on the Weiskirchen brooch is an integral part of a decorative design. The same duality is present in Britain, though here human representation is much rarer in the Iron Age. Two of the Tal-y-Llyn plaques (Fig. 100), found in a first century BC/AD hoard in Powys, bear two human faces joined by a long neck common to them both, as part of an essentially abstract pattern. But on the Aylesford (Kent) and Marlborough (Wilts) buckets of first century BC date, the heads stand out as heads *per se*, even though stylisation is present.

Most of the numerous depicted heads occurring in Gaul and Britain are of the Romano-Celtic period. The stone examples very frequently have schematised features and it is likely that they portray a number of different gods. The majority of British finds come from the Brigantian hegemony of North Britain where a plethora of local indigenous deities is recorded. Such heads are exemplified by a recent find from Lemington (Tyne & Wear) near Hadrian's Wall: the head here is a roughly-shaped, irregular rectangle with a mask-like face and coarse features – a thick, moustached mouth, wide flat nose, incised oval eyes and a fringe of hair. Perhaps the most interesting head from outside North Britain is that from Caerwent, Gwent (Fig. 99): carved in local stone, it has round open eyes and mask-like features. Its context is particularly illuminating in that it was found on a platform in a chamber which was evidently a shrine, situated in a remote part of the grounds belonging to a late Roman house. Boon has suggested that since the setting is late in the Roman period, the owner of the house may have been Christian while the old Celtic beliefs, perhaps followed by his staff, were banished to a position as far as possible from the house. The presence of a shrine specifically for the head-image argues strongly for its having represented a deity; such an occurrence may be paralleled in Gaul, for instance at the Forêt d'Halatte shrine (Oise) where stone and wooden heads formed a major part of the evidence for cult-activity. Romano-Celtic pots in the form of human heads or faces may also be part of the same tradition. Their sometimes overt function as cremation-receptacles connects them with funerary ritual, but they may on occasions represent deities. In a related context, the presence of

101   Face-pot; Caerwent, Gwent. Copyright: National Museum of Wales.

tongs on a pot from Colchester may denote a smith-god; a Lincoln face-urn was dedicated unequivocally to Mercury.

The practice of representing a god by the head alone appears to be the result of a complex set of thought-processes. We have seen (Chapter One) that Celtic deities were less bound by functional definition than Graeco-Roman gods; thus overt identification on images was less important. Anonymous anthropomorphic depictions where the whole body is portrayed but without distinctive attributes are recorded at, for example, Redruth and Cirencester. Likewise, deities depicted merely as heads needed no positive physical means of definition: both god and devotee knew who was being invoked. But the head-image had additional properties: set against the proven background of head-ritual, the depiction of the head on its own seems to embody several concepts. It could represent

219

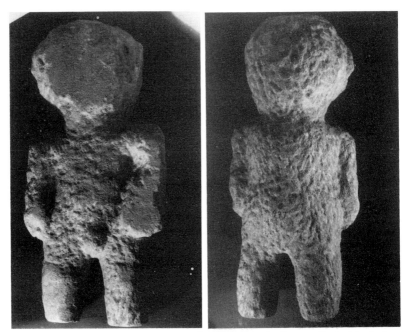

102    Stone figure; Cirencester; the rear view indicates that a kind of pelt may be worn; Cirencester. Photograph: Betty Naggar. Corinium Museum.

the god *pars pro toto*: thus the power of the image would have been positively enhanced because the symbolism was concentrated on the part of the body considered most important. Portrayal of the divinity by a head alone may thus have been a deliberate method of honouring a god. Allied to this is the concept of raising the image above the mundane simply because the whole body was not copied from life. The god represented by a head alone could have been as effective a way of de-secularising the image as schematised abstraction, enlargement or multiplication.

*Miniaturisation*

The practice of offering miniature replicas of tools, weapons and other 'secular' objects to the gods did not originate in the Celtic world nor was it confined to it. The tradition was widespread in antiquity: Near Eastern vehicle-models were made for religious purposes at least as early as 2000 BC and, at the same time, Cretans fashioned as offerings gold and bronze double-axe models. Model agricultural implements were buried in Egyptian tombs (so that the *shabti* of the deceased could do his work in the afterlife); in Britain, miniature halberd-pendants were being made in the Wessex Early Bronze Age.

Miniature objects appear to have had a particular sanctity in the Celtic world. The presence of pre-Roman models assures their indigenous origin: Late Bronze Age axe- and wheel-models occurring in continental contexts give way in the Iron Age to a much wider variety of models, which are distributed as far apart as Britain and Austria. Axe-models from Long Wittenham, Oxon and Arras, Yorks are just two examples from British Iron Age sites. On the other side of the Celtic world, at the *oppidum* of the Dürrnberg in Austria, several graves contained model objects placed with the dead as apotropaic symbols for the otherworld. The sword and shield and group of three shield-models from Frilford, Oxon and Worth, Kent are significant in coming specifically from pre-Roman religious sites. It is not until the Romano-Celtic period that we have large-scale evidence for the use of miniature replicas for cult-purposes. In Britain especially, there are numerous axes, spears and other implements which were offered in shrines, as at Woodeaton, Oxon and Harlow, Essex and many others; in Switzerland axe-models were dedicated to specific deities and have inscriptions on the blades, and in some instances, axe-models bear ritual signs – swastikas, crosses and cosmic motifs.

The precise function of models as votive objects and their symbolism is not at all obvious. The custom of dedicating a small replica of a working implement need only have some such pragmatic purpose as convenience or economy.

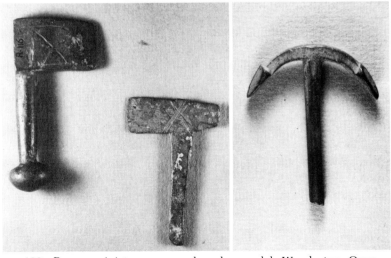

103   Bronze miniature axes and anchor-model; Woodeaton, Oxon.
Photograph: Betty Naggar. Ashmolean Museum.

Certainly, in cases where a model was worn as a talisman, the size-factor is self-evident. But where miniature items were not designed for amuletic use, the question of the role of miniaturisation must be raised. Cost may sometimes be a factor, but there is often more to it than that: model objects are frequently of an expensive metal such as bronze or silver and, more significantly, there is evidence that, in many instances, meticulous care was taken to copy life-size objects in miniature down to the last detail. The recently-discovered axe-model from Tiddington (Warws) is a case in point: here the craftsman took the trouble to cast the shaft and the blade separately in faithful imitation of a real axe of wood and iron, whilst the simplest technical procedure would have been merely to cast the bronze in one piece. The exact replication of detail is here taken even further in that there is skeumorphic decoration on the shaft to imitate the wood-grain. If the substitution of a miniature for a full-size object did have a cost-element, then it was realised that if it were to be acceptable to the gods, it must be a good copy.

The choice of specific types for miniaturisation could be in part due to the appropriateness of a particular tool to symbolise a particular god or devotee – a soldier might dedicate a sword-model to a war-god, a hunter a spear to a hunter-deity, or a wheel to a sun-god – but the general concept of miniaturisation itself may imply a sacred significance and the faithful replication of objects suggests this. Seen in this light, the practice of model-making can be interpreted as part of the same tradition as exaggeration, plurality and, indeed, ritual breakage which we have seen was a recurrent practice with full-size objects (and indeed model spears at Woodeaton were themselves bent double as a ritual act (Fig.52)). Miniaturisation could have been a positive expression of cult and an essential part of ritual. The diminutive size of model objects might actually have enhanced their cult-significance and their potency as symbols. The act of making something too small for normal use could have been a deliberate act of consecration or dedication, in which an item was sanctified through a conscious denial of utility. As with the other types of image-distortion we have looked at, we may have once again in model objects an example of deliberate removal to the 'unreal' world of the supernatural.

## Ambiguity and Obscurity in Cult Expression

Many Celtic images are based upon deliberate ambiguity

and double interpretation. La Tène art is described as 'telling much and concealing much' (Sandars 1968, 226). In Iron Age metalwork for instance, faces are frequently depicted employing geometric patterns – circles, crescents and other curvilinear forms, with characteristic stress upon pattern. Sometimes it is unclear whether a human face is intended or not and, in any case, there appears to be a deliberate 'see what you want to see' element in interpretation. A face can be a face on one level but a set of abstract motifs on another. The literary evidence of classical writers bears this out: 'in conversation they ... speak in riddles, for the most part hinting of things and leaving a great deal to be understood' (Diodorus Siculus V, 31, 1). This deliberate flexibility in interpretation may be seen not only during the Iron Age but later in the Roman period. We have already observed this in the *Genii cucullati* carving from Cirencester, where the very starkness of the relief may open up its significance to personal interpretation; indeed one could argue that the bare outline only was represented in order to facilitate this flexibility in religious symbolism. A different kind of ambiguity may be seen with some horned beings. For instance, at Uley, Emberton (Fig. 98), and on the Smithfield altar in London, Mercury occurs apparently with horns. The London altar is worn and unclear, but at Uley a bronze plaque shows a bust of the god with well-defined horns, and the Emberton stone similarly depicts the messenger-god. But the presence of horns on Mercury-depictions cannot be unequivocal; the classical deity traditionally wears a winged *petasos* (cap) or has wings sprouting from his hair. In Celto-Roman representation, however, it may be difficult to determine whether horns or wings are intended, and it may be that there is a conscious ambiguity and flexibility here – the worshipper or spectator saw what it was appropriate for him to see – and the god himself, whether horned Celtic deity or Roman winged Mercury, would be content with his image. That such vagueness and substitution may be important is perfectly valid in the context both of the composite symbolism discussed above and in that of the wider issue of schematic and understated expression.

## The Survival of the Celtic Tradition

The nature of Celtic religious art, when uncontaminated by the Graeco-Roman artistic and sacral tradition, being often highly stylised, aniconic and abstract, raises the question as to whether the introduction to Celtic lands during the Roman period of classical artistic and religious influences resulted in the demise or, rather, the metamorphosis of Celtic art and religion. Critics of Celtic representation after the Roman occupation accuse indigenous art of having been smothered by the presence of Rome '. . . with the gradual advance of Rome a heavy, monumental, rather spiritless classicism engulfs the Continent . . . Rome was moving in and the native arts prepared to go underground' (Sandars 1968, 273, 233). There are a number of points at issue here: it is recognised that Romano-Celtic stone-carvers were working in an unfamiliar medium, but it has yet to be argued cogently that the results of such superimposition were incompetent. It must also be realised, from a study of Romano-British stone representations – especially in North Britain and the West Country – that a non-Roman sculptural tradition was active and flourishing. Allied to this is the need to acknowledge the continued, albeit altered, existence of Celtic religious cults and concepts. Celtic religion did not die with the Romans. Britain was in the Roman Empire but only just. The Gods were, after all Celtic Gods. Sulis for example, may have been conflated with Roman Minerva, 'but her Celtic pedigree remains blazoned for all to see' (Cunliffe 1979, 158). I would argue, as have others, that the Iron Age abstract Celtic art-tradition continued to some degree after the Roman conquest of Britain. After AD 43 the introduction to Britain of new crafts, such as monumental stone-carving, produced a change of direction in that tradition. In discussing the northern British carvings of a Celtic warrior-deity, Ross comments on the style, admitting iconographic simplicity (in modern or Graeco-Roman terms at least), but acknowledging that individuality and vigour 'which is immediately impressive reflecting the attempt of local British craftsmen to give visual expression in an unfamiliar medium, to their concept of the local war-god' (Ross 1967a, 157). There seems to be substantial evidence that whilst Celtic art may have changed direction quite dramatically and radically, it was by no means entirely swamped by the presence of Rome but rather, perhaps, received new stimuli. 'In Britain, when the artists were of Celtic origin, and had a Celtic stylistic tradition behind them, the use of copy-books did not kill, or even stultify, their native genius' (Toynbee 1962, 16). Her view, which seems to me to be justified, is that Celtic artists, who possessed a long and distinctive heritage of their own as a backdrop, 'responded to the challenge of the classical tradition'.

The evidence we have looked at above bears out the

argument for the survival of a live Celtic religion and art-tradition into the Roman period. Schematic iconography, suggestive of skilful reduction to essentials, the presence of deliberate understatement, ambiguity and interpretative flexibility, and the practice of visual emphasis, all point to a continued flourishing of Celtic religion and its physical expression in art. There existed craftsmen who knew the significance of this iconography and patrons and gods who appreciated these specific qualities. Consideration needs to be given to ability versus choice on the part of Celtic artists. The Welshpool ox-head escutcheon 'a piece that is as splendidly and bluntly stylised as any representation of a beast could be' (Toynbee 1962, 17), proclaims survival of late La Tène tradition deep into the period of the Roman occupation in Britain. This surely points to the extreme diversity both of artistic capability and British patronal taste. Even where iconographic themes are essentially classical in origin – as in the east Gaulish Jupiter-columns – variations in style, technique and content produce hybrid forms whose originality owes much to the interpretation of indigenous talent; the conflation of ethnic tradition, arising from the interaction of two very different cultures, produced a new and often lively tradition entirely its own, born of the varied response made by British and Gaulish craftsmen to classical forms and themes. The mutual superimposition of Celtic abstract, symbolic and pattern-stressing concepts upon the naturalistic, representational and copy-stressing art of the Graeco-Roman world produced a tradition of physical religious expression that cannot, given its own context and assessed on its own terms, be dismissed as inferior art: 'judged on their own merits and in the light of the aesthetic ideas that shaped them, these ... carvings can claim to be regarded as the most impressive and original manifestations of art ...' (Toynbee 1964, 9).

Hand in hand with Celtic art, this book has sought to demonstrate that Celtic religion was a lively and individual phenomenon during the Romano-Celtic period. More than that, I hope I have shown that this fully-fledged religious expression had deep and complex roots in European prehistory. Whilst it is only in the Roman period that we can name and classify deities, there existed before that time a physically-expressed and complicated series of religious rituals which argue for the Celts' possession of a deep sense of the natural world and a deliberate desire to come to terms with the vagaries and capricious elements of the supernatural.

225

# REFERENCES

The references are to page and line : 1.9 refers to page 1, line 9. Chapter headings and sub headings do not count as lines. The reference is usually to the sentence which ends on the cited line.

Prologue

| | |
|---|---|
| 1.9 | Cunliffe 1979, 8 |
| 1.11 | Herodotus, *Histories*, II, 35 |
| 1.13 | Herodotus, *Histories*, IV, 48 |
| 1.13 | Herodotus, Histories, IV, 48 |
| 2.2 | Duval 1977, Fig 449 |
| 2.16 | Wiseman and Wiseman 1980, 12 |
| 2.19 | Piggott 1968, 35, Fig 1 |
| 2.23 | Champion *et al* 1984, 270–271 |
| 2.30 | Harding 1974, 86; Megaw 1970a, 13; Cunliffe 1979, 15 |
| 2.34 | Coles and Harding 1979, 366 |
| 3.2 | Burgess 1974, 196–7 |
| 3.10 | Megaw 1970a, 13 |
| 3.22 | Piggott 1965, 169ff |
| 3.27 | Champion *et al* 1984, 270–273 |
| 3.38 | Burgess 1980, 277 |
| 4.5 | Champion *et al* 1984, 270–273 |
| 4.14 | Vouga 1923 |
| 4.35 | Cunliffe 1983, 155–171 |
| 4.43 | Jackson 1964; Cunliffe 1983, 155–171 |
| 5.4 | Phillips 1980, 257 |
| 5.14 | Burgess 1974, 196–197 |
| 5.23 | Piggott 1976, 284 |
| 5.37 | Megaw 1970a, 22 |
| 5.38 | Powell 1966, 185 |

Chapter One: The Celts and Religion

| | |
|---|---|
| 7.23 | Piggott 1968, 22 |
| 8.11 | Megaw and Simpson 1979, 299 |
| 8.15 | Cunliffe 1974, 295 |
| 8.33 | Powell 1966, 160 |
| 8.42 | Megaw 1970a, 23 |
| 9.1 | Powell 1966, 190, ill.184; 218, ill.213 |
| 9.2 | Megaw 1970a, 38 |
| 10.3 | Powell 1966, 220–222 |
| 10.6 | Megaw 1970a, nos 187, 188, 252 |
| 10.9 | Powell 1966, 225, 236, 247 |
| 10.17 | Megaw 1970a, no. 237, no. 232 |
| 10.26 | Allen 1980 |
| 10.31 | Allen 1976a, 265, 266 |
| 10.36 | Allen 1976a, 270ff |
| 11.1 | Phillips 1980, 257 |
| 11.5 | Filip 1960, 155ff |
| 12.4 | Benoit 1955 |

| | |
|---|---|
| 12.31 | Megaw 1970a, nos 78, 118 |
| 12.36 | Cunliffe 1979, 26 |
| 12.43 | Cunliffe 1974, 287–299 |
| 13.5 | *Pharsalia* III, 399–417 |
| 14.21 | Piggott 1968, 99–101 |
| 14.25 | Caesar, VI, 17. Lucan, *Pharsalia* I, 444–446 |
| 15.14 | Bémont 1983–84, 130–132 |
| 15.30 | Champion 1985, 11 |
| 16.8 | Jackson 1964 |
| 16.12 | Champion 1985, 11 |
| 16.20 | Piggott 1968, 26–27 |
| 16.23 | MacCana 1983, 15 |
| 16.39 | Jackson 1964, 1–2 |
| 18.5 | Drury 1980, 45–78, fig 3.6 |
| 18.46 | Cunliffe 1974, 287–299; Harding 1974, 96 ff |
| 19.3 | Harding 1974 |
| 19.10 | Frere 1984, 298 |
| 19.18 | Downey et al 1980, 289–304 |
| 19.22 | Cunliffe 1983; South Cadbury – Alcock 1972 |
| 19.30 | Cunliffe 1974, 287–299 |
| 19.33 | Harding 1974, 96–112 |
| 19.36 | Piggott 1968, 56 ff |
| 19.41 | Muckelroy 1976, 188 |
| 19.47 | Henig 1984, 21–2 |
| 20.4 | Rodwell 1980 |
| 20.10 | Green 1976 |
| 20.23 | Harding 1974, 96–112 |
| 20.30 | Piggott 1968, 71 |
| 20.36 | Ross 1968 |
| 20.37 | Collis 1975, 101 |
| 20.42 | Cunliffe 1979, 92 ff |
| 21.6 | Allen 1976b, 200–201; Harlow – Henig 1984, 23 |
| 21.11 | Adkins and Adkins 1985, 69–75 |
| 21.20 | Strabo XII, 5, 1 |
| 21.26 | Tacitus, *Annals* XIV, 30 |
| 21.26 | Dio Cassius LXII, 2 |
| 21.28 | Lucan, III, 399–452 |
| 21.33 | Zwicker 1934–36, 50 |
| 21.24 | Strabo IV, 1–3 |
| 21.44 | Strabo, VI, 17 |
| 21.47 | Caesar, VI, 17 |
| 22.23 | de Vries 1963 |
| 22.28 | *CIL* XIII, 33, 223–225 |
| 22.29 | Pliny, *Natural History* XVI, 95 |
| 22.31 | Turner 1982 |
| 22.45 | de Vries 1963, 122 |

23.7    Green 1976, 46
23.15   Green 1976, 210
23.16   Green 1975b
24.4    Wickenden 1985
24.8    Pobé and Roubier 1961, 52
24.16   Henig and Taylor 1984
25.7    Green 1983a, 45
25.15   Olmsted 1979
25.24   Collis 1984, 12
26.11   Piggott 1968; Le Roux and Guyonvarc'h 1978
26.12   Strabo, IV, 4, 4; Diodorus Siculus V, 31, 2–5
26.13   Caesar, VI, 13, 14
26.15   Tierney 1959–60, 189–275
26.23   Tierney 1959–60; Harding 1974, 96ff
26.26   Nash 1976, 124
26.36   Drinkwater 1983, 38–9
26.37   Tacitus Histories IV, 54
26.40   Scriptores Historiae Augustae 2, XXII, 1
26.43   Commemoratio Professorum Burgigalensium IV, 7f
26.46   Jackson 1964
27.4    Caesar VI, 13
27.9    Caesar VI, 13
27.16   Pliny, Natural History XVI, 249
27.23   Piggott 1968, 123
27.25   Cunliffe 1979; 1983
27.29   Jackson 1964
27.39   Diodorus V, 31, 2–5; Strabo VII, 2, 3
27.45   Tacitus, Annals XIV, 30
28.4    Lucan, Pharsalia I, 450–458
28.7    Lucan, Pharsalia I, 444–446
28.10   Zwicker 1934–36, 50
28.16   Lucan, Pharsalia III, 399–417
28.23   Caesar VI, 16
28.37   Strabo VII, 2, 3
29.3    Cunliffe 1983, 155–171
29.10   Waite 1985
29.18   Alcock 1972, 103
29.26   Cunliffe 1983, 155–171
29.30   Ross 1967a, 65ff
29.33   Filip 1960, 157
30.1    Lambrechts 1954; Benoit 1955
30.5    Duval 1977, 111 pl 100
30.6    Collis 1984, 110
30.13   Miles 1970, 9
30.20   Livy XXIII, 24
30.22   Diodorus V, 29, 4; Strabo IV, 4, 5
30.24   Livy X, 26
31.3    Diodorus XIV, 115; Strabo IV, 4, 5
31.7    Ross and Feacham 1984, 338–352
31.9    Jackson 1964
31.20   Jones and Jones 1949
32.10   Caesar VI, 16

32.16   Anati 1965, 151ff
32.31   Duval 1957, 6
32.34   Megaw 1970a, 20
32.36   Sjoestedt 1940
33.13   Powell 1958, 115–162
33.16   Lambrechts 1942
33.26   Jackson 1964
33.29   Cunliffe 1979, 74
34.2    Gimbutas 1965, 341–2, pl 64
34.10   Lucan, Pharsalia III, 412
34.13   Megaw and Simpson 1979, 477
35.12   Diodorus Siculus, Frag. XXII, 9, 4
35.46   Szabó 1971, 62
36.25   Bober 1951
36.26   for example Caesar VI, 17
36.37   Rhodes 1964, 28
37.2    Henig 1984, 22
37.7    Zwicker 1934–36, 50
37.10   Wightman 1970, 208
37.14   Brogan 1973, 192–219
37.22   Boucher 1976, 160–164
38.10   Jackson 1953, 101

Chapter Two: Cults of Sun and Sky

For references to material in this chapter and additional details, see Green 1984a.

Chapter Three: Fertility and the Mother Goddesses

72.35   Gimbutas 1982
73.10   Megaw 1970a nos 79–83; Megaw 1970a, 45
74.10   Pliny, Natural History XVI, 249
74.11   Helm 1976, 143; Cunliffe 1979, 106–108; 74.16 Cunliffe 1979, 110.
74.40   Gimbutas 1982
75.1    Sandars 1957, 38; Thevenot 1968, 165ff
75.5    Powell 1966, 102, ill.98
75.7    Piggott 1954, 42
75.14   Thevenot 1968, 165
75.19   Gimbutas 1965, 342
75.23   Glob 1974, 162, 167, pl. 72
76.7    Megaw 1970a, 14; Cunliffe 1979, pl on 77
76.15   Piggott 1965, 184, fig 102; Pobé and Roubier 1961, 5
76.20   de Vries 1963; Grenier 1970, 248ff; Szabó 1971, 65–66
76.26   Dio LXII, 2
76.30   Ammianus Marcellinus XV, XII; Dillon and Chadwick 1967, 154.
76.34   Hodson and Rowlett 1973, 157–191
76.36   Linduff 1979, 817ff

227

76.41    Bémont 1983–84, 206, no 269
76.45    Megaw and Simpson 1979, 477; Arts Council 1970, no 82, 17; Piggott and Daniel 1951, no 33
77.4    Olmsted 1979, 120
77.7    ibid., 129
77.18    Tacitus, *Germania*, 40; Olmsted 1979, 130–132
77.29    Thevenot 1932, 101ff
77.33    Mont Bego – Briard 1979, 161–66. Val Camonica – Anati 1965
77.38    de Manteyer 1945
77.41    Anati 1965, 168ff
77.45    Breuil et al 1929
77.47    Gelling and Davidson 1969
78.4    Alcock 1972, 80–84
78.38    de Vries 1963; Duval 1957; Haverfield 1892, 314ff
78.47    Haverfield 1892, no 1
79.2    Ibid., no 11
79.3    for example the Homeland – Chichester; Hassal and Tomlin 1979, 339–40; Henig 1984, 49–50. Overseas – Lowther; Haverfield 1892, no 14
79.5    Nîmes – Thevenot 1968, 165ff
79.6    Treverae – de Vries 1963
79.8    Matres Glanicae – Salviat 1979, 30, 36
79.11    Smith and Wright 1847, 239ff
79.15    Babelon 1919
79.17    Colin 1927, 173ff. Matronae Aufaniae – e.g. *CIL* XIII, 8021
79.20    Hassall and Tomlin 1979, 339–340; Rüger 1983, 210–221
79.22    Comedovae – de Vries 1963
79.23    Suleviae – Szabó 1971, 65–66; Wightman 1970, 213ff; *RIB* 105, 106; *RIB* 192; Green 1976, 216
80.3    Wightman 1970
80.7    Hassall and Tomlin 1983, 337, fig 40, 342
80.10    Ross 1967a, 207
80.36    Chichester – Hassall and Tomlin 1979, 339–340; York – Henig 1984, 49–50
80.38    London – *RIB* 2; Green 1976, 225, pl XVIc
80.45    Henig 1984, 49–50
80.46    de Vries 1963
81.2    Anon 1965
81.3    Haverfield 1892, 319
81.12    Alesia – le Gall 1980, 161
81.13    Vertillum – Pobé and Roubier 1961, 70
81.14    Autun – Lewis 1883, 29–50
81.18    Colin 1927, 173ff
81.19    Thevenot 1968, 165ff
82.5    Toynbee 1978, 129–148, fig 1,

no 39
82.7    Ancaster – Green 1976, pl XVf. Cirencester – Toynbee 1964, 171
82.10    Merrifield 1983, 167–170; 180
82.15    Toynbee 1964, 171
83.2    Rüger 1983, 210–221
83.12    Cirencester – Toynbee 1964, 172. Maryport – Ross 1967a, 214
83.22    Haverfield 1892, 315
83.27    Szabó 1971, 65–66
83.28    Backworth – Green 1984b, 25–33
84.5    Toynbee 1978, 129–148
84.9    Bonn – Rüger 1983
84.10    Pesch – Lehner 1918–21, 74ff
84.16    Wightman 1970, 213ff
84.20    Clébert 1970, 254
84.23    Toynbee 1964, 101–103
84.24    Henig 1984, 49–50
84.27    *RIB* 2
84.28    Marsden 1980, 115; Green 1976, pl XVIa, Merrifield 1983, 167–170
84.41    Bonn – Rüger 1983. Baden – Alfs 1940
85.3    Colin 1927, 173ff
85.6    Wellow – Green 1976, 186, pl XVd; Cirencester – Wilson 1973, 324
85.12    de Vries 1963; Duval 1957
85.13    Deonna 1954, 403–428
85.19    Salviat 1979, 30; Thevenot 1968, 165ff
85.34    Ross 1967a; Cunliffe 1979
85.38    Wightman 1970, 213ff
85.40    Aveta – Wightman 1970, 217, pl 21d
85.47    Daglingworth – Green 1976b, pl XVIIe
86.8    Crozant – Thevenot 1968, 165ff
86.9    Cirencester – Green 1976, 173
86.13    Wightman 1970, 213ff
86.19    Thill 1978, 8, no 8
87.21    Van Aartsen 1971, 57
88.6    Lydney – Green 1976, 170; Ross 1967a, 207–208
88.9    Wheeler 1932
88.14    Green 1976, 183; Nash-Williams 1952–54, 18ff
88.18    Ross 1967a, 204–205; Richmond and Gillam 1951, 30
88.19    Dieburg – Toynbee 1964, 102
88.21    Linduff 1979
89.2    Jenkins 1957; 1978, 149–162; Rouvier-Jeanlin 1972
89.7    St Ouen – de Vesly 1909, Trier – Wightman 1970, 217
89.8    Colin 1927, 173ff
89.15    Alesia – Le Gall 1963, 161, 174

89.17   Boon 1983, 33–55
89.19   Ballerstein – Lickenheld 1929,
        67; Colin 1927, 173ff
89.22   Jenkins 1956
89.23   Titelburg – Thill 1978, no 46.
        Trier – Wightman 1970, 213ff
89.29   Linckenheld 1929, 72, 85
90.4    Drury and Wickenden 1982,
        239–243, pl XVIII, 4
90.5    Culverhole Cave – Green 1976,
        181. Owmby – Goodburn 1979,
        295
90.8    Green 1976, 193
90.10   Magnen and Thevenot 1953,
        no 79
90.25   Green 1976, pl XVIIe
91.3    Anon 1952, pl XIII
91.5    Green 1976, 173, pl XVIIIc
91.9    Toynbee 1976, 68ff
92.3    Magnen and Thevenot 1953,
        27
92.10   Ibid., 16–18
92.10   Ibid., 21–23
92.12   Ibid., 227
92.13   Ibid., no 5
92.16   Thevenot 1968, 185ff
92.19   Magnen and Thevenot 1953,
        no 90
93.1    Thevenot 1968, 165ff
93.2    Essay – Espérandieu no 2325
93.4    Magnen and Thevenot 1953,
        no 190
93.5    Hogondange – Ibid., no 117
93.10   Thevenot 1968, 185ff
93.12   Linduff 1979, 817–837
93.13   Linduff, after Markale 1975, 25
94.1    Friedl 1975, 51–55
94.15   Green 1984b, 25–33
94.17   Jenkins 1958, 61; Blanchet
        1890; Lambrechts 1942, 170ff
95.2    Linkenheld 1929, 70
95.6    Vichy – Lambert 1914, 225ff.
        Springhead – Detsicas 1983,
        66–76
95.9    Walbrook Valley – Green 1976,
        225, pl XIV, a-e
95.15   Jenkins 1958, 70
95.18   Bailey 1932, 119; Ferguson
        1970, 26, 71
95.22   Green 1984b, 25–33
95.41   Thevenot 1968, 165ff
95.43   Espérandieu, no 1564
95.46   Duval 1957
97.5    de Vries, 1963
97.11   Lambrechts 1942
97.17   Green 1976, 166
97.27   de Vries 1963
97.38   Green 1976, 171; Toynbee
        1964
97.42   Green 1976, 171; Rhodes 1964
97.47   Wedlake 1982, 137
99.8    Boon 1983

99.9    Espérandieu 1924, 38, no 139
99.11   Schindler 1977, 37
99.13   Armand-Galliat 1937, 43
99.16   e.g. Jenkins 1958
99.21   Blanchet 1890, type 10; Green
        1984b, 25–33
100.3   Johns 1982
100.12  Broadway – Green 1976, 200,
        175
100.33  Marshall 1984, 212–215
100.37  Green 1976, 217
101.6   MacCana 1983, 82–93
101.9   Olmsted 1979
101.23  MacCana 1983, 82–93
101.27  Linduff 1979, 817–837
101.36  Cunliffe 1979, 74
102.9   Toynbee 1976, 68–69
102.13  Bémont 1983–84, 132
102.20  Nyon – Green 1976, 17–19

Chapter Four: War, Death and the
Underworld

103.5–9 Caesar, de Bello Gallico VI, 14;
        Wiseman and Wiseman 1980,
        121
103.14  Wiseman and Wiseman 1980,
        120
104.9   Pobé and Roubier 1961, no 5
104.15  Anati 1965, 61ff; 194
104.19  Ibid., 158ff
104.21  Gelling and Davidson 1969,
        9–38
104.24  Gelling 1969, fig 14j
104.27  Megaw and Simpson 1979,
        299
104.30  Burgess 1974, 209–211
104.35  Fitzpatrick 1984
104.37  Neuchâtel – Powell 1958, 148;
        Vouga 1923; Llyn Cerrig –
        Savory 1976
106.2   Alcock 1972, 163
106.4   Downey et al 1980
106.5   Fitzpatrick 1984, 186
106.8   Caesar, de Bello Gallico VI, 17
106.10  Green 1975a; 1981
106.14  Green 1976, 194
106.19  Breedon – Wacher 1979, 44;
        Garton Slack – unpublished
106.23  Green 1976, 177–178
106.26  Harlow – Green 1976, 196.
        Lamyatt Beacon – Wilson
        1974, 422
106.29  Williams 1985
107.6   Hodder 1982
107.8   Polybius II 22.2
107.14  Diodorus Siculus V, 30
107.16  Olmsted 1979, 19
107.22  Orange Arch – Amy et al 1962;
        Duval 1977, 25; Anon 1980b,
        Abb 14, 123
108.2   Anon 1980a, 8, 16
108.8   Laing 1969, 159–61

229

108.14   Allen 1980, 92
108.17   Allen 1980, 76, no 222, pl 16
108.22   Caesar, *de Bello Gallico*, IV, 33
108.25   Allen 1980, 139–140
108.29   Allen 1980, 142–143
108.33   Dio Cassius LXII, 2
108.36   Anon 1980a, 15–21; Phillips 1980, 257
108.41   Duval 1977, 136–37; 190
108.45   Pobé and Roubier 1961, no 45
108.47   Hodson and Rowlett 1973, 190
109.2    Bémont 1983–84, 175
109.10   Olmsted 1979, pl 3
109.14   Brewster 1976, fig on 113; Frere 1977, 384
109.19   Megaw and Simpson 1979, 333, fig 6.42
110.6    Harding 1978, 17–18
110.12   Piggott 1965, 241
110.20   Ceasar, *de Bello Gallico* VI, 17
110.27   *Pharsalia* I, 444–446
110.31   Zwicker 1934, 50
111.2    Lambrechts 1942
111.4    Toynbee 1978, no 26
111.5    Hassall and Tomlin 1978, 478
111.7    Rodwell 1973, 265–67, pl XXIXa
111.9    de Vries 1963
111.13   de Vries 1963
111.15   Thevenot 1955
111.23   Leucetius – *CIL* XIII, 3087
111.33   Fairless 1984, 224–242
111.43   Fairless 1984
111.44   Thevenot 1955
111.45   Wightman 1970, 219
112.2    Ross 1967a, 176
112.8    Fairless 1984
112.12   Duval 1957
113.9    Fairless 1984; Tomlin 1985
113.10   Toynbee 1978, nos 35–36
113.11   Green 1983a, pl 16
113.14   Green 1976, 177–178
113.15   Charlton and Mitcheson 1983, 143–153
113.33   Maryport – Ross 1967a, 193–197
113.38   Segontium Museum
113.43   Hassall and Tomlin 1978, 473
113.46   Ross 1967a, 197
114.1    Housesteads – ibid.
114.10   Caesar, *de Bello Gallico*, V, 12
114.12   Stow on the Wold – Green 1976, 176, pl IIc
114.13   Lower Slaughter – Ibid., 175
116.1    Southbroom – Ibid., 191
116.7    Martlesham – Green 1976, 218
116.15   Rodwell 1973, 265–67 pl XXIXa
116.18   Olmsted 1979, pl 3
116.21   Zwicker 1934–36, 50
116.22   Kelvedon – Hassall and Tomlin 1978, 478
116.25   Wilson 1974, 452
116.26   Ross 1967a, 188–90
116.40   West Coker – Collingwood 1931, figs 1, 2
117.3    Thevenot 1951
117.16   Thevenot 1968, 46–47
119.3    Rhodes 1964, 27–30
120.2    MacCana 1983, 94
120.3    MacCana 1983, 86ff; Dillon and Chadwick 1967, 143
120.25   Powell 1958, 123
120.30   MacCana 1983, 86ff
121.10   Caesar VI, 19
121.20   Lucan, *Pharsalia* I, 446ff; MacCana 1983, 122
121.21   Caesar VI, 14
121.24   Diodorus Siculus V, 28, 6
121.39   Dillon and Chadwick 1967, 144
122.6    MacCana 1983, 97
122.34   MacCana 1983, 89, 122–128
123.14   Harding 1978, 86; Coles and Harding 1979, 366
123.21   Piggott 1968, 87–88
123.26   Megaw 1970a, 14; Collis 1984, 82
123.39   Megaw 1970a, no 7
123.42   Ebberston – Cunliffe 1974, 287–299
124.11   Megaw 1970a, no 35
124.31   Piggott 1965, 215
124.32   Collis 1984, 118, 138
124.42   Hodson and Rowlett 1973, 184–185
124.44   Stead 1979, 92
124.45   Cunliffe 1974, 287–299
125.8    Stead 1979, 22
125.10   Cunliffe 1974, 287–299
126.2    Anon 1984, 302–306; Dent 1985, 85–92
126.31   Cunliffe 1974, 287–299
126.33   Collis 1984, 130
126.40   Megaw 1970a, no 73
126.43   Ibid., no 41
126.44   Powell 1958, 144–145
126.45   Brewster 1976
127.4    Cunliffe 1974, 187–99
127.5    Wightman 1970, 242
127.8    Caesar VI, 19
127.15   Waite 1985
128.3    Waite 1985
128.9    Hawkes 1976, 4
128.14   Stead and Turner 1985, 25–29; BBC 1985
128.21   below, Chapter Five
128.24   Brewster 1976, 115
129.9    Cunliffe 1979, 23; Megaw 1970a, 21
129.13   Wightman 1970, 242–246
129.34   Collis 1984, 163–65
129.37   Collis 1984, 172
129.42   Piggott 1965, 247; 1968, 88

| | |
|---|---|
| 130.2 | Henig 1984, 190–192 |
| 130.7 | Biddle 1985 |
| 130.15 | Henig 1984, 190–192 |
| 130.19 | Toynbee 1971, 34–39; Walker 1985, 10 |
| 130.44 | MacDonald 1979, 415–424 |
| 131.5 | Simco 1984, 56–59 |
| 131.7 | Goodburn 1975, 336 |
| 131.8 | Kenchester – Goodburn 1978, 438. Stanton Harcourt – Ibid., 444 |
| 131.10 | Wilson 1975, 252 |
| 131.13 | Goodburn 1975, 331 |
| 131.16 | Green 1976, 228 |
| 131.21 | Green 1976, 48–49 |
| 131.27 | Green 1976, 202 |
| 131.40 | Leech 1981, 195–201 |
| 131.42 | MacDonald 1979, 404–407 |
| 131.47 | Anon 1978, 57–60 |
| 132.3 | Williams 1985; Lankhills – MacDonald 1979, 415ff |
| 132.6 | Brampton – Rankov 1982, 369–370 |
| 132.7 | Frilford – Green 1976, 194. Springhead – Ibid., 228 |
| 132.13 | Green 1983a, 18 |
| 132.15 | Green 1976, 49 |
| 132.19 | Toynbee 1971 |
| 132.24 | Wightman 1970, 242–246 |
| 132.27 | Linckenheld 1927 |
| 132.29 | Hatt 1970, 7–97 |
| 133.2 | Altheim 1938, 120f |
| 133.6 | Wilsford – Ashbee 1963, 116–120. Swanwick – Megaw and Simpson 1979, 272 |
| 133.14 | Piggott 1968, 80–82 |
| 133.19 | Cunliffe 1983, 156ff |
| 133.30 | Brogan 1973, 192–219 |
| 133.32 | Helm 1976, 161 |
| 133.38 | Paris – Espérandieu, no 3132. Trier – 4929; Wightman 1970, 210–211 |
| 133.45 | Ross 1968 |
| 134.7 | Cambridge – Anon 1978, 57–60 |
| 134.9 | Ross and Feacham 1976, 230–237 |
| 134.11 | Waite 1985 |
| 134.14 | Green 1976, 179 |
| 135.2 | Alcock 1972, 103 |
| 135.4 | Hatt 1970, 135 |
| 135.14 | Parfitt and Halliwell 1985 |
| 135.45 | Anati 1965, 181–83 |
| 136.2 | Bémont 1983–84, no 162 |
| 136.4 | Stead 1985, 40–42, pls I-III |
| 136.6 | Green 1976, 148, pl XXIXa |
| 136.9 | Toynbee 1964, 112–113; pl XXIXa |
| 136.12 | MacCana 1983, 36–37 |
| 136.15 | Caesar, de Bello Gallico VI, 18 |
| 136.23 | de Vries 1963; Linckenheld 1929, 65–66 |
| 136.24 | Wightman 1985, 179 |
| 136.26 | Linckenheld 1929, 84 |
| 136.30 | Tertullian, Ad Nationes 1.10 |
| 137.34 | Lambrechts 1942 |
| 137.37 | Reinach 1894, 137ff |
| 137.42 | Boucher 1976, 164ff |
| 137.43 | Duval 1957 |

Chapter Five: Water-Gods and Healers

| | |
|---|---|
| 139.13 | Merrifield 1983, 4–9 |
| 139.16 | Megaw and Simpson 1979, 299 |
| 139.18 | Coles and Harding 1979, 367–368 |
| 139.23 | Coles and Harding 1979, 254 |
| 139.27 | Burgess 1974, 196–197; 209–211 |
| 139.38 | Fitzpatrick 1984, 180–182 |
| 140.2 | Ibid., 183; Hodder 1982 |
| 140.7 | Fitzpatrick 1984, 179 |
| 140.10 | Hawkes 1976, 4 |
| 140.12 | Fitzpatrick 1984, 180–182 |
| 140.12 | Manning 1972, 224–250 |
| 140.16 | Merrifield 1983, 4–9, 15 |
| 140.22 | Cunliffe 1975, 89–108 |
| 140.29 | Strabo IV, 3, 2 |
| 140.30 | Drinkwater 1983, 111 |
| 140.31 | Hatt 1970, 243–44 |
| 141.1 | Fairless 1984, 224–242 |
| 141.13 | Megaw 1970a, 20, no 134; Piggott 1968, 83ff |
| 141.16 | Fitzpatrick 1984 |
| 141.29 | Strabo IV, 1, 3 |
| 141.33 | Allen 1976b, 200–208 |
| 141.38 | Strabo, IV, 1, 3 |
| 142.1 | Gregory of Tours, In Gloria Confessorum 2 |
| 142.2 | Lynch 1970, 249–277 |
| 142.17 | Megaw 1970a, no 179 |
| 142.20 | Powell 1958, 148 |
| 142.28 | Savory 1976, 46; 1980, 58 |
| 142.31 | Information, Sabine Gerloff |
| 143.1 | Lynch 1970, 249–277 |
| 143.4 | Megaw 1970a, no 254; Savory 1976, 49, 57 |
| 143.6 | Downey et al 1980 |
| 143.9 | Fitzpatrick 1984, 183–186 |
| 143.11 | Savory 1976, 49 |
| 143.12 | Cunliffe 1979, 89 |
| 143.17 | Caesar, de Bello Gallico, VI, 17, 3–5; Diodorus V, 27, 3–4 |
| 143.24 | Lynch 1970, 249–77 |
| 143.31 | Tacitus, Annals XIV, 29–30; Agricola XIV, XVIII |
| 143.38 | Manning 1972, 224–250 |
| 143.44 | Ibid. |
| 144.4 | Cunliffe 1974, 287–299 |
| 144.18 | Olmsted 1979, 15–16 |
| 144.20 | Anon 1980b, 54 |
| 144.25 | Glob 1969b, pl 63; Megaw 1970a, no 203 |
| 144.40 | Stead and Turner 1985, 25–29 |

231

| | |
|---|---|
| 145.3 | Glob 1969b |
| 145.31 | Ashbee 1963 |
| 145.33 | Manning 1972, 224–250 |
| 145.36 | Piggott 1968, 85, fig 31 |
| 145.38 | Goodburn 1978, 311 |
| 147.1 | Bouzek 1977, 197–202; Coles and Harding 1979, 367–368 |
| 147.4 | Anon 1980a, 3.30 |
| 147.8 | Powell 1958, 122 |
| 147.15 | Strabo IV, 1, 13 |
| 147.17 | Piggott 1968, 84 |
| 147.22 | Zwicker 1934–36, 50 |
| 147.30 | Gimbutas 1965, 341–342 |
| 147.34 | Gelling and Davidson 1969, 117–135 |
| 147.36 | Harding 1978, 86 |
| 147.45 | Espérandieu no 7676 |
| 147.47 | Pobé and Roubier 1961, 28 |
| 148.2 | Green 1983a, 10, fig 6 |
| 148.6 | Glob 1969a, 286–318; Gelling and Davidson 1969, 9–26 |
| 148.16 | Gelling and Davidson 1969, 9–26 |
| 148.17 | Durrnberg – Anon 1980b, 230 |
| 148.21 | Harding 1978, 15 |
| 148.24 | Nydam – Cunliffe 1975, 89–92 |
| 148.29 | H S Green 1985, 116–117; Savory 1976, 16 |
| 148.32 | Megaw 1970a, no 284 |
| 148.34 | MacCana 1983, 93 |
| 149.11 | H J M Green pers. comm May 1984 |
| 149.14 | King and Soffe 1983, 264–265, fig 8a |
| 149.16 | Turner 1982 |
| 149.19 | Dillon and Chadwick 1967, 143–145 |
| 149.22 | Ross 1967a, 231 |
| 150.1 | Ross 1967a, 213 |
| 150.19 | Thevenot 1968, 200ff |
| 150.24 | CIL XIII, 2858–2865 |
| 151.4 | Brogan 1973, 192–219 |
| 151.19 | Sandars 1984, 148 |
| 152.9 | Vatin 1969, 320 |
| 152.16 | Brogan 1973 |
| 152.19 | Thevenot 1955 |
| 152.24 | Thevenot 1968, 200ff |
| 152.27 | Brogan 1953, 93–94; 1973, 192–219 |
| 152.29 | Pobé and Roubier 1961, 30 |
| 152.30 | Thevenot 1957, 311–314. |
| 152.31 | Thevenot 1968, 200ff |
| 152.39 | Thevenot 1951, 131 |
| 152.44 | Thevenot 1968, 97ff |
| 152.47 | Wightman 1970, 220–222 |
| 153.11 | Wuilleumier 1984, no 403 |
| 153.12 | Magnen and Thevenot 1953, no 227 |
| 153.30 | Pauli 1984, 151–157 |
| 153.45 | Lucan, Pharsalia III, 411–412 |
| 154.3 | Cunliffe 1979, 77ff |
| 154.13 | Detsicas 1983, 66–76 |
| 154.17 | Green 1976, 228 |
| 155.10 | Blagg 1979, 103–107 |
| 155.22 | Green 1983a, pl 27 |
| 155.26 | Green 1983a, 43–44 |
| 155.35 | Ross 1968, 263 |
| 155.38 | Green 1976, 183 |
| 155.42 | Ross 1968, 262–263 |
| 155.43 | Green 1983a, 60 |
| 155.46 | Ross 1968, 255–286 |
| 157.1 | Eddy pers comm 27.8.81 |
| 157.3 | Parfitt and Halliwell 1985 |
| 157.7 | Rhodes 1964; Green 1976, 175–176 |
| 157.10 | Green 1976, 178 |
| 157.12 | Anon 1956, 17–36; Green 1976, 179 |
| 157.20 | Manning 1972, 224–250; Ross 1968, 266–267 |
| 158.10 | Thevenot 1968, 65–69 |
| 158.12 | Ibid. |
| 158.20 | Wightman 1970, 211–217 |
| 158.22 | Green 1983a, 44, pl 7; Ross 1967a, 191 |
| 158.25 | Alcock 1966, 53 |
| 159.5 | Wightman 1970, 220 |
| 159.10 | Webster 1983, 5–20 |
| 159.15 | Wheeler 1932 |
| 160.2 | Green 1983a, 57–60 |
| 160.4 | RIB 305–308 |
| 160.14 | RIB 1694 |
| 160.22 | Wedlake 1982 |
| 161.2 | Merrifield 1983, 188, fig 46 |
| 161.12 | Green 1983a, 57–60; 1976, 169–170 |
| 161.36 | Grand – de Vries 1963. Aix – Thevenot 1968, 97ff |
| 161.44 | Szabó 1971, 66 |
| 162.6 | Dio Cassius, Historiae 77, 15.5 |
| 162.15 | Zwicker 1934–36, 105 |
| 162.21 | Tertullian, Apologeticus 24–7 |
| 162.22 | Herodian, History of the Empire after Marcus VIII, 3.6 |
| 162.31 | Thevenot 1968, 97ff |
| 162.32 | Aix – Dayet 1963, 167. Bourbonne les Bains – CIL XIII, 5924 |
| 162.42 | Thevenot 1968, 97ff |
| 162.45 | Le Gall 1963, 147–151; plan on p 148 |
| 163.15 | Henig 1984, 151–152 |
| 163.18 | Wedlake 1982 |
| 163.21 | Henig 1984, 154 |
| 164.8 | Wedlake 1982 |
| 164.27 | Thevenot 1968, 97ff |
| 164.31 | Thevenot 1951, 131 |
| 164.34 | Magnen and Thevenot 1953, 21–23 |
| 164.38 | Chabouillet 1880–81, 15ff |
| 164.39 | Green 1984b, 25–33 |
| 164.40 | Zwicker 1934–35, 302–303 |
| 165.6 | Lambrechts 1949, 145, 149 |

165.26  de Vries 1963; Wightman 1970, 211–217
165.29  Wightman 1970, 211–217
165.36  Wheeler 1928, no 16
165.41  Aix – Thevenot 1968, 165ff
165.42  Clébert 1970, 254
166.11  Thevenot 1968, 200ff
166.18  Megaw 1970a, 20
166.20  Merrifield 1969, 66ff
166.22  Green 1976, 226

Chapter Six: Animals and Animism

167.13  Green 1977, 297–98
167.18  Megaw 1970a, 23
167.19  Anati 1965
168.4   Harding 1974, 96–112
168.12  Cunliffe 1983, 46
168.16  Ibid., 156ff
168.34  Cunliffe 1979, 100
168.37  Pobé and Roubier 1961, 37ff
168.40  MacCana 1983, 50–53
168.46  Piggott 1965, 243
169.15  Thevenot 1968, 149
169.18  Pobé and Roubier 1961, 37ff
169.20  Powell 1958, 123
169.22  Ross 1967a, 378–446
169.25  MacCana 1983, 51
169.26  Cunliffe 1979, 80
169.31  Megaw 1970a, no 226
169.35  Pobé and Roubier 1961, 37ff; pl 29
169.38  Green 1977
171.5   Stuart 1982, 141
171.13  Glob 1974, 125
171.17  Allen 1976b, 206
171.18  Harding 1978, 15–16
171.21  Cunliffe 1979, 50
171.26  Megaw 1970a, 35
171.36  Fordington – Cunliffe 1974, 287–299
172.3   Piggott 1965, 226
172.7   Alcock 1972, 136–153
172.10  Bémont 1983–84, nos 152, 153
172.12  Duval 1977, 113, pl 102
172.15  Magnen and Thevenot 1953, 10–14
172.20  Mauvières – CIL XIII, 1318
172.21  CIL XIII, 2846; for example at Lyon; CIL XIII, 1675
172.23  Mars Mullo – for example at Nantes and Rennes; CIL XIII, 3096, 3148, 3149; Terouanne 1965, 209ff
172.25  Thevenot 1955
172.32  Magnen and Thevenot 1953, 15–16
172.33  Green 1976, 111
172.35  Green 1976, 163–64
172.36  Green 1978, 23ff
172.43  Ross and Feacham 1976, 230–237
172.45  Green 1976, 111

172.46  Ibid., 179
173.2   Ibid., 230
173.11  Anon 1980a, 3.58
173.17  Thevenot 1955
173.19  Tudot 1860, pl 35. Thevenot 1951, 129–141
173.27  Ambrose and Henig 1980, 135–138
173.46  Juvenal, Satire VIII; Minucius Felix, Octavianus XXVII, 7
174.3   Thevenot 1968, 185ff
174.4   Bémont 1983–84, no 256; Espérandieu, no 2046; Thevenot 1968, 190
174.10  Allen 1958, 51, pl IV, no 35
174.12  Johns 1971–72, 37–41
175.15  Thevenot 1968, 157
175.16  Green 1976, 167; Cirencester – ibid., 173
175.21  Espérandieu 1924, no 158
175.24  Linckenheld 1929, 84
175.32  Green 1976, 174; 190
175.33  Wedlake 1982; Green 1976, 190
175.38  Wheeler 1932
176.17  Turner 1982, 15
176.19  Green 1976, 230
176.21  pers comm F J Collins 24.8.70; Green 1976, 226
176.27  Rankov 1982, 292
177.2   Anati 1965, 158
177.4   Gimbutas 1965, fig 109, 1, p 145
177.8   Megaw 1970a, 35; Anon 1980a, 14.48
177.12  Megaw 1970a, 33, no 162
177.16  Hawkes 1951, 172–199
178.7   Espérandieu no 3132; CIL XIII, 3026; Espérandieu no 4929
178.13  MacCana 1983, 46
178.15  Thevenot 1968, 154
178.18  Thevenot 1968, 154
178.21  Green 1976, pl Xf, g, h; pl Xc, d
178.24  Green 1976, 195, 213; 1978, 23ff
178.28  Cunliffe 1979, 94
178.29  Alcock 1972, 80–84, 136–153, 163; Harding 1974, 96–112
178.39  Green 1976, 181, 183, 206, 220, 163
178.40  Anon 1978, 57–60
179.3   Pliny, Natural History XVI, 249
179.12  Piggott 1965, 243
179.18  MacCana 1983, 50
179.23  MacCana 1983, 117
179.26  Anon 1980b, Abb 13
179.35  Anati 1965
179.40  Toynbee 1973
180.3   Strabo, IV, 4, 3
180.13  Cunliffe 1974, 287–299
180.15  Hodson and Rowlett 1973, 184–85

233

| | |
|---|---|
| 180.22 | Ross 1967a, 308–321 |
| 180.28 | MacCana 1983, 51 |
| 180.32 | Downey et al 1980 |
| 180.35 | Laing 1969, 163 |
| 180.37 | Allen 1976a, 270–272 |
| 180.42 | Megaw 1970a, no 226 |
| 180.43 | Szabó 1971, 65 |
| 181.2 | Megaw 1970a, no 238 |
| 181.4 | Duval 1977, 163; Szabó 1971, 65 |
| 181.5 | Ibid., 68 |
| 181.7 | Megaw 1970a, no 225 |
| 181.11 | Thevenot 1957, 156–157 |
| 181.13 | Tacitus, *Germania*, 35 |
| 181.24 | Dayet 1954, 334–335 |
| 181.29 | Goodburn 1975, 342 |
| 181.30 | Green 1976, 212 |
| 181.33 | Green 1976, 204; Ross 1968, 258 |
| 182.9 | Briard 1979, 209ff |
| 182.14 | Gelling and Davidson 1969, 86–96 |
| 182.15 | Paspardo-Anati 1965 |
| 182.20 | Bémont 1983–4, 130; Anati 1965, 172 |
| 182.23 | Megaw 1970a, no 209 |
| 182.24 | MacCana 1983, 42–43 |
| 182.27 | MacCana 1983, 113 |
| 182.29 | Anon 1980b, no 76 |
| 182.30 | Ibid., no 175 |
| 182.31 | Green 1977, pl 12, VIII, c |
| 183.4 | de Vries 1963 |
| 183.13 | Ross 1967a, figs 112, 113 |
| 184.16 | Green 1976, 26, 215 |
| 184.17 | Green 1976, 174 |
| 184.18 | Green 1976, 111 |
| 184.14 | MacCana 1983, 50 |
| 184.23 | Frere 1984, 196; Hassall and Tomlin 1984, 337 |
| 184.38 | Anon 1980b, no 216 |
| 184.42 | Wightman 1970, 217; *CIL* XIII, 4113, 5160 |
| 184.43 | Thevenot 1968, 157 |
| 184.47 | Green 1978, 23ff |
| 185.3 | Dio Cassius LXII, 2 |
| 185.4 | Green 1976, 174 |
| 185.6 | Green 1976, 221 |
| 185.9 | Ibid., 218 |
| 185.14 | Green 1976, 202 |
| 185.20 | Espérandieu 1924, no 158 |
| 185.24 | Thevenot 1968, 163 |
| 185.26 | Thevenot 1955 |
| 185.29 | Ross 1967a, 150–151 |
| 186.8 | Cunliffe 1983, 46 |
| 186.12 | Brogan 1973, 192–219 |
| 186.34 | Cunliffe 1979, 89–91; Espérandieu no 7676 |
| 186.36 | Rolland 1965, 190 |
| 186.38 | Green 1976, 190 |
| 187.12 | Ross 1967a, 302–378 |
| 187.17 | Hodson and Rowlett 1973, 189 |
| 187.19 | Megaw 1970a, 17 |

| | |
|---|---|
| 187.25 | Espérandieu no 3132 |
| 187.31 | Espérandieu no 4929 |
| 187.35 | Ross 1967a, 302–378 |
| 187.38 | Green 1976, 206 |
| 188.1 | MacCana 1983, 52 |
| 188.9 | Ross 1967a, 302–78 |
| 188.13 | Linckenheld 1929 |
| 188.28 | Cunliffe 1979, 87 |
| 188.30 | Green 1978, 23ff |
| 188.32 | Green 1977, pl 12, VIII, a, b |
| 188.38 | Thevenot 1968, 159–162 |
| 188.41 | ibid. |
| 188.44 | ibid. |
| 190.14 | Colombet and Lebel 1953, 111, fig 22 |
| 190.16 | Green 1976, 217 |
| 191.1 | Green 1976, 200 |
| 191.6 | *CIL* XIII, 2656 |
| 191.29 | Megaw 1970a, 33, no 209 |
| 191.35 | Wightman 1985, 179 |
| 191.44 | Lambrechts 1942 |
| 191.45 | Espérandieu no 3919 |
| 193.1 | Thevenot 1968, 162–63; Espérandieu nos 2072, 2067 |
| 193.5 | Espérandieu no 3015 |
| 194.5 | Carlisle – Green 1978, 23ff. Trier – Menzel 1966, pl 102a |
| 195.19 | CIL XIII, 3026 |
| 195.35 | Megaw 1970a, 34; Boucher 1976, 173 |
| 195.36 | Megaw 1970a, no 2 |
| 195.40 | Megaw 1970a, no 209 |
| 196.6 | Wightman 1985, 179 |
| 196.12 | Bober 1951, 13–51 |
| 196.20 | Boon 1982, 276–280 |
| 196.27 | Green 1976, 173, pl XVIIg |
| 197.24 | Glob 1974 |
| 197.26 | Ross 1967a, 131 |
| 197.28 | Jacobsthal 1944, passim |
| 198.2 | Duval 1977, 25 |
| 198.5 | Espérandieu, no 3015 |
| 198.8 | Ross 1961, 59ff; Green 1976, 110 |
| 198.11 | Green 1976, 230; Megaw 1970a, no 210 |
| 198.12 | Green 1976, 182 |
| 198.13 | ibid, 213, pl XIXe |
| 198.14 | Ross 1967a, fig 103 |
| 198.15 | Wandsworth – Green 1976, 221. Uley – Ellison 1977 |
| 198.18 | Frere 1977, 392–394 |
| 203.25 | Susini 1973; Green 1982 |
| 204.4 | Parfitt and Halliwell 1985 |
| 204.5 | Turner 1982 |
| 204.14 | Green 1983a, pl 25 |
| 204.18 | Green 1983a, pl 35 |
| 205.5 | Rhodes 1964, 28 |
| 205.6 | Ambrose and Henig 1980 |
| 205.32 | Boardman 1973, 129 |
| 205.36 | Onians 1979, 202 |
| 205.37 | Richter 1955, 49 |
| 205.39 | Combrich 1968, 93, 141 |

205.42  Boardman 1973, 120
205.45  ibid., 135
205.47  Bonanno 1983, 82; Etruscan influence – Pallotino and Hurliman 1955, 18, 23
206.2  Pliny, *Natural History* XXXIV, 38; Pollit 1983, xviii
206.3  Vitruvius, VII, 5, 3
206.13  Rhodes 1964, 32–36, in speaking of sculptured reliefs from a well at Lower Slaughter
206.14  Henig 1984, 62
206.20  Piggott 1983, 79
206.30  Toynbee 1964, 9; Powell 1966, 185
206.32  Megaw 1970a, 1970b; Finley 1973, 20
207.2  Anati 1965, 111
207.13  Gimbutas 1982, 37–38
207.16  ibid., 38; Renfrew 1973, 175–176
207.18  ibid., 39
207.21  Megaw 1970a, 12; Gombrich 1968
207.32  Boas 1955, 78–79
207.36  Finley 1973, 56
207.38  Cunliffe 1979, 104
207.41  Gombrich 1968, 104
208.1  Gombrich 1968, 90
208.14  Boas 1955, 66–68
208.16  Powell 1966, 7
208.17  Green 1983a, pl 35
208.34  Haverfield 1892
208.39  Green 1983a, 45, pl 29; 1976, 189; Anon 1954, 233
208.41  Eleven such images – e.g. Espérandieu nos 3651–2
208.42  Ross 1967a, fig 50a
208.44  Wroxeter – Green 1976, pl XXd. Bradenstoke – Ross 1967b
209.1  Corleck – Harding 1974, 102
209.4  Deonna 1954
209.5  Dayet 1954
209.11  MacCana 1983; Ross 1967a
210.4  London – Green 1976, 225. Holzerlingen – Powell 1958, 137
210.8  Hobley et al 1977, 31–66
210.26  Green 1976, 173
210.27  Rüger 1983
210.28  for example at Ancaster, Green 1976, 167, pl XVf
211.8  Powell 1966, 16–17

211.12  Briard 1979, 164
211.15  St Clair Baddeley 1923
211.16  Blazquez 1983, no 158, top
211.17  Megaw 1970a, no 232
211.23  Cowie pers comm 1984
211.26  British Museum 1925, 147–148
216.21  see e.g. Ross 1967a; 1959
216.24  Lambrechts 1954
216.36  Megaw 1970a, no 171
216.37  Duval 1977, 137; Collis 1984, 110, pl 30b
216.39  Benoit 1970b
218.4  Megaw 1970a, no 76
218.6  Powell 1966, 198
218.8  Megaw 1970a, 24–25
218.15  Megaw 1970a, nos 187, 188
218.23  Ross 1959; 1967a
218.28  Smith 1984, 221–223
218.31  Boon 1976, 163–175, fig 1
218.38  Boon 1976
218.43  Ross 1967a, 63
218.44  Braithwaite 1984, 99–132
219.2  Green 1980, 174–183
219.11  Green 1976, 173, pl XXXa; 198, pl XXXd
221.4  Green 1975, 54–70; 1981, 253–269
221.9  Long Wittenham – Savory 1937, 3. Arras – Kirk 1949, 32ff
221.13  Pauli 1975, 18, Abb 3, 28; 21, Abb 5, 9
221.15  Harding 1974, 96–112
221.21  Green 1975, 54–70
221.22  Forrer 1948
222.10  Green 1985
223.1  Megaw 1970b; Finley 1973, 70; Sandars 1968, 226
223.2  Sandars 1968, 226
223.10  Megaw 1970b, 269–273; Cunliffe 1979, 87
223.13  Diodorus Siculus V.31.1
223.14  Uley – Ellison 1977. Emberton – Green 1983a, pl 25. Smithfield – Green 1976, pl XVIIIe
224.10  Sandars 1968, 273, 233
224.23  Cunliffe 1979, 158
224.28  Toynbee 1962, 1–2; Ross 1967a, 157
224.35  Ross 1967a, 157
225.13  Toynbee 1962, 17
225.35  Toynbee 1964, 9

# BIBLIOGRAPHY

AARTSEN, J van    1971 *Deae Nehalenniae* Middelburg.

ADKINS, L & ADKINS, R    1985 'Neolithic Axes from Roman Sites in Britain', *Oxford Journal of Archaeology* 4, no. 1, 69–75.

ALFÖLDY, G    1974 *Noricum* Routledge, London.

ALFS, J    1940 'A Gallo-Roman Temple near Bretten (Baden)', *Germania* 24, 128–140.

ALCOCK, J P    1966 'Some Aspects of Celtic Religion in Gloucestershire and the Cotswolds', *Transactions of the Bristol & Gloucestershire Archaeological Society* 85, 45–57.

ALCOCK, L    1972 *'By South Cadbury, is that Camelot. . .' Excavations at Cadbury Castle 1966–70* Thames & Hudson, London.

ALLEN, D F    1958 'Belgic Coins as illustrations of life in the late pre-Roman Iron Age in Britain', *Proceedings of the Prehistoric Society* 24, 43–63.

ALLEN, D F    1976a 'Some Contrasts in Gaulish and British Coins', in Duval & Hawkes eds., 265–282.

ALLEN, D F    1976b 'Wealth, Money and Coinage in a Celtic Society', in Megaw ed, 200–208.

ALLEN, D F    1980 *The Coins of the Ancient Celts* Edinburgh.

ALTHEIM, F    1938 *A History of Roman Religion* London.

AMBROSE, T & HENIG, M    1980 'A New Roman Rider-Relief from Stragglethrope, Lincolnshire', *Britannia* 11, 135–138.

AMY, R, DUVAL, P-M *et al.*    1962 *L'Arc d'Orange* (Supplément à *Gallia* 15) Paris.

ANATI, E    1965 *Camonica Valley* London.

ANON    1935 'Roman Britain in 1934', *Journal of Roman Studies* 25, pl 43.

ANON    1952 'Roman Britain in 1951' *Journal of Roman Studies* 41, pl 13.

ANON    1954 'A Roman Carved Stone', *Transactions of the Bristol and Gloucestershire Archaeological Society* 73, 233, pl 21.

ANON    1956 'Roman Discoveries at Goadby Marwood', *Leicestershire Archaeology and History Society Transactions* 32, 17–36.

ANON    1965 'A New Altar to the Mothers from Juliacum (Jülich)', *Epigraphische Studien* V, 4, 1ff.

ANON    1968 *Epigraphische Studien: Sammelund*, 18ff.

ANON    1978 'The Cambridge Shrine', *Current Archaeology*, no. 61, April 1978, 57–60.

ANON    1980a *Die Hallstatt Kultur*, Linz.

ANON    1980b *Die Kelten in Mitteleuropa*, Salzburg

ANON    1984 'Two Chariot Burials at Wetwang Slack', *Current Archaeology*, no. 93, vol 8, no. 10, August 1984, 302–6.

ARMAND-CALLIAT A    1937 *Le Chalonnais Gallo-Romain* Châlon-sur-Saône.

ARTS COUNCIL    1970 *Early Celtic Art* Edinburgh University Press

ASHBEE, P    1963 'The Wilsford Shaft', *Antiquity* 37, 116–120.

BABELON, E    1961 *Le Rhin – L'Antiquité Gaulois et Germains* Paris.

BADDELEY, St Clair    1923 'A Romano-Celtic Sculpture at Churcham', *Transactions of the Bristol & Gloucestershire Archaeology Society* 45, 91ff.

BAILEY, C    1932 *Phases in the Religion of Ancient Rome* Oxford.

BAUCHHENSS, G                 1976 *Jupitergigantensäulen* Stuttgart.

BAUCHHENSS, G &               1981 *Die Jupitersäulen in den germanischen Pro-*
NOELKE, P                     *vinzen* Köln/Bonn.

BEDWIN, O                     1980 'Excavations at Chanctonbury Ring, Wiston,
                              West Sussex in 1977', *Britannia* 11, 173–221.

BÉMONT, C                     1983–1984 *L'Art Celtique en Gaule* Collections des
                              Musées de Province; Ministère de la Culture Direc-
                              tion des Musées de France.

BENOIT, F                     1955 *L'Art Primitif Méditerranéen dans la Vallée
                              de Rhône* Aix-en-Provence.

BENOIT, F                     1970a *Art et Dieux de la Gaule.* Paris.

BENOIT, F                     1970b *La Symbolisme dans les sanctuaires de la
                              Gaule, Latomus* 105, Brussels.

BENOIT, F                     1981 *Entremont,* Paris.

BERTRAND, A                   1897 *La Religion des Gaulois* Paris.

BICKNELL, C                   1911 *The Prehistoric Rock Engravings in the Ita-
                              lian Maritime Alps* Bordighera.

BIDDLE, M                     1985 'The Archaeology of Death', in CBA 9 Annual
                              Conference *The Archaeology of Death,* Oxford
                              16.3.85.

BIRLEY, E *et al.*            1934 'Third Report on Excavations at House-
                              steads', *Archaeologia Aeliana* (4) 11, 185–206.

BLAGG, T F C                  1979 'The Date of the Temple of Sulis Minerva',
                              *Britannia* 10, 101–107.

BLANCHET, J A                 1890 'Etude sur les figurines en terre cuite de la
                              Gaule Romaine', *Mémoires de la Société des
                              Antiquaires de France* (6) 51, 65–224.

BLANCHET, J A                 1923 'Le Jupiter à la roue trouvé à Champagnat
                              (Creuse)', *Bulletin Archéologique du Comité des
                              Travaux Historiques et Scientifiques,* 156–160.

BLÁZQUEZ, J M                 1983 *Primitivas Religionas Ibericas, Tomo II Re-
                              ligiones Prerromanes* Madrid.

BOARDMAN, J                   1973 *Greek Art* Thames & Hudson, London.

BOAS, F                       1955 *Primitive Art* Dover, New York.

BOBER, J                      1951 'Cernunnos: Origin and Transformation of a
                              Celtic Divinity', *American Journal of Archaeology*
                              55, 13–51.

BONANNO, A                    1983 'Sculpture', in Henig, M ed *A Handbook of
                              Roman Art,* 66–96 Phaidon.

BOON, G C                     1972 *Isca* National Museum of Wales, Cardiff.

BOON, G C                     1976 'The Shrine of the Head, Caerwent', in Boon,
                              G C & Lewis, J M (eds) *Welsh Antiquity* National
                              Museum of Wales, Cardiff.

BOON, G C                     1982 'A Coin with the Head of the Cernunnos',
                              *Seaby Coin and Medal Bulletin,* no. 769, 276–282.

BOON, G C                     1983 'Some Romano-British Domestic Shrines and
                              their inhabitants', in Hartley, B & Wacher, J (eds)
                              *Rome and her Northern Provinces,* 33–55 Alan
                              Sutton, Gloucester.

BOUCHER, S                    1976 *Recherches sur les bronzes figurés de la
                              Gaule pré-romaine et romaine* Paris.

BOUZEK, J                     1977 *Archéologické Rozheldy* 29.

BRAEMAR, F                    1969 'Sculptures en métal battu et repoussé dans la
                              Gaule romaine et des regions limetrophes *Revue
                              Archéologique* 81.

BRAITHWAITE, G                1984 'Romano-British Face Pots and Head Pots',
                              *Britannia* 15, 99–132.

BREUIL, H *et al.*            1929 *Rock Paintings of Southern Andulusia* Ox-
                              ford.

BREWSTER, T C M               1976 'Garton Slack', *Current Archaeology* 5, no. 51,
                              104–116.

BRIARD, J                     1979 *The Bronze Age in Barbarian Europe* BCA,
                              London.

237

BBC 1985 'The Body in Question, Q.E.D., 10.4.85.

BRITISH MUSEUM 1925 *Guide to the Early Iron Age Antiquities* London.

BRITISH MUSEUM 1964 *Guide to the Antiquities of Roman Britain* London.

BRITISH MUSEUM 1969 *Introductory Guide to the Egyptian collections* London.

BROGAN, O 1953 *Roman Gaul* Bell, London.

BROGAN, O 1973 'The Coming of Rome and the Establishment of Roman Gaul', in Piggott, Daniel & McBurney (eds), 192–219.

BURGESS, C 1974 'The Bronze Age', in Renfrew (ed), 165–232

BURGESS, C 1980 'The Bronze Age in Wales', Taylor (ed) *Culture and Environment in Prehistoric Wales* British Archaeological Reports 76, 243–286.

CERQUAND, J F 1881–1883 'Taranus ou Taranis', *Revue Celtique* 5, 381–383.

CHABOUILLET, A 1880–1887 'Notice sur des inscriptions et des antiquités provenant de Bourbonne-les-Bains', *Revue Archéologique* 39, 18ff.

CHAMBERS, R A 1985 'Romano-British Burials', in CBA 9 Annual Conference *The Archaeology of Death*, Oxford 16.3.85.

CHAMPION, T C et al. 1984 *Prehistoric Europe* Academic Press.

CHAMPION, T C & MEGAW, J V S eds 1985 *Settlement and society: Aspects of West European Prehistory in the First Millennium BC* Leicester University Press.

CHANTRE, E 1880 *Etudes Paléoethiques dans le Bassin du Rhône: Premier Age du Fer* Paris.

CHARLESWORTH, D 1961 'Roman Jewellery found in Northumberland and Durham', *Archaeologia Aeliana* (4), 39, 1–37.

CHARLTON, D B & MITCHESON, M M 1983 'Yardhope, a Shrine to Cocidius?', *Britannia* 14, 143–153.

CHENET, G 1919 'Rouelles de plomb et persistance d'emploi des rouelles gauloises', *Bulletin Archéologique du Comité des Travaux historiques et scientifiques*, 243–251.

CLARKE, J & CLARKE, D 1971 *Camulodunum* Ginn & Co., London.

CLÉBERT, J-P 1970 *Provence Antique 2: L'époque gallo-romaine* Robert Laffont, Paris.

CLIFFORD, E M 1938 'Roman Altars in Gloucestershire', *Transactions of the Bristol & Gloucester Archaeological Society* 60, 297–307.

COLES, J M & HARDING, A F 1979 *The Bronze Age in Europe* Methuen.

COLIN, J 1927 *Les Antiquités de la Rhenanie* Paris.

COLLINGWOOD, R G 1931 'Mars Rigisamus', *Somerset Archaeology & Natural History Society* 77, 112–114.

COLLINGWOOD, R G & TAYLOR, M V 1932 'Roman Britain in 1931', *Journal of Roman Studies* 22, 206.

COLLIS, J 1975 *Defended Sites of the Late La Tène* British Archaeological Reports, Oxford SS 2, 101.

COLLIS, J 1984 *The European Iron Age* Batsford, London.

COLOMBET, A & LEBEL, P 1952 'Mythologie Gallo-Romaine', *Revue de l'Est et du Centre-Est* 4, 108–130.

COLOMBET, A & LEBEL, P 1953 'Les Taureaux á trois cornes', *Revue de l'Est. . . . . 4, 130ff.*

COOK, A B 1914 *Zeus: A Study in Ancient Religion I* Cambridge.

COURCELLE-SENEUIL, J L 1910 *Les Dieux Gaulois d'après les Monuments figurés* Paris.

CRAVAYAT, P 1955 'Les Cultes indigènes dans la cité des Bituriges', *Revue Archéologique de l'Est et du Centre-Est* 6, 210–228.

CUNLIFFE, B W — 1974 *Iron Age Communities in Britain* Routledge, London.

CUNLIFFE, B W — 1975 *Rome and the Barbarians* Bodley Head.

CUNLIFFE, B W — 1979 *The Celtic World* Bodley Head.

CUNLIFFE, B W — 1983 *Danebury: Anatomy of an Iron Age Hillfort* Batsford

CUNLIFFE, B W — 1984 *Danebury: An Iron Age Hillfort in Hampshire. Vol 2. The Excavations 1969–1978. The Finds* CBA Research Report 52 442–474.

DAYET, M — 1954 'Le Sanglier à trois cornes du Cabinet des Medailles', *Revue de l'Est et du Centre-Est* 5, 334–335.

DAYET, M — 1963 'Le Borvo Hercule d'Aix-les-Bains', *Revue Archéologique*, 167.

DÉCHELETTE, J — 1913 *La Collection Millon: Antiquités préhistoriques et Gallo-Romaines*, 260ff Paris.

DÉCHELETTE, J — 1914 *La Tène: Manuel d'Archéologie IV: Celtique et Gallo-Romaine 2*, Part 3 Paris.

DENT, J — 1985 'Three Cart Burials from Wetwang, Yorkshire', *Antiquity* 59, 85–92.

DEONNA, W — 1954 'Trois: superlatif absolu. A propos du taureau tricorne et de Mercure triphallique', *L'Antiquité Classique* 23, 403–428.

DETSICAS, A — 1983 *The Cantiaci* Alan Sutton, Gloucester

DILLON, M & CHADWICK, N — 1967 *The Celtic Realms* Weidenfeld & Nicolson, London

DOWNEY, R *et al.* — 1980 'The Hayling Island Temple and Religious Connections across the Channel', in Rodwell, W (ed) *Temples, Churches and Religion in Roman Britain* British Archaeological Reports, Oxford 77.

DRINKWATER, J — 1983 *Roman Gaul* Croom Helm, London.

DRIOUX, G — 1929 'Le Dieu "à la roue" chez les Lingons', *Revue des Etudes Anciennes* 31, 354–358.

DRIOUX, G — 1934 *Cultes Indigénes de Lingons* Paris.

DRURY, P J — 1980 'Non Classical Religious Buildings in Iron Age and Roman Britain: A Review', in Rodwell, W (ed) *Temples, Churches and Religion in Roman Britain* British Archaeological Reports, Oxford 77.

DRURY, P J & WICKENDEN, N P — 1982 'Four Bronze Figurines from the Trinovantian Civitas', *Britannia* 13, 239–243.

DUVAL, P-M — 1957 *Les Dieux de la Gaule* Paris.

DUVAL, P-M — 1961 *Paris Antique* Paris.

DUVAL, P–M — 1977 *Les Celtes* Gallimard.

DUVAL, P-M & HAWKES, C F C eds — 1976 *Celtic Art in Ancient Europe: Five Protohistoric Centuries* Seminar Press.

ELLISON, A — 1977 *Excavations at West Uley: 1977. The Romano-British Temple* CRAAGS Occasional Papers No. 3.

ESPERANDIEU, E — 1907–1966 *Recueil Général des bas-Reliefs de la Gaule Romaine* Paris.

ESPERANDIEU, E — 1917 'Le Dieu Cavalier de Luxeuil', *Revue Archéologique* 70 (5), 72–86.

ESPERANDIEU, E — 1924 *Le Musée Lapidaire de Nîmes: Guide Sommaire* Nîmes.

EYGUN, F — 1965 'Information-Archéologiques: Poitiers', *Gallia* 23, 349–387.

FAIRLESS, K J — 1984 'Three Religious Cults from the Northern Frontier Region', in Miket R & Burgess, C (eds) *Between and Beyond the Walls*, 224–242 John Donald, Edinburgh.

FERGUSON, J    1970 *The Religions of the Roman Empire* Thames & Hudson London.

FERGUSON, J    1976 *An Illustrated Encyclopaedia of Mysticism and the Mystery Religions* Thames & Hudson, London.

FILIP, J    1960 *Celtic Civilisation and Heritage* Prague.

FINLEY, I    1973 *Celtic Art: an Introduction* Faber & Faber, London.

FITZPATRICK, A P    1984 'The Deposition of La Tène Iron Age Metalwork in watery contexts in Southern England', in Cunliffe B & Miles, D (eds) *Aspects of the Iron Age in Central Southern Britain* Oxford University Committee for Archaeology no. 2, Oxford.

FLEMMING, H    1908–1909 'Les Objects a'Alésia. . . .' *Pro Alésia*, 391–395.

FORRER, R    1948 *Die Helvetischen und Helveto-römischen Votivbeilchen der Schweiz* Basle.

FORSTER, R H & KNOWLES, W H    1910 'Corstopitum: Report on the Excavations in 1909' *Archaeologia Aeliana* (3) 6, 205–272.

FOUET, G & SOUTOU, A    1963 'Une cîme pyrénéenne consacrée à Jupiter: Le Mont-Saçon (Hautes-Pyrénées)', *Gallia* 21, 75–295.

FRERE, S S    1977 'Roman Britain in 1976', *Britannia* 8, 356–425.

FRERE S S    1984 'Roman Britain in 1983', *Britannia* 15, 266–332.

FRIEDL, E    1975 *Men and Women: in Anthropological View* New York.

GAIDOZ, H    1884 'Le Dieu Gaulois du Soleil et le symbolisme de la roue', *Revue Archéologique* 2, 7–37.

GAIDOZ, H    1885 'le Dieu Gauloise du Soleil et le Symbolisme de la roue', *Revue Archéologique* 3, 180–203.

GALL, J Le    1963 *Alésia: Archéologie et Histoire* Fayard.

GASSIES, G    1902 'Cavalier et anguipède sur un monument de Meaux', *Revue des Etudes Anciennes* 4, 287–297.

GELLING, P & DAVIDSON, H E    1969 *The Chariot of the Sun: and other Rites and Symbols of the Northern Bronze Age* Dent.

GETTY, R J ed    1940 *M Annaei Lucani de Bello Civili, Liber I* Cambridge.

GILBERT, H    1978 'The Felmingham Hall Hoard, Norfolk', *Bulletin of the Board of Celtic Studies* 28, part 1, 159–187.

GIMBUTAS, M    1965 *Bronze Age Cultures in Central and Eastern Europe* Mouton & Co.

GIMBUTAS, M    1982 *The Goddesses and Gods of Old Europe* Thames & Hudson, London.

GLOB, P V    1969a *Helleristninger i Danmark* Copenhagen.

GLOB, P V    1969b *The Bog People* Faber.

GLOB, P V    1974 *The Mound People* Faber.

GLUECK, W    1965 *Deities and Dolphins* New York.

GOMBRICH, E H    1968 *Art and Illusion* London.

GOODBURN, R    1976 'Roman Britain in 1975', *Britannia* 7, 291–377.

GOODBURN, R    1978 'Roman Britain in 1977', *Britannia* 9, 404–472.

GOODBURN, R    1979 'Roman Britain in 1978', *Britannia* 10, 268–338.

GOODCHILD, R G    1938 'A Priest's Sceptre from the Romano-Celtic Temple at Farley Heath, Surrey', *Antiquaries Journal* 18, 391ff.

GOODCHILD, R G    1947 'The Farley Heath Sceptre Binding', *Antiquaries Journal* 27, 83ff.

GRAPINAT, R    1970 'Les Avatars d'un Culte Solaire', *Forum:*

|  |  |
|---|---|
|  | *Revue de Groupe Archéologique Antique* 1, 54–56. |
| GREEN, H S | 1985 'The Caergwrle Bowl – not oak but shale', *Antiquity* 59, 116–117. |
| GREEN, M J | 1974 'A Symbol of the Celtic Jupiter from Little Houghton, Northants' *Journal of the Northampton Museums & Art Gallery* 10, 2–6. |
| GREEN, M J | 1975a 'Romano-British non-ceramic model objects in south-east Britain', *Archaeological Journal* 132, 54-70. |
| GREEN, M J | 1975b *A Romano-British Ceremonial Bronze Object found near Peterborough* Peterborough City Museum Monograph no. 1. |
| GREEN, M J | 1975–1976 'A Romano-Celtic cult Symbol from Icklingham, Suffolk', *Proceedings of the Cambridge Antiquarian Society* 66, 55–61. |
| GREEN, M J | 1976 *A Corpus of Religious Material from the civilian Areas of Roman Britain* British Archaeological Reports, Oxford, no. 24. |
| GREEN, M J | 1977 'Theriomorphism in Romano-British Cult Art' in Henig, M & Munby, J (eds) *Roman Life and Art in Britain* British Archaeological Reports, Oxford no 41, 297–327. |
| GREEN, M J | 1978 *Small Cult Objects from the Military Areas of Roman Britain* British Archaeological Reports, Oxford, no. 52. |
| GREEN, M J | 1979 'The worship of the Romano-Celtic Wheel-God in Britain seen in relation to Gaulish evidence', *Collections Latomus* 38, fasc 1, 345–368. |
| GREEN, M J | 1980 'A Romano-British Face-Urn Fragment from the Bancroft Roman Villa, Milton Keynes, Bucks and other British Face-Urns', *Bulletin of the Board of Celtic Studies* 29, 174–183. |
| GREEN, M J | 1981a 'Wheel-God and Ram-Horned Snake in Roman Gloucestershire', *Transactions of the Bristol & Gloucestershire Archaeological Society* 99, 109–115. |
| GREEN M J | 1981b 'Model Objects from Military Areas of Roman Britain', *Britannia* 12, 253–269. |
| GREEN, M J | 1982 'Tanarus, Taranis and the Solar Wheel', *Journal of the Chester Archaeological Society* 65, 37–44. |
| GREEN, M J | 1983a *The Gods of Roman Britain* Shire Archaeology no. 34. |
| GREEN, M J | 1983b 'A Celtic God from Netherby, Cumbria', *Tansactions of the Cumberland & Westmorland Antiquarian & Archaeological Society* 83, 41–47. |
| GREEN, M J | 1984a *The Wheel as a Cult Symbol in the Romano-Celtic World* Latomus, Brussels. |
| GREEN, M J | 1984b 'Mother and Sun in Romano-Celtic Religion', *Antiquaries Journal* 64, part 1, 25–33. |
| GREEN, M J | 1984c 'Celtic symbolism at Roman Caerleon', *Bulletin of the Board of Celtic Studies* 31, 251–258. |
| GREEN, M J | 1985 'A Miniature Bronze Axe from Tiddington, Warwickshire', *Britannia* 16, in press. |
| GRENIER, A | 1970 *Les Gaulois* Haimond. |
| GRINSELL, L V | 1961 'The Breaking of Objects as a Funerary Rite', *Folklore* 72, 475–491. |
| HAFFNER, A | 1971, 1974, 1978 *Das Keltisch-römisch Graberfeld von Wederath-Belgium* 1–3 Mainz. |
| HARDING, D W | 1974 *The Iron Age in Lowland Britain* Routledge, London. |
| HARDING, D W | 1977 'The Celts', *Archaeology* 30, no. 6. |

| | |
|---|---|
| HARDING, D W | 1978 *Prehistoric Europe*, Phaidon. |
| HARDWICK, L | 1979 *Athenian Social History* Open University Units 7–8, A292. |
| HARMAND, J | 1970 *Les Celtes au second âge du fer* Paris. |
| HASSALL, M W C & TOMLIN, R S O | 1977 'Roman Britain in 1976. II Inscriptions', *Britannia* 8, 426–449. |
| HASSALL, M W C & TOMLIN, R S O | 1979 'Roman Britain in 1978. II Inscriptions', *Britannia* 10. 339–356. |
| HASSALL, M W C & TOMLIN, R S O | 1981 'Roman Britain in 1980. II Inscriptions', *Britannia* 12, 369–396. |
| HASSALL, M W C & TOMLIN, R S O | 1983 'Roman Britain in 1982. II Inscriptions', *Britannia* 14, 336–356. |
| HATT, J J | 1945 *Les Monuments funéraires gallo-romain du Comminges et du Couserans* Toulouse. |
| HATT, J J | 1951 ' "Rota Flammis Circumsepta": a propos du symbole de la roue dans la religion gauloise', *Revue de l'Est et du Centre-Est* 2, 82–87. |
| HATT, J J | 1964 'Circonscription de Strasbourg', *Gallia* 22, 355. |
| HATT, J J | 1967 'Sculptures Gallo-Romaines en Basse-Alsace', *Cahiers Alsaciens d'Archéologie, d'Art et d'Histoire*, 133–140. |
| HATT, J J | 1970a *Celts and Gallo-Romans* Barrie & Jenkins, London. |
| HATT, J J | 1970b 'Les Croyances funéraires des Gallo-Romains d'après des tombes, *Revue Archéologique de l'Est et du Centre-Est* 21, 7–97. |
| HAVERFIELD, F | 1892 'The Mother Goddesses', *Archaeologia Aeliana* (2) 15, 314ff. |
| HAWKES, C F C | 1951 'Bronzeworkers, Cauldrons and Bucket-Animals' in Grimes, W F (ed) *Aspects of Archaeology in Britain and Beyond* Edwards, London. |
| HAWKES, C F C | 1976 'Celts and Cultures: Wealth, Power and Art', in Duval, P-M & Hawkes, C F C (eds) *Celtic Art in Ancient Europe*, 1–27 Seminar Press. |
| HELM, G | 1976 *The Celts* Weidenfeld & Nicholson, London. |
| HENIG, M ed | 1983 *A Handbook of Roman Art* Phaidon |
| HENIG, M | 1984 *Religion in Roman Britain* Batsford, London. |
| HENIG, M & TAYLOR, J W | 1984 'A Gold Votive Plaque', *Britannia* 15, 246. |
| HETTNER, F | 1901 *Festschrift zur Feier des hundertjarhigen Bestehen der Gesellschaft für Nützliche Forschungen in Trier* Trier. |
| HINGLEY, R | 1982 'Recent Discoveries of the Roman Period at the Noah's Ark Inn, Frilford, South Oxon', *Britannia* 13, 305–309. |
| HODDER, I ed | 1982 *Symbolic and Structural Archaeology* Cambridge. |
| HODSON, F R & ROWLETT, R M | 1973 'From 600 BC to the Roman Conquest' in Piggott, S, Daniel, G & McBurney, C (eds) *France Before the Romans*, 157–191 Thames & Hudson, London. |
| HOOD, S | 1978 *The Arts in Prehistoric Greece* Harmondsworth. |
| HUBERT, H | 1925 'Divinités Gauloises – le mythe d'Epona', *Mélanges Vendryes*, 187. |
| HULL, M R | 1938 'An Epona Sculpture in the Colchester and Essex Museum', *Transactions of the Essex Archaeological Society* (2) 19, 198. |
| JACKSON, K H | 1953 *Language and History in Early Britain* Edinburgh. |
| JACKSON, K H | 1964 *The Oldest Irish Tradition: A Window on the* |

| | |
|---|---|
| | *Iron Age* Cambridge. |
| JACKSON, K H | 1970 *A Celtic Miscellany* Harmondsworth. |
| JACOBSTHAL, P | 1944 *Early Celtic Art* Oxford. |
| JENKINS, F | 1956 'Nameless or Nehalennia', *Archaeologia Cantiana* 70, 192–280 |
| JENKINS, F | 1957 'The Cult of the Dea Nutrix in Kent', *Archaeologia Cantiana* 71, 30ff. |
| JENKINS, F | 1958 'The Cult of the Pseudo-Venus in Kent', *Archaeologia Cantiana* 72, 60ff. |
| JENKINS, F | 1978 'Some interesting types of clay statuettes of the Roman period found in london', Bird, J *et al* (eds), *Collectanea Londinensia*, 149–162 London & Middlesex Archaeological Society. |
| JOHNS, C M | 1971–1972 'A Roman Bronze Statuette of Epona', *British Museum Quarterly* 36, no. 1–2, 37–40. |
| JOHNS, C M | 1982 *Sex or Symbol* British Museum, London. |
| JOHNSTON, P M | 1903 'Roman Vase fund at Littlehampton', *Sussex Archaeological Collections* 46, 233–234. |
| JONES, G & trans. JONES, T | 1949 *The Mabinogion* Dent. |
| JONES, G D B & CREALEY, S | 1974 *Roman Manchester* Manchester Excavation Committee. |
| KELLNER, H J | 1971 *Die Römer in Bayern* Munich. |
| KING, A & SOFFE, G | 1983 'A Romano-Celtic Temple at Ratham Mill, Funtington, West Sussex', *Britannia* 14, 264–66. |
| KIRK, J R | 1949 'Bronzes from Woodeaton', *Oxoniensia* 14, 32ff. |
| KROMER, K | 1959 *Das Gräberfeld von Hallstatt* Florence. |
| LABROUSSE, M | 1959 'informations-Archéologiques: Toulouse', *Gallia* 17, 409–449. |
| LAET, S J de | 1942 'Figurines en terre cuite d'époque romaine trouvées à Assche-Kalkoven', *L'Antiquité Classique* 2, 41–54. |
| LAING, L R | 1969 *Coins and Archaeology* Weidenfeld & Nicolson. |
| LAMBERT, L | 1914 'Recent Roman Discoveries in London', *Archaeologia* 66, 225ff. |
| LAMBRECHTS, P | 1942 *Contributions à l'étude des divinités Celtiques* Bruges. |
| LAMBRECHTS, P | 1949 'La colonne du Dieu-cavalier au géant et le culte des sources en Gaule', *Collections Latomus* 8, 145–158. |
| LAMBRECHTS, P | 1950 'Epona et les Matres', *L'Antiquité Classique* 19, 103–112. |
| LAMBRECHTS, P | 1951 'Divinités Equéstres Celtiques on Defunts Heroisés?', *L'Antiquite Classique* 20, fasc 1. |
| LAMBRECHTS, P | 1954 *L'Exaltation de la Tête dans la Pensée et dans l'Art des Celtes* Bruges. |
| LEBEL, P & BOUCHER, S | 1975 *Bronze figurés Antiques* Paris. |
| LEBER, P | 1965 'Fund eines votiv-Altars auf der Koralpe', *Pro Austria Romana* 15, 25f. |
| LEECH, R | 1981 'The Excavation of a Romano-British Farmstead and Cemetery on Bradley Hill, Somerton, Somerset', *Britannia* 12, 177–252. |
| LEHNER, H | 1918–1921 'Der Tempelbezirk der Matronae Vacallinehae bei Pesch', *Bonner Jahrbücher* 125–126, 74ff. |
| LELONG, C | 1970 'Note sur une sculpture gallo-romaine de Mouhet (Indre)', *Revue Archéologique du Centre* 9, 123–126. |
| LEWIS, B | 1883 'The Antiquities of Autun', *Archaeological* |

243

*Journal* 40, 29–50.

LINCKENHELD, E — 1927 *Les stèles funéraires en forme de maison chez les Médiomatriques et en Gaule* Paris.

LINCKENHELD, E — 1929 'Sucellus et Nantosuelta', *Revue de l'Historie des Religions* 99, 40–92.

LINCKENHELD, E — 1947 'Le Sanctuaire de Donon', *Cahiers d'Archéologie et d'Histoire d'Alsace* 38, 67–110.

LINDUFF, K — 1979 'Epona: A Celt among the Romans', *Collections Latomus* 38, fasc 4, 817–837.

LÖE, A de — 1937 *Belgique Ancienne: Catalogue Raisonné III: La Période Romaine* Brussels.

LOTH, J — 1925 'Le Dieu Gaulois Rudiobus, Rudianos', *Revue Archéologique*, 210.

LYNCH, F — 1970 *Prehistoric Anglesey* Anglesey Antiquarian Society.

MACALISTER, R A S — 1956 *Lebor Gabála Érenn*, part V Dublin.

MACCANA, P — 1983 *Celtic Mythology*, Newnes, London.

MACDONALD, J L — 1979 'Religion', in Clarke, G *The Roman Cemetery at Lankhills* Winchester Studies 3, Pre-Roman and Roman Winchester, 404–433 Oxford University Press.

MAGNEN, R & THEVENOT, E — 1953 *Epona* Bordeaux.

MAJOR, E — 1940 *Gallische Ausiedlung mit Gräherfeld bei Basel* Basle.

MANNING, W H — 1966 'A Hoard of Romano-British Ironwork from Brampton, Cumberland', *Transactions of the Cumberland & Westmorland Antiquarian & Archaeological Society* 66, 1–36.

MANNING, W H — 1972 'Ironwork Hoards in Iron Age and Roman Britain', *Britannia* 3, 224–250.

MANTEYER, G de — 1945 'Les Dieux des Alpes de Ligurie', *Bulletin de la société d'Etudes des Hautes-Alpes*.

MARKALE, J — 1975 *Women of the Celts* London.

MARSDEN, P — 1980 *Roman London* Thames & Hudson, London.

MARSHALL, A — 1984 'A Roman-Celtic Carved Stone Phallic Figure from Guiting Power, Gloucestershire', *Transactions of the Bristol & Gloucestershire Archaeological Society* 102, 212–215.

MEGAW, J V S — 1970a *Art of the European Iron Age* Harper & Row, New York.

MEGAW, J V S — 1970b 'Cheshire Cat and Mickey Mouse: analysis, interpretation and the art of the La Tène Iron Age', *Proceedings of the Prehistoric Society* 36, 261–279.

MEGAW, J V S ed — 1976 *To Illustrate the Monuments. Essys on Archaeology presented to Stuart Piggott* Thames & Hudson, London.

MEGAW, J V S & SIMPSON, D D A — 1979 *Introduction to British Prehistory* Leicester University Press.

MENZEL, H — 1966 *Die römischen Bronzen aus Deutschland. II Trier* Mainz.

MERRIFIELD, R — 1983 *London City of the Romans* Batsford, London. *Archaeologist* part 1, The Roman Period, 1, no. 3, 66ff.

MILES, H — 1970 'The Cosgrove Roman Villa', *Wolverton Historical Journal*, 9.

MORTILLET, G de — 1876 'Amulettes gauloises et gallo-romaines', *Revue d'Anthropologie* 9, 14, fig 2, 11.

MUCKELROY, K W — 1976 'Enclosed Ambulatories in Romano-Celtic Temples in Britain', *Britannia* 7, 173–191.

NASH, D — 1976 'Reconstructing Posidonius' Celtic Ethnography: some considerations', *Britannia* 7, 111–126.

NASH WILLIAMS, V E — 1952–1954 'The Roman Inscribed and Sculptured Stones found at Caerwent. . .'. *Bulletin of the Board of Celtic Studies* 15, 18ff.

OLMSTED, G S — 1979 *The Gundestrup Cauldron* Latomus, Brussels.

ONIANS, J — 1979 *Art and Thought in the Hellenistic Age* Thames & Hudson, London.

PALLOTINO, M & HÜRLIMANN, M — 1955 *Art of the Etruscans* Thames & Hudson, London.

PARFITT, K & HALLIWELL, G — 1985 'A Possible Underground Roman Shrine at Deal', *Dover Archaeological Group*, forthcoming.

PASCAL, C B — 1964 *The Cults of Cisalpine Gaul* Latomus, Brussels.

PERRIER, J — 1960 'L'Autel de Thauron (Creuse)', *Gallia* 18, 196–197.

PHILLIPS, E J — 1976a 'A Roman Figures Capital at Cirencester', *Journal of the British Archaeological Association* 129, 35–41.

PHILLIPS, E J — 1976b 'A Workshop of Roman Sculptors at Carlisle', *Britannia* 7, 101–110.

PHILLIPS, P — 1980 *The Prehistory of Europe* Allan Lane.

PICARD, G Ch — 1968 'Informations-Archéologiques: Centre', *Gallia* 26, 321–345.

PICHON, R — 1912 *Les Sources de Lucain* Paris.

PIETTE, J — 1981 'Le Fanum de la Villeneuve-au-Châtelot (Aube). État des recherches en 1970' *Mémoires de la Société Archéologique Champenoise* 2, 367–375.

PIGGOTT, S & DANIEL, G E — 1951 *A Picture Book of Ancient British Art* Cambridge University Press.

PIGGOTT, S — 1954 *Neolithic Cultures of the British Isles* Cambridge.

PIGGOTT, S — 1965 *Ancient Europe* Edinburgh.

PIGGOTT, S — 1968 *The Druids* Thames & Hudson, London.

PIGGOTT, S — 1976 'Summing up the Colloquy', in Duval & Hawkes (eds), 283–289.

PIGGOTT, S et al. eds — 1973 *France Before the Romans* Thames & Hudson, London.

PIGGOTT, S — 1983 *The Earliest Wheeled Transport: From the Atlantic Coast to the Caspian Sea* Thames & Hudson, London.

POBÉ, M & ROUBIER, J — 1961 *The Art of Roman Gaul* London.

POLLITT, J J — 1983 *The Art of Rome, 753 BC–AD337* Cambridge University Press.

POWELL, T G E — 1958 *The Celts* Thames & Hudson, London.

POWELL, T G E — 1966 *Prehistoric Art* Thames & Hudson, London.

RANKOV, N B — 1982 'Roman Britain in 1981', *Britannia* 13, 328–395.

REINACH, S — 1894 *Antiquités nationales: Bronzes Figurés de la Gaule Romaine* Paris.

REINACH, S — 1895, 1898 'Epona', *Revue Archéologique* 1, 113, 309; 2, 187.

REINACH, S — 1917 *Catalogue Illustré du Musée des Antiquités Nationales au Château de Saint-Germain-en-Laye*, I Paris.

RENAUD, J — 1956 'Le Dieu Gaulois accroupi de l'Oppidum de Crêt-Châtelard à Saint Marcel de Félines (Loire)', *Revue Archéologique de l'Est et du Centre-Est* 7, 292–296.

RENFREW, C — 1973 *Before Civilisation* Jonathan Cape, London.

RENFREW, C ed. — 1974 *British Prehistory : A New Outline* Duckworth, London.

RICHMOND, I et al. — 1951 'The Temple of Mithras at Carrawburgh', *Archaeologia Aeliana* (4) 29, 1–92.

RICHTER, G M A — 1955 *A Handbook of Greek Art* Phaidon.

RHODES, J F — 1964 *Catalogue of the Romano-British Sculptures in the Gloucester City Museum* Gloucester City Museum.

RISTOW, G — 1975 *Religion und ihre Denkmäler in Köln* Köln.

RODWELL, W — 1973 'An unusual pottery bowl from Kelvedon, Essex', *Britannia* 4, 265–267.

RODWELL, W ed — 1980 *Temples, Churches and Religion in Roman Britain* British Archaeological Reports, Oxford, no. 77.

ROOKE, H — 1809 'Roman Antiquities at and near Bradburn in the City of Derby', *Archaeologia* 12, 6ff.

ROSS, A — 1959 'The Human Head in Insular Pagan Celtic Religion', *Proceedings of the Society of Antiquaries of Scotland* 91, 10–43.

ROSS, A — 1962 'The Horned God of the Brigantes, *Archaeologia Aeliana* (4) 39, 59ff.

ROSS, A — 1967a *Pagan Celtic Britain* Routledge, London.

ROSS, A — 1967b 'A Celtic Three-Faced Head from Wiltshire', *Antiquity* 41, 53–56.

ROSS, A — 1968 'Shafts. Pits, Wells – Sanctuaries of the Belgic Britons?', in Coles, J M & Simpson, D D A (eds) *Studies in Ancient Europe*, 255–285 Leicester University Press.

ROSS, A & FEACHAM, R — 1976 'Ritual Rubbish The Newstead Pits', in Megaw, J V S (ed) *To Illustrate the Monuments* Thames & Hudson, London.

ROSS, A & FEACHAM, R — 1984 'Heads Baleful and Benign', in Miket, R & Burgess, C (eds) *Between and Beyond the Walls*, 338–352 Edinburgh.

ROUVIER-JEANLIN, M — 1972 *Les Figurines Gallo-Romaines en terre-cuite au Musée des Antiquités Nationales* Supplément à *Gallia* 24.

ROUX, F Le & GUYONVARC'H, G-J — 1978 *Les Druides* Rennes.

RUGER, G B — 1983 'A Husband for the Mother Goddesses – some observations on the Matronae Aufaniae', in Hartley, B & Wacher, J S (eds) *Rome and her Northern Provinces* Alan Sutton, Gloucester.

SALVIAT, F — 1979 *Glanum* Caisse Nationale des Monuments Historiques et des Sites.

SANDARS, N K — 1957 *Bronze Age Cultures in France* Cambridge University Press.

SANDARS, N K — 1968 *Prehistoric Art in Europe* Harmondsworth.

SANDARS, N K — 1984 Review of S Deyts: *Les Bois Sculptés des Sources de la Seine* Paris, *Antiquity* 58, 148.

SAUTEL, J — 1926 *Vaison dans l'Antiquité* Avignon/Lyon.

SAUTER, M R — 1976 *Switzerland* Thames & Hudson, London.

SAVORY, H N — 1937 'An Early Iron Age Site at Long Wittenham, Berks', *Oxoniensia* 2, 3.

SAVORY, H N — 1976 *Guide Catalogue of the Early Iron Age Collections*, National Museum of Wales, Cardiff.

SAVORY, H N — 1980 *Guide Catalogue of the Bronze Age Collection*, National Museum of Wales, Cardiff.

SCHINDLER, R — 1970 *Landesmuseum Trier Fürher durch dir Vorgeschichtliche un römische Abteilung* Trier.

SCHINDLER, R — 1977 *Führer durch das Landesmuseum Trier* Trier.

SIMCO, A — 1984 *Survey of Bedfordshire: The Roman Period* Bedfordshire County Council/Royal Commission on Historical Monuments.

| | |
|---|---|
| SJOESTEDT, M–L | 1940 *Dieux et Héros des Celtes* Paris. |
| SMITH, C R & WRIGHT, T | 1847 'On Certain Mythic Personages mentioned on Roman Altars found in England and on the Rhine', *Journal of the British Archaeological Association* 2, 239ff. |
| SMITH, D J | 1984 'A Romano–Celtic Head from Lemington, Tyne & Wear', in Miket, R & Burgess, C (eds) *Between & Beyond the Walls*, 221–223 Edinburgh. |
| SPROCKHOFF, E | 1955 'Central European Urnfield Culture and Celtic La Tène: an outline', *Proceedings of the Prehistoric Society* 21, 257–282. |
| STEAD, I | 1979 *The Arras Culture*, Yorkshire Philosophical Society. |
| STEAD, I & TURNER, R C | 1985 'Lindow Man', *Antiquity* 59, 25–29. |
| STEAD, I | 1985 'The Linsdorf Monster', *Antiquity* 59, 40–42. |
| STEBBINS, E B | 1929 *The Dolphin in the Literature and Art of Greece and Rome* Menasha, Wisconsin. |
| STUART, A J | 1982 *Pleistocene Vertebrae in the British Isles* Longman, London. |
| SVENSSON, K R | 1982 *Hällristninger I A'lvsborgs Län* Ölvsborgs. |
| SZABÓ, M | 1971 *The Celtic Heritage in Hungary* Corvina. |
| TAYLOR, M V | 1957 'A Roman Bronze Statuette from Northamptonshire', *Antiquaries Journal* 37, 71–72. |
| TEROUANNE, P | 1965 'Sur les traces de Mullo', *Revue Archéologique* 2, 209ff. |
| THEVENOT, E | 1932 *Autun*. |
| THEVENOT, E | 1949 'Les Monuments et le Culte d'Epona chez les Eduens', *L'Antiquité Classique* |
| THEVENOT, E | 1951 *'Le Cheval sacré dans la Gaule de l'Est'*, *Revue Archéologique de l'Est et due Centre-Est* 2, 129–141. |
| | 1955 *Sur les traces des Mars Celtique* Bruges. |
| THEVENOT, E | 1957 'Sur les figurations du "Dieu au Tonneau" ', *Revue Archéologique de l'Est et du Centre-Est* 8, 311–314. |
| THEVENOT, E | 1968 *Dieux et sanctuaires de la Gaule* Paris. |
| THILL, G | 1969 1978 *Les époques gallo-romaine et merovingienne au Musée d'Histoire et d'Art. . . .* Luxembourg. |
| TIERNEY, J J | 1959–1960 'The Celtic Ethnography of Posidonius', *Proceedings of the Royal Irish Academy* 60, 189–275. |
| TOMLIN, R S O | 1985 'Religious Beliefs and Practice: the evidence of inscriptions', in *The Roman Inscriptions of Britain*, conference, Oxford, April 1985. |
| TORBRÜGGE, W | 1972 'Vor- und Frühgeschichtliche Flussfunde. Zur Ordnung und Bestimmung einer Denkmälergruppe' *Berichte Römisch-Germanischen Kommision* 51–52, 1–146. |
| TOUTAIN, J | 1920 *Les Cultes Päiens dans l'empire Romain III* Paris. |
| TOYNBEE, J M C | 1962 *Art in Roman Britain* Phaidon. |
| TOYNBEE, J M C | 1964 *Art in Britain under the Romans* Oxford University Press. |
| TOYNBEE, J M C | 1967 'Romano-British Figurine from Baginton', *Antiquaries Journal* 4, 109. |
| TOYNBEE, J M C | 1971 *Death and Burial in the Roman World* Thames & Hudson, London. |
| TOYNBEE, J M C | 1973 *Animals in Roman Life and Art* Thames & Hudson, London. |
| TOYNBEE, J M C | 1976 'Roman Sculpture in Gloucestershire', in |

247

McGarth P & Cannon, J, *Essays in Bristol & Gloucestershire History* Centenary volume of the Bristol & Gloucestershire Archaeological Society, 62–100.

TOYNBEE, J M C 1978 'A Londinium Votive Leaf or Feather and its Fellows', in Bird, J et al (eds) *Collectanea Londinensia: Studies in London Archaeology and History*, 129–148 London & Middlesex Archaeological Society.

TUDOT, F 1860 *Collections de figurines en argile, oeuvres premières de l'art gaulois* Paris.

TURNER, R C 1982 *Ivy Chimneys, Witham: An Interim Report* Essex County Council Occasional Paper No 2.

TWOHIG, E J 1981 *Megalithic Art of Western Europe* Oxford.

USENER, H 1869 *M Annaei Lucani Commentaria Bernensia* Leipzig.

VAN ES, W A 1972 *De Romeinen in Nederland* Bussum: Fibula-van-Dishoeck.

VANVINCKENROYE, W 1975 *Tongeren Romeinse Stad* Tongeren.

VATIN, C 1969 'Ex-voto de bois gallo-romain à Chamalières', *Revue Archéologique*, 103.

VESLY, L de 1909 *Les Fana ou petits temples gallo-romains de la region Normande* Rouen.

VILLEFOSSE, H de 1881 'Note sur in bronze découvert à Landouzy-la-Ville (Ainse)', *Revue Archéologique* 41, fasc 1, 1–13.

VOUGA, A 1923 *La Tène* Leipzig.

VRIES, J de 1963 *La Religion des Celtes* Payot, Paris.

WACHER, J S 1979 *The Coming of Rome* Routledge, London.

WAITE, G 1985 'Human Burial and Animal Sacrifice in the Iron Age', in *The Archaeology of Death* CBA 9 Annual Conference, Oxford, 16.3.85.

WALKER, S 1985 *Memorials to the Roman Dead* British Museum, London.

WEBSTÉR, G 1983 'The Function of the Chedworth Roman "Villa"' *Transactions of the Bristol & Gloucestershire Archaeological Society* 101, 5–20.

WEDLAKE, W J 1982 *The Excavation of the Shrine of Apollo at Nettleton, Wiltshire 1956–1971* Society of Antiquaries, London.

WELLS, P S 1980 *Culture Contact and Culture Change: Early Iron Age Europe and the Mediterranean World* Cambridge.

WHEELER, R E M 1928 'Roman-Celtic Temple at Harlow....'. *Antiquaries Journal* 8, 300–327.

WHEELER, R E M 1932 *Report on the Excavations .... in Lydney Park, Gloucestershire* Oxford.

WICKENDEN, N P 1985 'A Copper Alloy Votive Bar and a Carved Bone Plaque from Chelmsford, Essex', *Britannia* 16, in press.

WIGHTMAN, E M 1970 *Roman Trier and the Treveri* Hart-Davis.

WIGHTMAN, E M 1985 *Gallia Belgica* Batsford, London.

WILHELM, E 1974 *Pierres sculptées et inscriptions de l'époque romaine* Musée d'histoire et d'art – Luxembourg.

WILKES, J J 1969 *Dalmatia* Routledge, London.

WILLIAMS, R 1985 'Bancroft Mausoleum, and Roman Burials', in *The Archaeology of Death* CBA 9 Annual Conference, Oxford 16.3.85.

WILSON, D R 1973 'Roman Britain in 1972: II Inscriptions', *Britannia* 4, 324.

WILSON, D R 1974 'Roman Britain in 1973', *Britannia* 5, 396–460.

WILSON, D R — 1975 'Roman Britain in 1974', *Britannia* 6, 220–283.

WISEMAN, A & eds
WISEMAN, T P — 1980 *The Battle for Gaul* Chatto & Windus.

WRIGHT, R P — 1966 'Roman Britain in 1965', *Journal of Roman Studies* 56, 224.

WRIGHT, R P &
PHILLIPS, E J — 1975 *Roman Inscribed and Sculptured Stones in Carlisle Museum* Carlisle.

WUILLEUMIER, P — 1984 *Inscriptions Latines des Trois Gaules* Supplément à *Gallia* 17.

ZWICKER, J — 1934–1936 *Fontes Historiae Religionis Celticae* Berlin.

# INDEX

Abandinus 149
Aericura 136
Aesculapius 101, 155, 162, 175
Afterlife 2, 17, 103, 121–137
Aigues Mortes 56, 57
Aillil 15, 173
Aix-la-Chapelle 161
Aix-les-Bains 79, 84, 88, 162, 165
Albaina 211
Albiorix 111
Alesia 4, 22, 42, 58, 81, 89, 162, 171, 188
Alisonus 22
Allerey 153, 164
Allier 50, 70, 90, 94
Allonnes 158
Altripp 22
Alzey 58
Ancamna 165
Ancaster 82, 175
Andraste 21, 76, 108, 185
Angers 111
Anglesey 21, 27, 143, 177
Animal ritual passim but esp. 167–199
Antefix 51, 52, 69
Antigney-la-Ville 152
Antre, Lake 152
Apollo 111, 152, 153, 158ff, 161ff, 172,
    173, 175
Appleby 8
Aquae Arnemetiae 21, 153
Arduinna 22, 37, 181
Argonne 42
Armançon 92, 165
Arnemetia 153, 165
Arras 221
Arras Culture 124, 171, 180
Artaios, Mercury 184
Artio 22, 37, 169, 184
Artomagus 22
Arvernus 98
Ashill 181
Assche-Kalkoven 172
Assingenehae 79
Atepomarus 172, 173
Athelney 198
Aufaniae 79, 84
Augst 46
Aulnay-aux-Planches 19, 20, 21, 167,
    178
Autun 77, 81
Auxy 192
Aveta 85, 89
Aveyron 75
Avrigney 181
Axes 41, 221ff

Aylesford 10, 218

Backworth 23, 46, 48, 59, 69, 83
Badb 101, 108, 120, 188
Bad Dürkheim 49
Baden 84
Balèsmes 47
Ballachulish 13, 34, 75
Ballerstein 89
Balzars 182
Banbha 101
Bancroft 106, 132
Barkway 111
Barton 10, 129, 176
Basle 41
Báta 181
Bath 23, 24, 37, 38, 79, 80, 81, 88, 91, 95,
    97, 102, 111, 153ff, 158, 164, 165, 209
Battersea 104–105, 139
Bear 22, 37, 169, 184, 185
Beaucroissant 184
Beaune 165
Beauvais 192
Begnères 56
Beire-le-Châtel 152, 190
Beisirissa, Jupiter 68
Bekesbourne 172
Belatucadrus 111
Belenus 152–53, 162ff, 164
Belginum 46, 129
Beltine 15, 74
Bergusia 95
Bewcastle 111–112, 113
Bibracte 77
Biddenham 187
Biel, Lake 142
Biesenbrow 197
Billhook 57
Bird 12, 33, 92, 107, 133, 145, 157, 181,
    186ff
Birdoswald 57, 58
Bisley 36, 116, 119
Blackburn Mill 143, 146
Blain 193, 198
Boann 149
Boar 9, 10, 22, 35, 41, 54, 107, 108, 159,
    168, 170, 179ff, 195, 211, 212
Boar, triple-horned 209, 215
Boats (see also Ships) 145, 146, 147
Böckingen 66
Bog, bog-burial 28, 128, 138ff, 144
Bolards 172, 173
Bollendorf 184
Bonn 79, 83, 84
Bootle 185

Bordeaux 58
Bormana 162
Bormanus 162
Bormo 95, 162, 165
Borre Fenn 144
Borvo 162, 185
Boudica 73, 75
Boughton Aluph 198
Bouray 10, 195, 211
Bourbonne-Lancy 162
Bourbonne-les-Bains 162, 164, 185
Bourges 75
Bourton Grounds 172
Brå 9, 146, 176
Bradenstoke 208
Bradley Hill 131
Brampton 132
Bran (Irish) 122
Bran (Welsh) 31
Branwen 147
Bredon Hill 29
Breedon-on-the-Hill 106
Bremevaque 59
Bres, King 73
Brescia 67
Bricta 95, 153
Brigetio 161
Brigstock 20, 23, 116, 178
Britannicae 78
Brixianus, Jupiter 67
Broadway 100
Broighter 148
Bull/ox 22, 27, 33, 35, 42, 44, 53, 70, 77, 100, 113, 132, 167, 168, 169, 170, 171, 172, 176ff, 182, 187, 188, 189, 195, 196, 197ff, 211
Bull, triple-horned 53, 181, 189ff, 209
Butterstadt 58
Býći Skala 124, 171, 176

Cadéac 68
Caergwrle 148
Caerleon 51, 52
Caernarfon 113
Caerwent 88, 114, 115, 155, 158, 165, 176, 178, 217, 218, 219
Calalzo 'Làgole' 153
Callirius, Silvanus 182, 183, 211
Cambridge 131, 134, 178
Camonica Valley 32, 77, 104, 135, 167, 179, 182, 193, 195, 207
Camulos, Mars 111
Canterbury 89
Carlingwark Loch 143, 146
Carlisle 83, 194
Carmarthen 31
Carnutes 27
Carrawburgh 80, 88, 149, 155
Cartimandua 73, 75
Carvoran 111, 197
Castlecary 183
Castleford 80
Castlesteads 57, 84

Catalauni 42
Cathbad 26
Caturix, Mars 111
Cauldron 4, 25, 28, 75, 129, 141, 142, 143, 146ff, 177, 178, 179, 195ff
Cavenham 23
Caves Inn 157, 166
Cerberus 136, 175, 190
Cernunnos 26, 33, 44, 170, 178, 180, 182ff, 189, 192, 193ff, 215
Chamalières 76, 151ff
Champagnat 59
Cart/chariot-burial 3, 4, 77, 123ff, 135, 171
Charon 136
Chedworth 140, 158, 159, 160, 182, 183, 185
Chelmsford 24, 181
Chester 66, 67, 210
Chesterholm 158
Chesters 214
Chichester 80
Chorey 174
Christians 56, 65, 86, 195, 218
Churcham 59, 69, 211
Cimbri 28, 140, 147
Circle, concentric 45, 55, 60
Cirencester 64, 65, 75, 79, 80, 82, 83, 85, 86, 90, 91, 175, 190, 192, 193, 196, 201, 204, 208, 210, 213, 219, 220, 223
Clarensac 57, 59, 99
Cocidius 111–112, 113, 183
Cockerel 169
Coins 7, 10, 43ff, 59, 108, 139, 140, 155, 168, 171, 174, 208
Colchester 79, 136, 182, 183, 190, 191, 211, 219
Coligny Calendar 27, 74
Colijnsplaat 87, 166
Collias 56
Cologne 56, 57
Comedovae, Matres 79, 165
Comminges 61
Conall Cernach 31, 185
Conchobar 15, 101
Condatis 99, 111, 140
Conifer 56
Conla 122
Coralli 64
Corbridge 50, 51, 58, 116, 136
Corleck 209
Corotiacus, Mars 116, 117
Cosgrove 30
Coventina 80, 149, 154, 155, 157, 165, 166, 172
Crane 133, 178, 187, 191
Crêt Châtelard 192
Crow 101, 108, 136, 170, 187f
Crozant 86
Cú Chulainn 31, 101, 120, 187, 188
Cuda 85, 91
Culverhole Cave 90
Cunomaglus 160, 163, 164, 175

Curbridge 131
Curgy 192, 196
Curse 24, 25, 37, 155
Custom Scrubs 37, 118, 205
Cwlhwch and Olwen, Tale of 16, 180

Dagda 33, 147, 149
Daglingworth 85, 90
Dalheim 86, 93
Damona 95, 162, 165, 185
Danebury 4, 8, 19, 28f, 127, 133, 168, 186
Danu 73
Deal 134, 135, 157, 204
Dea Nutrix 82, 89, 93
Death 31, 55, 60, 61, 64, 70, 73, 88, 90, 91, 93, 101, 103, 121–137, 144, 147, 166, 175, 182, 187, 194, 211
Decapitation 31, 130–131
Defixio 24, 25, 155
Dejbjerg 77, 144
Dhronecken 46, 89
Diana 66, 164, 175
Diarville 41
Die 162
Dieburg 88
Dijon 13, 147, 150, 186
Dispater 66–67, 69, 136
Divination 14, 27ff, 188
Divine Couples 95–97
Dog 82, 83, 85, 86–90, 92, 101, 130, 133, 155, 158ff, 166, 168, 170, 175ff, 182, 188, 211
Dolaucothi 23
Dolichenus 47, 68
Dolphin 53, 69
Domburg 86–87, 166
Domesticae 79
Dompierre 59
Don 73
Donn 122, 136
Double-axe 45, 47, 98, 220
Druid 14, 16, 17, 21, 22, 26ff, 32, 74, 103, 137, 143, 144, 179, 188
Drunemeton 21
Duchcov 141, 146
Duck 147, 148, 186f
Dürrnberg 4, 41, 148, 221

Eagle 39, 46, 50, 53, 58, 170, 178, 188ff, 192
East Stoke 97
Ebberston 123
Ebchester 112
Écury-le-Repos 126
Emberton 204, 215, 223
Emphasis 200ff
Entremont 12, 29, 30, 75, 108, 216
Epona 35, 37, 85, 87, 88, 90, 91–94, 153, 164, 169, 170ff, 211
Ériu 101
Essarois 164

Essay 93
Esus 14, 28, 37, 110, 133, 186
Euffigneix 10, 170, 180
Evreux 10, 180
Ewell 185
Exaggeration 201ff, 211ff
Eype 100

Face-pot 100, 218–219
Farley Heath 23, 54, 55, 69, 208
Fates 81
Feasting esp. 129ff
Feather Plaques 25, 82
Felmersham 177
Felmingham Hall 23, 46, 47, 69, 188
Fertility passim, but esp 72–102
Fódla 101
Fontaines Salées, Les 152
Fordington, Dorchester 171
Forêt d'Halatte 181, 218
Fortuna 81, 85, 97, 99
Fox-Amphoux 48
Frilford 18, 19, 20, 21, 106, 132, 221
Frog/Toad 168, 185ff

Gallicae 78
Gannat 90
Garton Slack 106, 109, 126, 128–129, 180
Genius 92, 118, 208
Genius cucullatus 90–91, 97, 102, 154, 155, 157, 158, 201, 208, 223
Genius loci 22
Gévaudan, Lake 142
Gilly 57
Glanum, Glanicae, Glanis 79, 85, 152, 165
Gloucester 97–99
Goadby 134, 157
Goat 100, 169, 189, 197, 198, 211, 212
Godmanchester 149
Godramstein 66
Goldberg 20
Goloring 20
Goose 113, 114, 126, 187
Gournay-sur-Aronde 106, 143
Grand 161, 162
Grand-Jailly 49, 53
Grannus, Apollo 161, 162, 164
Grauballe 144
Grave passim but esp 122–137
Gravettian 211
Gréoulx 84, 165
Grézean 108
Grimes Graves 75
Grimston, North 126
Griselicae 84, 165
Grove (see nemeton)
Guilden Morden 131
Guiting Power 100
Gundestrup 25, 35, 44, 49, 71, 77, 107, 109, 116, 144, 146ff, 178, 179, 180–182, 192, 195, 198

Gusenberg 46

Hadad 47, 68
Haddenham 19
Hainault 49
Hajduböszörmény 147
Halstatt (site) 3, 40, 42, 108
Ham Hill 177
Hammer 54, 57, 97, 175
Hare 168, 182, 184, 185
Harlow 21, 106, 221
Hassocks 89
Hausen-an-der-Zaber 62, 63
Hayling Island 18–22, 29, 106, 143, 180
Head, head-hunting 12, 14, 28ff, 35, 100, 108, 110, 120, 124, 127, 154, 157, 166, 172, 173, 180, 186, 188, 198, 211, 212, 216ff
Head, triple 85, 175, 188, 192, 196, 208, 211
Healing 22, 80, 88, 89, 97, 99, 101, 112, 118, 138, 148–166, 172, 175, 176, 185, 189, 194, 195
Heathrow 20
Heidelberg 11
Hercules 162
High Rochester 198
Hirschlanden 10, 108
Hjortspring, Als 148
Hobnail-boots 130–131
Hochscheid 152, 161, 185
Hockwold 23, 181
Hogondange 93
Höhmichele 123
Holyhead 177
Holzerlingen 11, 12, 35, 198, 210
Holzhausen 20, 28, 133
Hoppstädten 127
Horns 11, 12, 32, 35, 42, 44, 60, 69, 75, 100, 106, 107, 113, 114, 144, 147, 169–70, 179, 189, 192, 193, 195ff, 197ff, 209, 211, 212ff, 223
Horse 3, 8, 35, 40, 43, 49, 59, 63, 70, 88, 91–94, 101, 117, 124, 164, 168, 170ff, 178
Horseman 33, 35, 58, 59, 61ff, 90, 116–118, 136, 165, 171ff, 182, 205
Hounslow 41, 211
Housesteads 49, 84, 114
Hradiste 42
Hultenhause 89
Human Sacrifice 14, 20, 21, 27ff, 109, 127, 128, 131, 134, 139, 144ff, 147
Hunter (see also Silvanus, Stag) 160ff, 169, 175, 182, 185, 198, 222

Icklingham 46, 47, 100, 178, 198
Icovellauna 85, 165
Imbolc 74
Infant-burial 19, 28, 131, 132
Interpretatio romana/celtica 36ff
Iovantucarus, Lenus 158

Ipswich 185
Iunones 80
Ivy Chimneys 22, 149, 176, 204, 207

Jabreilles 92
Janiform, Janus 12, 198, 204, 210
Jordan Hill 157
Juno 58
Jupiter 39–71, 99, 111, 116, 117, 121, 136, 164, 179, 188
Jupiter-Giant (columns) 50, 58, 61ff, 116, 153, 165, 173, 185, 194, 225
Juthe Fen 144–145

Kelvedon 111, 116, 145, 156
Kenchester 131
Key 96
Kimmeridge 131
Kingscote 90, 116
King's Stanley 119
Klein Aspergle 126
Kleinklein 173
Koralpe 68

Ladicus, Jupiter/Mount 67
La Gorge-Meillet 124, 180
La Horgue-au-Sablon 93
Lake 138ff
Lakenheath 43
Lamyatt 106, 116
Landouzy-la-Ville 52
Lankhills 130, 131, 132
Lansargues 56, 65
La Tène (site) 4, 104, 142
Latis 149
Latobius 68
Le Châtelet 49, 51, 52
Le Donon 183
Lemington 218
Le Mont Saçon 56
Lenus 36, 84, 114, 115, 158ff, 165, 188
Lexden 9, 177, 211
Libeniče 19, 20, 167
Lichterfelde 139, 145
Limbs, votive 150ff, 154, 155, 160, 163, 164, 166
Lincoln 219
Lindow Moss 28, 128, 144
Linsdorf 136
Little Houghton 49
Llyn Cerrig 104, 142, 143, 146
Llyn Fawr 142, 146
Loire 42, 164
London 80, 82, 94, 105, 140, 160, 166, 175, 176, 210, 223
Long Wittenham 221
Loucetius, Mars 37, 111, 155, 158, 164
Lower Slaughter 114, 115, 156, 208, 211
Lug 16
Lugdunum (see Lyon)
Lugnasad 74
Luncani 181

Luxeuil 59, 92, 95, 153, 165
Luxembourg 92, 183
Luxovius 95, 153, 165
Lydney 88, 140, 158, 159ff, 163, 165, 175
Lyon 96, 140
Lypiatt 63, 194

Mabinogion 16, 73, 101, 147, 187
Mabon 73
Mac Da Tho 122
Macha(s) 101, 120
Magic 27, 146, 180, 188
Maiden Castle 8, 19, 21, 28, 191
Mahlinehae 79
Mainz 37, 43, 49, 161
Malton 49, 184
Manannan 121
Manchester 49
Maponus 158
Margidunum 117
Marlborough 10, 218
Marne 19, 42, 46, 124, 126, 147, 164, 180
Mars 36, 37, 90, 98, 103–121, 152, 155, 158ff, 160, 172, 173, 185, 192, 193, 194, 205, 208, 211
Marseille 12, 28, 153
Martigny-en-Valais 178
Martlesham 116, 117, 173
Maryport 57, 58, 83, 198
Mask 23, 24, 203
Mauvières 172
Mavilly 109, 152, 158, 185, 192
Meaux 59
Medb 15, 27, 73, 77, 120
Mercury 36, 37, 84, 85, 95, 97–99, 111, 155, 169, 184, 192, 194, 198, 204, 215, 219, 223
Merten 62
Metamorphosis (see Shape-changing)
Metz 48, 85
Milber Down 148, 182, 183, 186f
Mildenhall, Suffolk 171
Milton 23
Minerva 154ff
Miniaturisation (see also Models) 202, 213, 216, 220–223
Mistletoe 27, 28, 74, 144, 179
Mithras 88
Moccus, Mercury 181
Model Objects 18, 40ff, 46ff, 61, 106, 107, 113, 148, 213, 220–223
Modron 73, 101
Mont Bego 77, 176, 179
Mont Beuvray 77
Montbuoy 145
Montmaurin 55
Montpellier 56
Moon 8, 23, 39, 43, 46ff, 51
Moritasgus 162ff, 165
Mórrígan 101, 120, 170, 184, 188

Mother-goddesses 32, 33, 35, 37, 38, 46, 57, 59, 69, 70, 72–102, 121, 155, 161, 165, 170, 175, 178, 194, 201, 204, 208, 209, 210, 211, 213
Mouhet 59
Mountain 22, 67–68, 176
Mouriès 172
Msěcké Žehrovice 11, 216
Mullo, Mars 158, 172
Muntham Court 18, 19, 20, 134, 155, 159, 160, 176, 178, 181, 211

Nages 170
Naix 59, 86
Nantosuelta 95, 97, 140, 188
Nehalennia 86–87, 166, 169, 170ff, 175ff
Nemausicae 79, 84, 165
Nemausus 38, 84, 152, 165
Nemeton 21, 22, 27, 28, 111–112
Nemetona 22, 37, 111, 155
Neolithic Axes 21
Neptune 160
Néris 192
Nerthus 77
Netherby 59, 60
Nettleton Shrub 97, 160, 163ff, 175
Nauchâtel (see La Tène)
Neuvy-en-Sullias 10, 168, 181, 182
Newstead 134, 172
Nijmegen 47
Nîmes 38, 56, 57, 59, 84, 108, 152, 165, 175
Nodens 16, 88, 140, 158, 159, 160ff, 175ff
Nors Thy 148
Northmavine, Shetland 172
Noves 135, 218
Nuada 16, 159, 160
Nydam 148
Nymph 80, 149, 154, 164
Nyon 102

Obernburg 59
Ocelus 115
Odell 131
Oise 46, 164
Olloudius, Mars 37, 112, 119
Orange 42, 44, 48, 107, 140, 198
Orăstie 147
Orgon 66–67
Orléans 42, 145
Orton Longueville 131
Ospringe 131
Owmby 90
Oxen (see Bull)

Palm 56, 82, 88
Paris 133, 178, 187, 191, 195
Parthinus 68
Paspardo 182
Peacock 186

Pesch 84
Peterborough 118
Petersfield 44, 196
Petit-Morin 75
Pfalzfeld 11, 12, 216
Phallus 85, 98, 100, 109, 113, 184, 193, 195, 197, 198, 209, 212
Pig (see also Boar) 4, 106, 122, 125, 126, 129, 168, 180, 181
Pillar 11, 29, 61–64, 170
Pit 19, 20, 28, 29, 127, 132ff, 145, 157, 168, 172, 173, 176, 178, 181, 183, 184, 185–187
Plessis-Barbuise 47
Plurality 42, 102, 106, 201ff, 208ff
Poeninus, Jupiter 68
Pogny 42
Pommern 159
Pool 149, 150, 152, 154, 155
Popeşti 195
Port 142
Priest 5, 10, 23ff, 140, 158, 162, 163, 195, 203
Puech-Real 104
Puig-Castelar 29
Pyrenees 22, 49, 55, 56, 61

Quémigny-sur-Seine 59

Rain 39
Ram 97, 98, 169, 189, 194, 197, 198, 213
Ram-horned Snake 26, 63, 109, 116, 152, 185, 189, 190, 192ff, 201, 213
Rappendam 144
Rat 176, 196, 197
Ratham Mill, Funtington 149
Raven 54, 69, 89, 97, 101, 108, 120, 136, 158, 187f
Ravenna Cosmography 113
Realism 200ff
Rebirth 61, 120, 175, 182, 189, 211
Redruth 219
Regalia 23ff, 52, 53, 54, 71, 192, 203
Reims 65, 178, 183, 196, 197
Reinheim 73, 126
Rézé 89, 99
Rhiannon 101, 188
Ribble 170, 178, 188
Richborough 198
Rigisamus, Mars 111, 116
Rigonemetis, Mars 112
Risingham 113, 183
Ritona 85, 165
River 138–141, 149
Ritual Damage 18, 21, 106, 107, 124, 129, 143, 155, 222
Rodenbach 8
Rödingen 80
Romulus 37, 119, 205
Roos Carr 109, 148
Roquepertuse 12, 30, 172, 187, 188
Rosette 45, 55, 56, 60, 75, 157

Rosmerta 37, 85, 95, 97, 98–99, 155
Rotherley Down 186
Rouen 49
Rynkeby 9, 177

S-sign 45, 49, 52
Saalfelden 182
Sablon 165
Sainatis Trumusiatis 153
Saint Bernard 68, 133
Saint Blaise 29
Sainte Fontaine 161
Saintes 178
Sainte Sabine 152, 164, 172
Saint Germain-les-Rocheux 19
Saint Margarethen-am-Silberberg 19
Saint Michel de Valbonne 173
Saint Moritz, Engaden 153
Saint Ouen de Thouberville 89, 165
Saint Vulbas 162
Salzbach 136
Samain 15, 74, 122
Santenay 92
Sarapis 162
Sarrebourg 89
Saulon-la-Chapelle 164
Saverne 60–61
Scardona 66, 67
Schematism passim but esp 200ff
Sea 138, 160, 166
Segomo, Mars 111, 172
Séguret 58, 63, 70, 116
Seine 13, 46, 140, 147, 150ff, 163, 164, 166, 175, 186
Sequana 37, 140, 147, 150ff, 175, 186, 187
Severn 140, 160
Shape-changing 33, 108, 121, 169–170, 178, 180, 184, 191, 197, 199
Sheep (see also Ram) 168, 180
Ship 8, 148
Shrinkage 216ff
Silchester 49, 53, 100, 178
Silvanus 57, 97, 112, 137, 160, 161, 164, 176, 182–183, 211
Simpelveld 132
Sirona 152, 161, 165, 169, 185
Sky-god 39–71, 99, 111, 116, 164, 165, 188, 192
Slänge 75
Smith-god 54, 219
Snake 58, 59, 63, 70, 155, 162, 169, 173, 175, 185ff, 194, 196, 198
Snake, ram-horned (see under Ram-horned)
Sommerécourt 192, 196
Sopron 177, 181
Sougères-en-Pulsaye 172
Southbroom 116, 193
South Cadbury 8, 19, 21, 29, 78, 104, 134, 172, 178
South Ferriby 178

Spring 22, 70, 95, 138ff, 141, 149ff, 158ff, 165
Springhead 91, 95, 131, 132, 154, 165, 172
Stag 10, 26, 44, 54, 77, 133, 135, 161, 167, 168, 169, 178, 180, 182ff, 187, 189, 193, 195ff, 211, 215
Staines 176
Stanton Harcourt 131
Stanwick 29
'Stèles-maisons' 60–61, 132
Stonehenge 145
Stow-on-the-Wold 114
Stragglethorpe 173, 205
Strettweg 34, 76, 77, 173, 182
Sucellus 33, 54, 95, 96, 136, 140, 152, 175, 185, 188
Suleviae 79, 80, 81, 82, 84, 155
Sulis 24, 38, 153, 154ff, 158, 164, 165
Sun 8, 23, 35, 39–71, 80, 94, 95, 99, 104, 116, 147, 148, 153, 155, 160, 161ff, 164ff, 171, 172, 182, 189, 222
Sutherland 211
Suttee 121, 127
Swan 147, 186f, 197
Swanwick 20, 28, 133
Swarling 10
Swastika 44, 45, 49, 55, 56, 59, 221
Symonds Hall Farm 208

Tal-y-Llyn 217–218
Taranis 14, 28, 66–67, 69
Tarbes 22, 24, 179
Tarn 75
Tarvostrigaranus 178, 187, 191
Territorial gods 22, 37, 78, 95, 101
Teutates 14, 28, 37, 110, 111, 116, 147
Teutones 140
Thames 105, 106, 139, 140
Thatcham 145
Thauron 66–67
Thealby 53, 169, 170, 178, 188
Thil Châtel 92
Thincsus, Mars 114
Thistleton Dyer 185
Three (see also Triplism) 85, 86, 90–91, 98, 136, 187, 190ff, 208ff
Thunder/bolt 39, 45, 50, 54, 57, 58, 66–67, 138
Thundersley 90
Tiddington 222
Titelburg 89
Toad (see Frog)
Tollund Man 144
Tongres 58, 85, 98
Tongs 54
Torc 10, 12, 42, 108, 109, 147, 180, 192, 193, 195
Torrs 144
Tortoise 169
Toulon 89
Toulouse 21, 49, 141, 143

Tours 59, 66
Toutatis (see Teutates)
Toutenant 99
Transmigration of souls 121
Tree 21, 22, 63, 112, 119, 133, 168, 187, 188
Trègnes 47
Tre-owen 113
Tresques 56
Trier 46, 79, 81, 84, 85, 86, 89, 99, 129, 133, 158ff, 161, 165, 178, 185, 187, 188, 194
Triplism 32, 78ff, 93, 101, 102, 114, 115, 149, 175, 188, 192, 201ff, 208ff
Troyes, La Charne 9
Trundholm 8, 40, 171
Tuatha Dé Danann 73
Turbelsloch 196

Ucuetis 95
Uley 37, 198, 223
Ulster Cycle 15, 16, 27, 33, 110, 119, 170, 187, 188
Underworld 20, 53, 58, 61–65, 69, 89, 90, 91, 101, 102, 103, 117, 121–137, 147, 157, 166, 175, 176, 185, 194, 195, 197
Unterseebach 136
Upchurch 176
Uxellinus, Jupiter 68

Vacallinehae 84
Vachères 108
Vaison 186
Valais 41
Varhély 93, 136, 175
Vellaunus 115
Vendoeuvres 196
'Venus' 94–95, 99, 132, 154, 165, 198
Verbeia 140, 149
Vernostonus 112
Vertillum 81
Verulamium 95, 132, 178
Vessel 2, 25, 30, 49, 71, 109, 116, 139, 145ff
Vichy 95, 152, 158, 165
Viereckshanzen 133, 216
Villeneuve-au-Châtelot 41
Villeneuve-Renneville 135
Vinča Culture 207
Vindonnus 164
Visucius, Mercury 98
Vix 73, 75, 77
Vorocius, Mars 158
Vosegus 22

Walbrook, 95, 140, 165, 166
Waldalgesheim 12, 218
Wall 198
Wandlebury 29, 127
Wandsworth 198
War/warrior 3, 4, 12, 21, 30, 42, 48, 50,

52, 54, 58, 61ff, 73, 75, 101, 102, 103–121, 126, 139, 143, 185, 188, 189, 198, 222
Wasperton 184
Water-bird 8, 35, 40, 70, 75, 138ff, 145ff, 186
Water-cult 3, 21, 22, 32, 42, 48, 85, 88, 97, 101, 104, 138–166
Waterloo 104, 106, 139
Weapons, armour (see War)
Wederath-Belginum 46
Weiskirchen 218
Well 88, 145, 149, 155ff, 176, 215
Wellow 85
Welwyn/Garden City 129
Welshpool 177, 225
West Coker 116
Wetwang Slack 109, 125–126
Wharfe, river 140, 149
Wheel/wheel-god 33, 35, 39–71, 107, 116, 147, 153, 164, 192, 194, 196, 211, 222

Willingham Fen 23, 53, 69, 188, 191
Wilsford 20, 133, 145
Wincheringen 129
Winchester 78, 90, 129, 131
Winterbourne Kingston 185
Witchcraft 131
Witham 9, 10, 139, 181
Woodeaton 106, 107, 113, 188, 189, 212, 221, 222
Woodendean 181
Worth 18, 21, 106, 221
Wroxeter 163, 172, 178, 208, 210
Wycomb 91

Xulsigiae 84

Yardhope 113
York 79, 80, 96, 97, 132

Zeus 52
Zürich (Altstetten) 8, 40, 182